# MORE JUSTICE
# MORE PEACE

# THE BLACK PERSON'S GUIDES

# MORE JUSTICE MORE PEACE

## THE BLACK PERSON'S GUIDE TO THE AMERICAN LEGAL SYSTEM

■

### NEDRA D. CAMPBELL

Lawrence Hill Books

Library of Congress Cataloging-in-Publication Data

Campbell, Nedra D.
  More justice, more peace : the Black person's guide to the
American legal system / Nedra D. Campbell.—1st ed.
      p.   cm.
Includes index.
ISBN 1-55652-468-4
  1. Justice, Administration of—United States—Popular works.
  2. Law—United States—Popular works.  I. Title.
    KF8700.Z9 C28 2003
    349.73—dc21

                                                        2002009450

*Cover and interior design: Monica Baziuk*
*Cover Photograph: Steve Belkowitz/Getty Images*

©2003 Nedra D. Campbell
First edition
Published by Lawrence Hill Books
An imprint of Chicago Review Press, Incorporated
814 North Franklin Street
Chicago, Illinois 60610
ISBN 1-55652-468-4
Printed in the United States of America
5  4  3  2  1

■

*This book is dedicated to my father, Arthur Charles Campbell,
who taught me how to dream, and my mother, Gwendolyn McZeek
Campbell, who taught me how to work to make my
dreams materialize.*

# CONTENTS

■

# ACKNOWLEDGMENTS

■

SOME STORIES REMAIN in our hearts forever. For me, one of these is a simple story about a young black girl and a bicycle told in *Lemon Swamp and Other Places: A Carolina Memoir*, by Mamie Garvin Fields with Karen Fields, a book describing growing up in Jim Crow South Carolina. Little Mamie had a bike her grandfather had been teaching her to ride. One day, when she finally learned how to ride the bike, she ran into the house exclaiming, "I *did* it! I did it *all by myself!*" Her grandfather was not pleased. He suggested to her that many people, from her parents who had bought her training wheels to the other children who had shown her how to ride, had in some way or another made it possible for her to now ride by herself.

As little Mamie learned, I realize this book would not have been possible without the assistance of numerous people. I would like to acknowledge all of you who have in some way made valuable contributions. From those who pried open the doors of previously white-only institutions like Duke University and Georgetown University Law Center so I could get a first-rate education, to the numerous black lawyers, both past and present, who by your existence alone make my job easier on a daily basis, I say thank you. I would also like to thank the other lawyers who assisted with the manuscript and in particular Erika Campbell-Harris and Josh Goldfein. Special thanks go to former police officer Jeffery Harris for providing me with an insider's view. I would also like to acknowledge my editor, Yuval Taylor, who not only recognized the need for a book like this, but who provided valuable assistance throughout the process. Finally, I would like to thank my parents, Arthur and Gwendolyn Campbell, who bought me several "training wheels"; my grandmother, Kathryn Hannon; and my brother, Nicholas Campbell, for their support. I can finally say, "I did it! I did it *with you all!*"

# INTRODUCTION

■

"NO JUSTICE, NO PEACE. No justice, no peace," chanted the marching crowds on April 29, 1992, after an all-white jury had acquitted all four of the white police officers on trial for using excessive force against Los Angeles motorist Rodney King. More than a year earlier on March 3, 1991, Rodney King had been stopped by the Los Angeles Police Department in what was initially a routine traffic stop. An area resident videotaped King enduring more than fifty baton blows, several kicks, and paralyzing electric taser shocks. King was hospitalized after the beating, which left him with a bruised kidney, eleven skull fractures, and brain damage. Shortly thereafter, four of the police officers involved were charged with assault with a deadly weapon and the use of excessive force. The trial was moved away from Los Angeles, where the alleged crime occurred, to a predominantly white suburb. The videotape, which was aired throughout the world, apparently had no influence on the jury.

"No justice, no peace" became the battle cry resonating from the city of Los Angeles, which was a riotous battlefield for almost a week. More than fifty people were killed and thousands were injured. The property damage to the city was estimated at more than $700 million. Several demonstrators practiced nonviolence and banded together in marches, shouting, "No justice, no peace." Demonstrations spread to other major metropolitan cities such as Atlanta and Detroit, where demonstrators there joined the chant.

One of the first people arrested during the 1992 Los Angeles riots was Donald Coleman, a black man who was convicted of tossing a Molotov cocktail into a 7-Eleven store. He fared far worse than the white police officers acquitted of charges of assault with a deadly weapon and use of excessive force. Coleman was sentenced to nineteen years and eight months in prison.

In a less publicized beating four years later, Jonny E. Gammage, pulled over by Pittsburgh police for "driving erratically," was less fortunate than King. These police officers, trying to restrain a man they deemed was "out of control," beat Gammage to death. They too were acquitted. The four undercover New York police officers who put more than forty bullets in Amadou Diallo after mistaking him for a suspect were acquitted on February 24, 2000. And on September 26, 2001, the police officer who shot and killed an unarmed teenager, Timothy Thomas, making him the fourth person in five months to be shot to death by a Cincinnati police officer, was also acquitted.

An ABC News report, *Rich, Famous, but Not Equal,* showcased the less threatening but equally demoralizing acts of discrimination that many blacks regularly suffer. Darius Rucker, the lead singer of the rock group Hootie and the Blowfish, recounted how he, the only black member of the band, was stopped and questioned by a Secret Service agent before his band was to play at Vice President Albert Gore's inaugural ball. Actor Danny Glover, a frequent visitor to New York, publicized his inability to hail a cab as he stood with his daughter on the streets of New York. Christopher Darden, one of the prosecutors in the O. J. Simpson trial, recounted how he was unable to purchase a Jaguar because the sales staff ignored him.

White Americans do not always recognize what is a daily reality for black Americans. In fact, according to a poll publicized along with the ABC News report, almost half of the white Americans interviewed believed that black Americans exaggerate accounts of discrimination (fortunately, that means that more than half of the white Americans interviewed acknowledge that black Americans do suffer discrimination). This should come as no surprise. And even less surprising is that this type of collective white unconsciousness has infested our laws and our legal system. It was not until I was a student at the Georgetown University Law Center that I began to recognize the extent to which this is the case.

I was a first-year law student, studying with my study group, when we began discussing a question that dealt with a lawyer who had provided legal advice to his cousin. The question asked what would happen if the cousin didn't want to pay his lawyer-cousin for his services. Would the cousin have the burden of proving his lawyer-cousin meant to provide him with *free* legal advice? Or would the lawyer-cousin have to prove his cousin had agreed to pay him for his services?

At last, I thought, an easy question. Of course the lawyer-cousin would have to prove he had made it clear he was going to charge a *relative*. But Robert, a white guy in my group, claimed that I was obviously wrong. He "knew" that whenever a lawyer gave advice, regardless of whether she or he gave it to a family member, the presumption was that the lawyer would be paid.

According to the law, Robert was right. But in the black community, family is family, and lawyers don't just go around charging family like that. Because I had failed to consider that the law does not typically reflect our community, but the white community instead, I got the question wrong.

That was not the last time in law school I realized how the American legal system fails to reflect and protect the values and interests of the black community. Later I was introduced to this creature called the "reasonable man" and discovered that the American legal system is based on him. The reasonable man has never been called the "n" word or been viewed as a thief. He's never been turned down for a job he was qualified to do, and he has never been pulled over by the police. This reasonable man always has enough money to pay his bills on time, and even has enough money to pay costly attorneys' fees and court fines. In short, this reasonable man has got it going on.

Of course I never actually met this reasonable man, but I know he's not black, and if he resembles anyone I do know it would probably be Robert. In one two-week period during my D.C. stint, I was pulled over by police officers at least five times. Robert, two years older than me, hadn't been pulled over that many times during his entire life.

Like it or not, the American legal system was created by white men for white men. It was not created *by* us. It was not created *for* us. But today, hundreds of years after slavery and decades after Jim Crow, we can use this imperfect system to our advantage. *More Justice, More Peace: The Black Person's Guide to the American Legal System* is your compass to making this system work for you. In an 1849 letter, abolitionist Frederick Douglass wrote, "Power concedes nothing without a demand." The notion of us *having* rights is flawed. You only truly have rights you choose to exercise. This book will arm you with enough information to empower you to demand that those in power respect your rights.

You can gain valuable information from this book without reading it cover to cover. Of course, doing so won't hurt. First, if you doubt the need for a book that addresses the legal system for the black person, all you need to do is read the first chapter on civil rights. This chapter tracks the path black people have had to take to become entitled to any rights. The chapter also outlines your civil rights and explains how they can be enforced.

The next three chapters deal with issues that affect almost everyone—crime and punishment, your rights as an employee, and your rights as a consumer—as does the final chapter, on voting rights. The information contained therein is invaluable, since you could be confronted with these issues at any time.

The remaining chapters can be consulted on an as-needed basis. If, for example, you are considering beginning your own business, you should refer to Chapter 7, which addresses legal issues for the aspiring entrepreneur or entertainer.

Naturally, this book does not address every legal issue, and it won't enable you to handle every aspect of your particular legal issue. Rather, it has been designed as a practical guide that will help you understand your rights, exercise your rights, and find more information about your rights. I hope that by reading and using the information in this book, you will find a little more justice and a little more peace in our legal system.

# FREE AT LAST

## Your Civil Rights

■

"What is striking is the role legal principles have played throughout America's history in determining the condition of Negroes. They were enslaved by law, emancipated by law, disenfranchised and segregated by law; and, finally, they have begun to win equality by law."

—JUSTICE THURGOOD MARSHALL, speech on the occasion of the two-hundredth anniversary of the United States Constitution

## STONY THE ROAD WE TROD: BECOMING PEOPLE WITH CIVIL RIGHTS

From the very beginning, America has been shrouded in clouds of hypocrisy. The self-evident truth declared in the Declaration of Independence that all men are created equal was not so evident when the Supreme Court issued its infamous *Dred Scott* decision in 1857. One of the main questions addressed in this case was whether a black slave who had lived on Northern free soil could sue for his freedom.

The answer from the Court was an unequivocal "no." For almost 250 years, Africans had been captured from their native land and brought to America to become slaves. Although the preamble of the Constitution begins, "We the People," Chief Justice Taney, reflecting on the history of the African people in this country and asking whether this phrase included them, remarked, "We think they are not, and that they are not included, and were not intended to be included. . . . They had for more than a century before been regarded as beings of an inferior order, and altogether unfit to associate with the white race. . . . a Negro of the African race was regarded . . . as an article of property, and held, and bought and sold as such."

The Supreme Court also ruled that the Missouri Compromise, which sought to balance the number of free and slave states, was unconstitutional because Congress had no right to deny white citizens the right to their black property even on free soil. What the *Dred Scott* decision meant was that, under our Constitution, black people were not "people" but property that whites had a right to enjoy wherever they pleased, in free states and slave states. Today, this Constitution, which was never meant to consider us black people as "people," with its attendant amendments, remains the cornerstone of American lawmaking.

During our early history, people of African descent fought numerous battles to become recognized as "people." Almost as soon as one law was declared unconstitutional, one door finally cast open, another appeared and was firmly closed to keep black people from enjoying the same rights and freedoms as those of the white race. Soon after the Fourteenth Amendment was passed in 1868, states once again reacted and began to ratify "separate but equal" laws. In yet another infamous decision, the Supreme Court in 1896 interpreted the Constitution and the Fourteenth Amendment to permit States to pass these "separate but equal" laws in *Plessy v. Ferguson*. The *Plessy* decision would become "the law" for the next sixty or so years.

When the Supreme Court declared in *Plessy* that it was constitutional for states to pass laws segregating people solely on the basis of race, mandatory segregation throughout the country, including the North and Midwest, became more commonplace. What became known

---

### ■ NOTABLE SUPREME COURT DECISIONS AFFECTING THE LEGAL STATUS OF BLACKS

---

DRED SCOTT (1857): *Black people are not "people" under the Constitution.* Blacks are not *people* as that word was meant in the Constitution. Blacks are property and it is unconstitutional for whites to be denied their black property on Northern soil.

PLESSY V. FERGUSON (1896): *Black people are relegated to "separate but equal" accommodations.* Even though the Fourteenth Amendment provides for the equal protection of the laws, state laws providing for "separate but equal" accommodations—like requiring railroad patrons to sit in certain seats based on race—are declared constitutional.

HOLLINS V. OKLAHOMA (1935): *Trial by a jury of our peers finally includes having black jurors.* The Court finally recognizes that the right of black criminal defendants to be tried by a jury of their peers includes the right to have black jurors on the jury. The Court therefore overturns the convictions of black criminal defendants by all-white juries.

SMITH V. ALLWRIGHT (1944): *Black people gain the right to participate in primary elections.* Preventing black people from participating in a primary election, a practice that further stifles the practically nonexistent black vote, is unconstitutional. Notably, even after this decision it remains dangerous for black people to exercise the right to vote, as reflected by the number of murders arising from their attempts to do so.

SHELLY V. KRAEMER (1948): *Black people gain the right to purchase houses in white neighborhoods.* In a residential housing case, the Court rules that restrictive covenants aimed at keeping residential areas segregated are not enforceable.

BROWN V. BOARD OF EDUCATION OF TOPEKA, KANSAS (1954): *"Separate but equal" in public education is declared unconstitutional as black people gain the right to send their children to public schools previously reserved for white children.* The Court overrules its "separate but equal" 1896 *Plessy* decision, ruling that, under the Fourteenth Amendment of the Constitution, states cannot continue the practice of maintaining separate public schools for whites and blacks. In direct response to this decision, Governor Oliver Faubus of Arkansas closes all the schools in Little Rock to protect white

---

*continued*

---

■ **NOTABLE SUPREME COURT DECISIONS AFFECTING THE LEGAL STATUS OF BLACKS** *(continued)*

---

children from black ones. The schools are closed for an entire school year until the Supreme Court orders them to reopen.

BOYNTON V. VIRGINIA (1960): *The "separate but equal" doctrine is successfully attacked in interstate commerce as black people gain the right of access to the same accommodations as white people.* The Court, ruling that buses and trains traveling through different states are "interstate transportation," uses its power under the commerce clause to determine that they have to be integrated. This decision leads to the Freedom Rides of the 1960s, in which black and white activists ride together throughout the South, forcing local governments to either implement this decision or openly refuse. Incidentally, the riders are met with great resistance and, despite the Court's decision, several riders are jailed under outdated state laws.

---

as *Jim Crow* laws gained an even firmer footing in the South. "Separate but equal" was quickly translated into separate but unequal, as blacks were banned altogether from certain places, and relegated to the less desirable portions of others (like the balconies of movie theaters). The entire American legal system, from the lawmakers who drafted these laws, to the police officers who enforced them, to the judges who interpreted them and declared them constitutional, was involved.

Crucial to understanding the legal plight of blacks is recognizing, as Thurgood Marshall reflected, how "the law" has had a powerfully negative impact on the basic civil rights of black people. When we joined with sympathetic whites to integrate interstate transportation throughout the South, it was "the law" we had to confront. Police officers used water hoses and tear gas to disperse nonviolent protesters and permitted angry white mobs to openly assault us. When the bus boycott began in Montgomery, Alabama, in late 1955, "the law" arrested many organizers on random charges just to thwart our efforts. And in 1956, when Governor Oliver Faubus of Arkansas refused to implement a school district's desegregation plan, he used "the law," and the strength of the state's National Guard, to keep black children out of white schools.

As a direct result of these events and many others in American history, "the law" has now been changed and strengthened. Racist whites who purposefully read the Fourteenth Amendment to prevent blacks from enjoying basic civil rights must now contend with several civil rights statutes passed to shore up unintended loopholes. Now the Fourteenth Amendment, federal civil rights statutes, and state civil rights statutes protect the civil rights of blacks. But, as mentioned earlier, you only truly have those rights that you demand. The following sections show you how to demand your civil rights.

## WHAT ARE THESE RIGHTS WE CALL "CIVIL" RIGHTS AND WHICH LAWS PROTECT THEM?

OK, I am not trying to bust anybody out, but if the shoe fits. . . . My people, every time somebody does something to you that you don't like, that does not mean he or she has violated your civil rights. I know, people violate our civil rights so much we think that every violation of a right has gotta be of one of those "civil" rights. But that just ain't so. Civil rights are personal liberties that the federal and state governments, and in a few rare instances private individuals or organizations, must respect. They are those personal freedoms either contained in our Constitution or derived from the Constitution. In the next few sections, I'm going to break down just what "civil" rights are so if anyone ever accuses you of violating her civil rights you can "smoke 'em with your intellect" and tell her she is clearly on the wrong page.

Civil rights are found in the United States Constitution, state constitutions, and a number of statutes passed by both our federal and state governments. Many people have heard of the rights found in the Fifth and Fourteenth Amendments that prohibit the government from

---

■ **WHAT IS A CIVIL RIGHT?**

---

Many people think of "civil" rights as the rights black people fought for during the civil rights movements, like the right to be free from racial discrimination in public places, housing, employment, and education. These are civil rights. But the term "civil rights" is actually a little broader. Civil rights are civil liberties, which are personal rights guaranteed by the Constitution. These include the right to vote, the right to free speech, and the right to be free from racial discrimination.

Broadly speaking, civil rights include all personal rights guaranteed and protected by the Constitution. Unless there is a specific statute that provides otherwise, only a government can violate civil rights. For example, say you work for a private fast-food chain. According to Title VII of the Civil Rights Act of 1991, which prohibits racial discrimination in employment, your boss would violate your civil rights if she refused to promote you because of your race. She would not violate your civil rights for discriminating against you on other bases, like negative information in a credit report. Nor would there be a violation of your civil rights if you were fired and had problems getting unemployment compensation benefits. Your right to unemployment benefits, as well as other government benefits, is a "statutory right," a right provided for in a state or federal statute, as opposed to a "civil right."

---

denying us life, liberty, or property without due process. These amendments are basically the same, except the Fifth Amendment applies to the federal government and the Fourteenth Amendment applies to the state governments (see sidebar, "Blacks, Civil Rights, and the Constitution: The Road to Personhood").

In this country, it is widely accepted that government should not infringe on a person's right to life, liberty, and her pursuit of happiness. Laws protecting civil rights therefore protect basic rights of citizenship and personhood. Generally, these laws are found in the Civil Rights Act of 1866, the Civil Rights Act of 1871, the Civil Rights Act of 1964, and the Civil Rights Act of 1991.

The Civil Rights Act of 1866 was enacted to give all persons the same set of rights "as is enjoyed by white citizens." Sometimes referred to as "1981" rights, short for the section of the United States Code it appears in (42 USC § 1981), this law provides that all persons, including black people, have the right to make and enforce contracts, sue, and be subjected to other punishments and enjoy the same privileges as white citizens. Part of this same Act are "1982" rights, listed at 42 USC § 1982, which give all citizens the same property rights as white citizens, including the right to inherit, purchase, sell, and lease property. These statutes, as suggested by the language used in them, were specifically passed to give blacks the same rights as white citizens.

The Civil Rights Act of 1871 was enacted to further protect the rights of black people by specifically providing that individuals may sue the government for damages when their rights are violated. Civil rights attorneys rely on a section of this Act, Section 1983 (42 USC § 1983), perhaps more than any other statute in cases involving a state entity that has deprived someone of rights "under color of law," as in police brutality cases. As you may expect, these rights are often referred to as "1983" rights. This section allows a private individual—a person like you or me—suing in his own name, rather than a government entity suing on behalf of the people, to sue the government for depriving him of his civil rights. It provides that a private individual may sue for damages, including monetary damages, when a government official "under color of any statute . . ." deprives a person of "any rights, privileges or immunities secured by the Constitution." Along with this section are "1985" rights, 42 USC § 1985(c), which permits actions to be brought against two or more people or agencies or organizations that come together to conspire to deprive a person of equal protection, privileges, or immunities under the law.

While most of our discussion of civil rights relates to civil remedies, there are some federal civil rights statutes that provide for criminal penalties when civil rights have been violated. For example, after the all-white jury acquitted the white police officers for beating black motorist Rodney King, the federal government intervened and brought federal criminal civil rights actions against the police officers. Under 18 USC § 242, a person may be subjected to fine or imprisonment if "under color of law" he or she "willfully deprives another" of any rights protected by the Constitution or federal statutes, on account of color or race. Just like the civil statute, there is also a criminal counterpart, 18 USC § 241, that provides that conspiracies to deprive a person of such rights "under color of law" may result in criminal penalties. During seminars I have given on police brutality, people have often asked me what they can do to the person responsible for the death or injuries of their loved ones. They tell me straight up that they are not interested in money, but want the offending officer to pay for what he has done. These statutes are the answer.

Unfortunately, though, private citizens like you or me cannot bring a criminal action against anyone. All we can do is pressure federal prosecutors to bring an action against the responsible government officials. If they have enough facts to get a conviction, they should bring this type of action. If you find yourself in this situation, gather as many facts as possible to make it difficult for prosecuters to ignore your claims. Your only other alternative, as unsavory as it may sound, is to file a civil action for monetary damages and an injunction against the offending officials and government entity. And don't deny the power of money— while you won't be bringing the action to seek monetary damages, if you are successful and the government is forced to pay a significant monetary award, you may serve to change government policies and procedures that could save someone else's loved one.

The above statutes, all enacted during the nineteenth century, deal with government agencies and officials. During the twentieth century, statutes were enacted that deal with the problem of private discrimination—discrimination from private individuals or organizations rather than those affiliated with a local, state, or federal government. The Civil Rights Act of 1964 is the most sweeping civil rights law ever passed. The Public Accommodations Title of the Civil Rights Act of 1964, 42 USC § 2000a, prohibits discrimination in public accommodations, which include hotels, motels, concert halls, theaters, and shopping malls. Places like the Holiday Inn, which used to have a "whites only" policy, can now no longer refuse to provide blacks with rooms. Title III of the Act prohibits discrimination in public facilities like jails and courthouses. Title IV prohibits racial discrimination in public schools, and Title VII prohibits racial discrimination in employment.

The Voting Rights Act of 1965, 42 USC § 1973, was a further attempt to ensure that blacks have the right to vote. Portions of this statute prohibit the use of literacy tests like those used in Alabama prior to this Act. Title VIII of the 1968 Civil Rights Act contains fair housing protections. This law prohibits private white individuals and entities from refusing to sell or rent housing to blacks. Also part of the Civil Rights Act of 1968 is a "violent interference" prohibition. This prohibits a person, even a government official, from "violently" interfering with a person's enjoyment of his civil rights.

The Civil Rights Act of 1991 was passed to strengthen other civil rights laws and to increase civil rights protections in the employment arena. If you are wondering why this Act was needed to strengthen rights that had already been guaranteed by previous laws, recall my suggestion in the beginning of this chapter that blacks have historically suffered a backlash once they gained rights. The Civil Rights Act of 1964 "guaranteed" that blacks would no longer suffer discrimination on the basis of race. But just as soon as this law was passed, white conservatives obsessed with thwarting the attempts of blacks to gain equal opportunity took to the courts and began crafting legal arguments to convince willing judges to misconstrue the Act to limit the rights of blacks. The Civil Rights Act of 1991 was designed to combat the weakening of civil rights legislation. This Act requires that all federal "laws protecting the civil rights of persons shall be interpreted consistent with the intent of such laws, and shall be broadly construed to effectuate the purpose of such laws to provide equal opportunity and provide effective remedies."

As you can see, your civil rights are protected by a number of different laws. In addition to the civil rights protected by the various civil

## ■ BLACKS, CIVIL RIGHTS, AND THE CONSTITUTION: THE ROAD TO PERSONHOOD

The Preamble of the Constitution begins "We the People . . . " This phrase was interpreted to not include black people in the landmark *Dred Scott* decision in 1857. The rights of black people began to be recognized only as amendments to the Constitution were passed. While some white people believe that these amendments were passed to protect the rights of all individuals, the historical reality is that the rights of white American men have always been assumed and never been contested. The rights of black American men, as evidenced by the laws enacted prior to amendment of the Constitution, have never been assumed and frequently been contested.

### FUGITIVE SLAVE ACT OF 1793

Congress enacted this Act to ensure that slave owners had the legal authority to reclaim their lost "property." Many non-Southern whites tend to view slavery as something that occurred only in the South and that cannot be imputed to the entire federal government. But our laws indicate that the institution of slavery received considerable encouragement and protection from the federal government. It was not just passively tolerated but legislatively protected.

### FUGITIVE SLAVE ACT OF 1850

Congress enacted this Act to give the courts more power to enforce the fugitive slave laws. It provided that more resources be committed to assist slave owners in securing the return of any lost "property." Again, this Act demonstrates that the federal government was heavily involved in protecting the institution of slavery.

### EMANCIPATION PROCLAMATION

On September 22, 1862, President Abraham Lincoln, who reportedly believed in white supremacy, officially made slavery an issue of the Civil War. This proclamation is often misconstrued as the proclamation that set slaves free, and Lincoln is frequently viewed as the man who freed the slaves. But as you can imagine, slavery was not abolished by one proclamation. Slavery officially ended when the Thirteenth Amendment was passed—after thousands of people, white and black, lost their lives in the Civil War, largely fought over the issue of slavery.

### Article I, Section 3 of the United States Constitution (1788): Blacks as Three-Fifths of a Person

"Representatives and direct Taxes shall be apportioned among the several States which may be included within this Union, according to their respective Numbers, which shall be determined by adding to the whole Number of free persons, including those bound to Service for a Term of Years, and excluding Indians not taxed, three fifths of all other Persons."

### Fourth Amendment (1791)

"The right of the people to be secure in their persons, houses, papers, and effects, against unreasonable searches and seizures, shall not be violated, and no Warrants shall issue, but upon probable cause, supported by Oath or affirmation, and particularly describing the place to be searched, and the persons or things to be seized."

### Fifth Amendment (1791)

"No person shall be held to answer for a capital, or otherwise infamous crime, unless on a presentment or indictment of a Grand Jury, except in cases arising in the land or naval forces, or in the Militia, when in actual service in time of War or public danger; nor shall any person be subject for the same offence to be twice put in jeopardy of life or limb; nor shall be compelled in any criminal case to be a witness against himself, nor be deprived of life, liberty, or property, without due process of law; nor shall private property be taken for public use, without just compensation."

### Thirteenth Amendment (1865)

" . . . Neither slavery nor involuntary servitude, except as a punishment for a crime whereof the party shall have been duly convicted, shall exist within the United States, or any place subject to their jurisdiction."

### Fourteenth Amendment (1868)

" . . . No State shall make or enforce any law which shall abridge the privileges or immunities of citizens of the United States; nor shall any State deprive any person of life, liberty, or property, without due process of law; nor deny to any person within its jurisdiction the equal protection of the laws. . . ."

*continued*

---

■ **BLACKS, CIVIL RIGHTS, AND THE CONSTITUTION: THE ROAD TO PERSONHOOD**
*(continued)*

---

**FIFTEENTH AMENDMENT (1870)**

" . . . The right of citizens of the United States to vote shall not be denied or abridged by the United States or by any State on account of race, color, or previous condition of servitude. . . ." By the way, this amendment applied only to black men. In 1870, women did not have the right to vote. It was not until 1920, when the Nineteenth Amendment was adopted, that all women gained the right to vote.

---

rights acts and the federal Constitution are those civil rights protected by state constitutions and statutes. A review of all the civil rights, both federal and those protected by individual states, is beyond the scope of this book. However, guidelines to enforcing those civil rights which blacks are frequently denied are set forth either below or later in this book. (For example, civil rights in employment are discussed in Chapter 3, and your civil right to vote is discussed in Chapter 10.)

## ENFORCING YOUR CIVIL RIGHTS

Both federal and state laws guarantee a person's civil rights. If there is a state statute that provides more rights than a federal statute, then the state statute will govern the particular situation. In a situation that involves a state agency or state officials, like the North Carolina Sheriff's department, you should first seek to address the issue by following state procedures. For example, if you feel that your civil rights were denied by a local police officer, first see if your state Attorney General's office has a Civil Rights Division that can handle your complaint. If the state fails to resolve your problem, contact the federal agency responsible for these issues, which in this case would be the Department of Justice. You may be unsure whether you have a state or federal issue. Often, both a state and a federal agency may be able to address your complaint. When you are unsure, do not hesitate to contact both state and federal agencies. Also consider contacting your local NAACP office for further direction. (Although the NAACP does not provide legal advice, it can provide helpful information and help you determine which agency to contact to file a complaint.) Below are descriptions of actual cases detailing how blacks have taken action after being deprived of their civil rights. Some of these scenarios involve well-publicized circumstances, and none are in any way fictitious.

## DWB (Driving While Black) and Racial Profiling: Presumed Guilty

It's late Thursday night and I'm returning home from an enjoyable night in Windsor, Canada. I live only miles from the U.S.–Canadian border and expect to be home within the hour. As I make my way across the Ambassador Bridge, sipping my warm latte on this cool night, I am relieved to see that the lines through Customs are short. It is only weeks after the September 11, 2001, attacks on the World Trade Center and Pentagon and on other occasions since then I have waited at least three hours to get through Customs. This time there are only two vehicles in front of me—one vehicle, which I cannot really see, and the one directly in front of me, which is a white flatbed truck driven by a thirty-something white male.

Without having to provide any type of identification, the white male is waved through. When I get to the booth, I lower my window and am asked the standard questions: "Citizenship?" "What were you doing in Canada?" Then, I am given several instructions, which include: (1) place your vehicle in park, (2) provide me with proof of citizenship (which usually means provide me with your birth certificate or passport), (3) pop your trunk, and (4) turn off the engine. No problem. Even though the person in front of me did not have to go through the same routine, at that time I think Customs is just randomly checking for contraband. I have no reason to be upset or alarmed.

I tried to comply with these requests as best as I could. I drive a hatchback; it does not have a trunk. I placed my car in park and fumbled for my passport. By that time, one of the officers had exited the booth and traveled around my car with his flashlight, peering inside presumably to check for contraband. I closed my window as I expected to be there for a little while until they had completed their search. The Customs officer in the booth apparently felt offended that I had closed my window. She yelled something to the effect that she was still talking to me. I then, with my passport in hand, opened my door (to exit my car and open my hatchback. I have done this on several occasions for Customs officers who have asked me to "pop" my nonexistent trunk). The rest is a blur.

The Customs officer rushed out of her booth. She grabbed my left arm and twisted it back, grabbing my passport from my left hand. The other Customs officer who had been in the rear waiting for me to "pop my trunk" came around and twisted my other arm back. I was handcuffed, roughed up, and searched. I was escorted to an office where I was detained and questioned for at least an hour.

I did not resist. But naturally I quietly asked, "Why me, Lord?" I am an honorably discharged officer of the United States Army who, having completed the requirements of Georgetown University Law Center, now practices law. I am a citizen of the United States with a valid United States passport and Michigan driver's license. I do not have a police record and I pay my taxes. But suddenly, I found myself, attorney, former U.S. Army officer, and law-abiding U.S. citizen, handcuffed, searched, surrounded, and then detained by United States Customs officers. "Why me?"

The stories of countless other brothers and sisters, anywhere from the straight-up 'hood to the big house on the best street in the most affluent neighborhood, can attest that the reason is quite simple—I am black. Some argue that the black community is less united since improvements gained by the 1960s Civil Rights movement were mostly enjoyed by middle-class blacks. People think that some folks have "forgotten where they came from" and may be part of an "uppity" black crowd. Well, if there is one thing that'll yank your ass back into reality it is the reality of racial profiling. Black is black whether you're a Yale graduate or a jail graduate. Racial profiling sees only color.

In 1992, Washington, D.C., lawyer Robert Wilkins, a graduate of Harvard law school and a public defender, was pulled over by the now infamous Maryland State Police as he and his family returned from a funeral. They were forced out of the car as the officers had dogs sniff throughout the vehicle for drugs. Fortunately, Wilkins sued the Maryland State Police for violating his family's civil rights, and part of the settlement forced the department to track the racial identity of the motorists it stopped for three years. The information amassed proved what most of us already know: Blacks make up a disproportionate amount of all traffic stops. Of 732 motorists who were stopped and detained in Maryland for those three years, 75 percent were black.

In "DWB," his April 1999 *Esquire* article, Pulitzer Prize–winning journalist Gary Webb, who has studied this phenomenon for some time, described the factors law enforcement officers have used when deciding to conduct a stop and search. These include whether the person makes eye contact; whether he wears loose clothing, earrings, nose rings, or eyelid rings; and whether there is a tree-shaped air freshener hanging from the car's rearview mirror, which is supposedly used to mask drugs. Some officers indicate that they will conduct a stop whenever someone appears "suspicious." I apparently looked suspicious when I was stopped at 2:00 A.M. in Alexandria, Virginia, about fifteen miles from my law school's library. I had been studying all day and night and was extremely tired. As I made the turn into my apartment complex, a police officer in a car followed me and turned on his lights. I was detained, only feet from the comfort of my bed, while he ran my information. When he let me go, he told me that I looked suspicious because when he looked my way, I looked away. Apparently, he was taught to look for the factors mentioned above. Most police officers, including my brother-in-law, who has been an officer for over ten years, admit that racial profiling occurs. However, they disagree as to whether it should be legal.

If looking away from a police officer makes people suspicious enough to warrant being stopped, then a lot of brothers and sisters out there can be deemed suspicious. Many of us fear "Five-O"—and with good reason. My sister, who has locks, was stopped by a police officer who had drawn his gun and was waving it in her face. He said she "fit the profile." According to our legal system Jonny Gammage, a motorist who was stopped in a routine traffic stop, was not denied his right to due process even though he lost his life in the process. The problems blacks face in dealing with the police, other law enforcement agencies, and racial profiling are quite significant.

This problem is amplified by the difficulty in tracking the fact that blacks are regularly treated differently from other motorists. In 1999, Congressman John Conyers (D-Michigan) supported a bill requiring that police agencies keep track of the race of the people it stops. The bill was approved by Congress but died in the Senate. Fortunately, some agencies began to amass this much-needed information absent a legal mandate. Conyers has once again garnered support for a new bill and in a June 6, 2001, speech delivered to Congress, he reported that racial profiling has "gone from anecdote and theory to well-documented fact." Describing racial profiling as "a double-barreled assault on our social fabric," Conyers argues that support for the bill is now overdue.

Since September 11, 2001, many of us fear how the terrorist attacks may affect not only this bill but other rights seeking to protect blacks against racial profiling. During times like these we are at an even greater risk of having our rights violated. It is important for us to take action like Robert Wilkins and protect both others and ourselves from this "assault on our social fabric." Here is a list of things you can do when you have been stopped for "driving while black," or have been the victim of racial profiling:

1. Be calm. Remember that, although an officer may be in the process of violating your rights, there are certain steps you can take

after the incident to vindicate yourself. Many of us have had to endure more than our share of stops, and at some point you may find it hard to keep your composure. It's one thing to remain calm during the first or second stop but, for me at least, by the time I had been stopped for the seventh time in two weeks, I was beginning to lose my patience. But try not to. Your life depends on your ability to remain calm.

2. Take notes. During the incident, take mental notes. When I entered the area where Customs detained me, I immediately looked for a clock so I could pinpoint precisely what time I was being detained. When I finally heard the words, "you're free to leave," I again looked at the clock. I also got the name of the officer who questioned me and attempted to get the name of the arresting officers. Later, I wrote down this information.

3. Report the incident. I am not saying you should report incidents when you have been stopped or detained and you believe the officers acted legitimately. But report incidents where you believe you have been subjected to racial profiling. I have made this suggestion before at seminars and some people have responded that if they reported every single incident they would be making reports constantly. Hey, maybe that's what it will take. But since you likely won't make a complaint every single time, I do encourage you to make a complaint in cases you suspect are blatant. For example, say you are traveling from Jamaica to Atlanta. When you arrive at Customs at Hartsfield International Airport, you notice that all of the black travelers you flew with are now being subjected to extensive searches. You should write a letter to the customs director and send a copy to the U.S. Department of Justice, Civil Rights Division. It should include the date, time, and location of the searches and indicate that you believe these searches were based on race and a violation of your civil rights (see the Resource Guide for a sample letter).

4. Document the incident. Don't expect your report to the offending agency to have any observable effect. But if you do send a letter

like the sample letter, consider also sending a copy of the letter to
the American Civil Liberties Union (ACLU) and your local
NAACP office. The ACLU Web site (www.aclu.org) has a specific
complaint form for racial profiling that you may file on-line.

5. Get more information. Submit a Freedom of Information Act
   (FOIA) request to obtain more information on your particular
   situation and on stops in general. Because you will be submitting
   this request to a law enforcement agency, you may find that the
   request is denied or that you receive limited information. But it is
   still worthwhile to seek the information. After my incident with
   Customs, I quickly sent a FOIA request to the Port Director (see
   sample letters in the Resource Guide).

6. Consider filing a lawsuit. If the situation is serious, consider filing a lawsuit against the agency and officers for violating your
   civil rights. The lawsuit would likely be what is referred to as a
   "Section 1983 suit" and would allege that your constitutional
   rights to liberty were violated when the government official
   detained you without cause. If you truly are the victim of racial
   profiling, then it has happened to many other black people,
   maybe even hundreds or thousands in the same location. A case
   like this could be quite extensive and retaining a civil rights
   lawyer could benefit you, others who have suffered, and ultimately your community.

Racial profiling is not something we should have to tolerate. Some
people, even black people, have argued that racial profiling is or should
be legal because blacks commit a disproportionate number of crimes.
To use a phrase worn out by my kinfolk, "Now, ain't that just puttin'
the cart before the horse." Racial profiling is generally described as stop-
ping a person based on that person's race. If you put the cart before the
horse and think that blacks are more likely to be guilty, then stop them
75 percent of the time and at a much greater proportion than you do
whites, you will find ample support for your argument that blacks commit more crimes. During my time at Duke University, I saw more whites

commit crimes. I never saw Grant Hill drink alcohol or do anything illegal for that matter. But I saw several white guys using drugs. Racial profiling means that Grant Hill, a.k.a. Mr. Goodboy, gets pulled over. At the same time, white boys high on drugs are permitted to freely enjoy their constitutional rights and move around in this society without the least bit of suspicion.

We have these rights too. As black folks, we must demand that they are respected. In the case of racial profiling, to help ensure that both your rights and those of other minorities in your community are protected, you should at the very least report suspicious incidents to the proper organizations. By doing so, you will be amazed how often you discover that the "isolated" incident you endured has actually happened numerous times to other people just like you.

### Police Brutality and Excessive Force

Have you ever heard of a white man being beaten to death by a group of black police officers, who were then acquitted of any wrongdoing by an all-black jury? No, you have not. But you probably have heard of a black man being beaten to death by a group of white police officers, who were then acquitted by an all-white jury of any wrongdoing. Jonny Gammage, Dion Hinnant, Michael Taylor, and Edward Mallet are just a few young black men who were denied their right to life without due process in the name of giving police officers the undeniable right to kill.

Police brutality, or, as our legal system calls it, "excessive force," is a problem that the black community has had to contend with for years. During my work with this issue, I had the opportunity to deliver a seminar for Amnesty International with Ronald Hampton, a retired police officer who has served as the executive director of the National Black Police Association. Hampton has suggested that these cases exist due to the prevalence of racism, which he characterizes as an "endemic disease" in our police departments. Both Hampton and other black police officers have suggested that our legal system unfortunately protects those few police officers who regularly use excessive force.

In excessive force cases, our legal system, including police departments and courts, protects police officers, not victims. The phrase
"excessive force" is defined as the use of more force than necessary to
arrest a person. Unfortunately, the term "arrest" has been interpreted
to mean "dead or alive," and police officers have been able to legally
arrest a person by killing him. So, even though the Fifth Amendment of
the United States Constitution states that "no person . . . shall be
deprived of life . . . without due process of law," our United States
Supreme Court has ruled that excessive force cases must be analyzed by
using the Fourth Amendment. This amendment states that the "right of
the people to be secure in their persons . . . against unreasonable searches
and seizures, shall not be violated." By relying on the Fourth Amendment, the Court has ruled that excessive force cases must be judged by
determining whether the search or seizure was "unreasonable."

Take the case of brother Gammage, for example, a black man
allegedly pulled over because he was driving erratically. The court will
instruct a jury to determine if the seizure of his life was "unreasonable"
in order to find the police officers were at fault. It is hard to accept that
killing a citizen in an ordinary traffic stop of this kind could ever be
reasonable, but this is the way the law works today.

What can we do about this? First, in terms of our own safety, it
is extremely important that we understand and remember that the law
in excessive force cases does not side with the victims. This has made
some police officers perfectly comfortable with using excessive force.
They know the law is on their side. So, even though they could arrest
you without pushing, shoving, and roughing you up, they do it because
they can.

While safety is of paramount importance during an incident of
excessive force, once the incident is over, report it. Because "excessive
force" is generally defined as using more force than necessary to arrest
a person, officers can be guilty of using excessive force in various con-
texts. One police officer confided in me that he believes an officer uses
excessive force when he uses vulgar and/or derogatory language, unnec-

essarily pushes and shoves people especially when handcuffing them, or physically assaults the person by hitting and beating him. Naturally, the steps you will take will depend on the seriousness of the incident. However, if we are going to combat this evil as a community, it is important to report these incidents: to the local police department, the Civil Rights Division of your state's attorney general's office, and the following organizations:

**United States Department of Justice**
Civil Rights Division
Criminal Section
10th Street & Constitution Avenue, NW
Washington, DC 20530
(202) 514-1412
(800) 869-4499
Fax: (202) 514-3003
www.usccr.gov

**NAACP (National Association for the Advancement of Colored People)**
4805 Mount Hope Drive
Baltimore, MD 21215
(410) 521-4939
(877) NAACP-98
www.naacp.org

**ACLU (American Civil Liberties Union)**
Public Education Department
132 W. 43rd Street
New York, NY 10036
(212) 944-9800, ext. 422
Fax: (212) 869-9065
www.aclu.org

**National Black Police Association**
3251 Mt. Pleasant Street, NW
Washington, DC 20010-2103
(202) 986-2070
www.blackpolice.org

**Rainbow/PUSH Coalition**
930 East 50th Street
Chicago, IL 60615
(773) 373-3366
Fax: (773) 373-3571
www.rainbowpush.org

If you feel that the incident was serious enough—for example, you were beaten by police officers and now have medical bills due to their conduct—consider suing the police. Hire an attorney, who will likely file a suit not only for monetary damages but also for "injunctive" relief to prevent the police officers from continuing to engage in this type of conduct.

Even if you have never been the victim of police brutality or excessive force, you can still take steps in your community to combat this problem. Some communities have called for greater accountability of its police officers and have instituted civilian review boards. These boards operate on various levels. They frequently try to coerce police departments into keeping detailed records of all alleged uses of excessive force. By doing this, both the police department and the board can readily pinpoint repeat offenders. The boards' aim is to hold individual officers, their supervisors, and the department accountable for these incidents.

Also consider participating in community education workshops designed to inform people how to remain safe when confronted by the police. The National Black Police Association publishes a pamphlet that offers instruction on how to keep incidents from escalating.

## Accommodations

Picture this. A group of black coworkers head to an all-night restaurant before work to get breakfast. They're waiting when an all-white group of their coworkers show up. The white group gets seated. The black group is forced to wait, and wait, and wait. When they finally get seated, the service is terrible and, unlike the white coworkers who were served quickly and able to return to work on time, the black group is now about to be late for work. The group didn't think much about the incident the first time it happened, but it kept happening again, and again, and again.

Another group of coworkers, this time black and white, go to the same restaurant. Reportedly, one of the restaurant employees tells them they are out of food. The manager tells the group they "don't look right together" and says the restaurant is closed. The employees refuse to serve them.

Another group of friends go to a private club. The group includes two white people and three black people. The white people are permitted to enter, but the black people are asked to wait outside. A man, proudly displaying a KKK pin on his jean jacket, tells the black people it is for their own protection.

The Public Accommodations Act, passed as a part of the Civil Rights Act of 1964, was designed to deal with the first two scenarios. This Act forbids public accommodations, which include restaurants, hotels, ski resorts, and movie theaters, from discriminating against people based on race. So, in the first two instances, both groups could sue the restaurant for racial discrimination.

The third instance, which involved a private club, is different. Because the United States Constitution protects the freedom of private individuals to associate with whomever they please, the federal government cannot pass a statute to force white people to let black people into their private clubs. Some organizations have either tried to pretend they are private, or have actually become private, just to keep black people out. To be successful, the organization must be truly private. It can't call itself private, then let every Tom, Dick, and Harry in while keeping the brother man out. If it does and gets sued, it will be treated just like other public accommodations and found liable for race discrimination.

As is true for racial profiling, your complaints are especially valuable because they can help demonstrate a pattern of discrimination at an establishment. To file a complaint, contact your state's attorney general's office, as well as your region's United States attorney general's office. You may also want to send a letter to the local media, like a local newspaper or radio hosts. Negative publicity can be an effective way of motivating establishments to change their policies.

## Housing

During the late 1960s to early 1970s, my father worked for the Southern Regional Council (SRC), a nonprofit organization in Atlanta, Georgia. He likes to hold onto things, and years later I discovered that he had an official poster with a circle, a lightning bolt down the center, and the words "ZONED AS A WHITE COMMUNITY." This, he told me, was just one of the posters SRC members removed as they tried to end racial discrimination in housing.

They were backed by a statute called the Fair Housing Act, which is part of Title VIII of the Civil Rights Act of 1968. This Act doesn't just prohibit racial discrimination in the sale or leasing of housing. It also prohibits discrimination in the financing of housing. Like private accommodations, there are certain instances where a private party can legally engage in racial discrimination. However, these situations are limited and most people who sell, buy, or lease housing are covered by the Act.

Here are a few things the Fair Housing Act prohibits:

1. Claiming a house for sale is sold just because a black person asks about the house
2. Refusing to provide home loans to people because they are black or because they want to purchase a home in a "black" area

3. Refusing to rent an apartment because a person is black
4. Making housing available but only on different terms to blacks—like increasing the sale price or requiring a larger down payment than they would from others
5. Advertising housing for sale but limiting it on a racial basis

Contact your local Fair Housing Enforcement Center of the Department of Housing and Urban Development (HUD) to report any of these types of discrimination. You can get more information on how to file a complaint by contacting the HUD Housing Discrimination Hotline at (800) 669-9777. The national HUD office can be reached at:

**U.S. Department of Housing and Urban Development**
Office of Fair Housing and Equal Opportunity
451 7th Street, SW, Room 5204
Washington, DC 20410-2000
(202) 619-8041
(800) 669-9777
TDD (800) 927-9275
Fax: (202) 708-1425

There may be private nonprofit organizations in your area, like the Southern Regional Council, that can assist you if you have been discriminated against when seeking housing. Two national organizations you may wish to contact are:

**National Fair Housing Alliance**
927 15th Street, NW
Washington, DC 20005
(202) 898-1661
Fax: (202) 371-9744
www.nationalfairhousing.org

**National Housing Law Project**
614 Grand Avenue, Suite 320
Oakland, CA 94610
(510) 251-9400
Fax: (510) 451-2300
www.nhlp.org

**National Low Income Housing Coalition**
1012 14th Street, NW, Suite 610
Washington, DC 20005
(202) 662-1530
Fax: (202) 393-1973
www.nlihc.org

If you believe the racial discrimination you have suffered is part of an ongoing problem, contact the United States Department of Justice. Say you discover an apartment complex refuses to rent to black people. The complex advertises vacancies, but whenever you or some of your black friends ask to see an apartment, the complex says it doesn't have any vacancies. And yet every Saturday during the summer you see white people moving into the complex. The U.S. Department of Justice (DOJ) does not handle all claims of racial discrimination in housing, but these types of cases suggest that there is a "pattern and practice" of discrimination, which it does handle. That office can be reached at:

**U.S. Department of Justice Civil Rights Division**
Housing and Civil Enforcement Section
P.O. Box 65998
Washington, DC 20035-5998
(202) 514-4713
Fax: (202) 514-1116
www.usdoj.gov/crt

## Education

> "It is very appropriate then that from this Cradle of the Confederacy, this very Heart of the Great Anglo-Saxon Southland, that today we sound the drum for freedom. . . . In the name of the greatest people that have ever trod this earth, I draw the line in the dust and toss the gauntlet before the feet of tyranny . . . and I say . . . segregation today . . . segregation tomorrow . . . segregation forever."
>
> —GEORGE WALLACE, Governor of Alabama Inaugural Speech, 1963

A 1970 Gallup Poll reported that George Wallace, the governor who stood in the door of the University of Alabama to prohibit two blacks from attending, was the seventh most liked person in the country—following immediately behind the Pope. So, when the United States Supreme Court cases and the federal anti-discrimination laws were passed to prohibit racial discrimination in education, it almost goes without saying that much of the country did not fully embrace integration. And yet as a result of several thousands of courageous people who banned together in the name of integration, Title IV of the Civil Rights Act was passed to prohibit racial discrimination in public schools.

Today, all programs that receive federal financial assistance from the Department of Education, including public, private, or parochial schools, are prohibited from engaging in racial discrimination. Racial discrimination in the context of education can appear in various forms and may include:

1. Segregating you or your child from others on the basis of race, like having seats designated for blacks only
2. Admitting white students who are outside the local school district lines but refusing to admit black students who are also outside the lines

3. Providing poor service to you or your child, like having the bus stop for your child far away from home while maintaining better bus stops for white children

4. Engaging in any other conduct that has the effect of discriminating against you or child on the basis of race, like encouraging only white children to take classes that will prepare them for college while encouraging only black children to take manual labor classes like shop.

The United States Department of Education handles complaints dealing with discrimination in education. You do not have to be the parent of the child who may have suffered the discrimination; you may be a schoolteacher and think that a certain school is acting in a racially discriminatory way. In either case, you should contact the U.S. Department of Education at:

**United States Department of Education**
Office for Civil Rights
330 C Street, SW, Suite 5000
Washington, DC 20202
(202) 205-5413
(800) 421-3481
Fax: (202) 205-5381
www.ed.gov

## Prisoners' and Institutionalized Persons' Civil Rights

Prisoners have very limited civil rights. These rights include the right to be free from cruel and unusual punishment and the right to exercise religious practices such as praying, worshipping with other inmates, and reading religious texts. Any complaint that your civil rights as a prisoner have been violated should be reported to your institution within fifteen days following the incident. If you believe you would somehow be punished for reporting the incident to your institution, report the incident to your area's Regional Director of the Bureau of Prisoners (see Resource Guide). You may also wish to contact the ACLU at:

**American Civil Liberties Union**
National Prison Project
1875 Connecticut Ave., NW, Suite 410
Washington, DC 20009
(202) 234-4830
www.aclu.org

The Civil Rights of Institutionalized Persons Act was passed to protect all people institutionalized by the government, including prisoners, disabled persons, and elderly persons in government facilities. The purpose of the Act was to make sure people who were being forced to live in government-run facilities, including prisoners, certain disabled persons, and elderly persons living in government nursing homes, do not have to live in unconstitutional conditions. While it may be hard to pinpoint just what is an "unconstitutional" condition, chances are you'd know such a condition if you saw it. If you go to visit old grandma in a government nursing home and the roaches there are so big she thought they were baby hamsters and has adopted them as pets, you're looking at an unconstitutional living condition. First, you should report the incident to the director of that particular institution. Write a letter explaining the conditions you believe are unconstitutional. You may also wish to send a copy to the Department of Justice at:

**United States Department of Justice**
Civil Rights Division
Special Litigation Section
P.O. Box 66400
Washington, DC 20035-6400
(202) 514-6255
www.usdoj.gov/crt

Several organizations are dedicated to protecting civil rights. Some of the national organizations dedicated to protecting civil rights are listed below. If you have a civil rights issue and don't know how to proceed, think about contacting at least one of these organizations.

**NAACP (National Association for the Advancement of Colored People)**
4805 Mount Hope Drive
Baltimore, MD 21215
Toll free: (877) NAACP-98
(410) 521-4939
www.naacp.org

**NAACP Legal Defense and Educational Fund, Inc.**
1275 K St., NW, Room 301
Washington, DC 20005
(202) 682-1300
Fax: (202) 682-1312
www.naacpldf.org

**Rainbow/PUSH Coalition**
930 East 50th Street
Chicago, IL 60615
(773) 373-3366
Fax: (773) 373-3571
www.rainbowpush.org

**Southern Poverty Law Center**
400 Washington Avenue
Montgomery, AL 36104
(334) 264-0286
www.splcenter.org

# 2

# CRIME AND PUNISHMENT

## Criminals, Suspects, and Victims

■

PERHAPS YOU ARE one of the lucky ones who will never have to deal with the criminal system, also known as the criminal "justice" system, which for some of us sounds a bit wrong. But most of us will at some time be forced to confront this system, whether it be for a minor traffic offense or something as major as a felony. Unfortunately, many of us first experience the legal system when forced to confront the criminal aspect.

When I told one of my boys I was writing a FUBU-like book about the legal system, he told me that he thought of the "legal system" as the "criminal system." Now, I'm not saying that all black people will at some point in their lives be handcuffed or locked up. But it's more than likely you or someone you are close to will need help in dealing with this system.

To make this system work for you, you must have a grasp of certain key information: who the players are, what the steps are in the process, what tactics you can use to your advantage. This chapter will break it down for you.

## The Players

In no particular order, the players are:

### The Criminal Defendant

The criminal defendant is the person charged with the violation or crime. For the purposes of this chapter, it could be you, someone you're close to, or the person who injured you.

### The Prosecutor

The prosecutor is the attorney for the government. The prosecutor is not your attorney. Depending on where the supposed violation was committed or, in legalese, the "jurisdiction where the crime occurred," prosecutors may handle all types of cases, including traffic citations. Whatever their assignment, it is their job to prosecute. In our criminal system, that means they'll attempt to make you pay the fine, send you to jail, or both.

Sometimes, prosecutors have political aspirations and seek to show how hard they can be on criminals. Or they may already be elected officials with campaign promises to fulfill. If you face a prosecutor who ran a "tough on crime" campaign during which she made a public promise to prosecute each and every alleged drug offender she can, you may have a battle on your hands if you've been charged with a drug offense.

Now, you might be thinking that if our system is a criminal "justice" system, then the prosecutor should try to make sure only those people who are truly guilty of a crime are prosecuted. Think again. Our system is what lawyers call an "adversarial" system, the kind that forces two parties to fight against each other with the thought that the end result will be justice. While prosecutors, especially the nice ones, may be willing to refuse to prosecute you if you can convince them that justice will be served by letting you go, this is highly unlikely. Try stepping to them with the reasons they don't have a case; show them some credible evidence of your innocence prior to your case being called. Then you just might be in business.

## The Defense Attorney

The defense attorney is your attorney. If you are dealing with a basic traffic ticket, then you will need to hire your own attorney if you want one. In cases where you are facing jail time or prison, you have a right to an attorney and if you cannot pay for one you can ask the court to appoint you one. One woman I was talking with recently said to me, "I thought I had a 'right' to an attorney. Why do I have to pay?" Well, my people, there are many rights you may have in this country, but they're not necessarily free. (We now have a right to sit anywhere we want to on a public bus, but I haven't seen the government shell out any money for bus fare.) Unless you are "indigent"—as defined by the court, not by you—you more than likely will be forced to pay for a defense attorney.

In one of the areas, or jurisdictions, where I practice, there is a big sign in the courtroom notifying people that they can use the court-appointed attorney if they want, but that they will be forced to pay for these services unless the court finds they are indigent. Whether you decide to use these services should depend on your type of case. Court-appointed criminal defense attorneys are a lot like schoolteachers; they don't get paid much, but many of them are passionate about their work and good at their job. Plus, they probably have the added benefit of having spent a lot of face time in front of the judge and may know the prosecutor pretty well. If you are unsure about your needs and are dealing with a situation that could cause severe penalties like prison, a court-appointed attorney may be your best bet, even if it is only for a short period of time until you or your family retains an attorney.

Don't underestimate your need for an attorney when dealing with the criminal system. Say you have a basic speeding ticket. You may have heard that an attorney could cost you anywhere from $500 to $1,500. Since you're educated and articulate you think you can handle the situation and keep the money. You might be right. But always consider the costs of proceeding without an attorney.

Chances are, if you are representing yourself, you will be shuffled into the courtroom with a group of other people and may spend an entire day waiting for your case to be called. You may have to take the whole day off from work, which can mean money out of your pocket. There will probably be no chance for negotiating with the prosecutor prior to your case being called. When your case is finally called, there will be you on one side, the prosecutor on another, and probably the police officer who gave you the ticket or had you arrested. The police officer probably has worked with these prosecutors and regularly attends court at designated times to testify in these types of cases. You may get a chance to tell the judge your side of the story—maybe you can offer a Shaggy "it wasn't me" plea—but chances are this story won't help your cause. You will probably be found guilty and forced to pay whatever fine and do whatever time. The damage to your driving record may mean you will have to pay more for car insurance. The money you thought you saved by not hiring an attorney could be spent on higher insurance premiums within a year. Also, the damage to your record could have repercussions if you are faced with another ticket or violation.

A criminal defense attorney is the solution. Now don't think that I'm just saying this because I'm an attorney. Ask someone who has tried it both ways. One of my friends was charged with a DUI (driving under the influence). It was his second offense and he had to spend time in jail. He didn't hire an attorney the first or second time. He told me there were guys in jail with him with their third and fourth offenses doing less time than he was doing for his second offense. They all had attorneys. He lost more money from being off from work than he would have spent to hire an attorney. He did hire an attorney for his third DUI. Had he hired an attorney the first time, he probably would have gotten a lighter sentence in terms of jail time and would have been forced into rehab sooner, which could have saved him from getting these other tickets.

In a perfect system, everyone would be treated the same, with or without an attorney. But our system isn't perfect. A criminal defense attorney is able to approach the prosecutor to negotiate for you. She knows the criminal law in your area. She will talk with you and hear your side of the story. In doing so, she may realize that the police officer who wrote you the ticket charged you with a much greater violation than necessary. Your attorney will then approach the prosecutor and explain that you should have been charged with a lesser violation. The prosecutor may even agree to dismiss your case. Since you have an attorney, your case will be one of the first ones called. Depending on the type of case, you may not even have to miss a day from work if your attorney can appear on your behalf. And even if you do appear, you will probably be in and out of court with less damage to your record and a lesser fine.

If you are charged with a serious crime like murder or attempted murder, I strongly suggest the use of a criminal defense attorney. Remember the brother who was charged with killing the people on the train, Colin "The Long Island Railroad gunman" Ferguson? He dismissed two criminal defense attorneys in order to represent himself. This man was charged with killing six people and injuring several others, all during daylight hours on a crowded commuter train, so there were several eyewitnesses. He tried to use the "it wasn't me" plea, and it didn't work so well for him. Ferguson ended up being sentenced to about 200 years in prison.

I thought his refusal to use the help of two criminal defense attorneys, specialists in this area of the law, was enough to show he was probably insane and certainly too crazy to represent himself. I may not tell you you're crazy for choosing to represent yourself if you're charged with a serious crime, but that's just because my momma always told me that if you can't say something nice, don't say anything at all. Consider this: former President Bill Clinton, a lawyer himself, hired a team of attorneys to defend him. You should at least hire one.

## The Victim

In our system, the victim isn't just who you think it is, the person who directly suffered from the violation or crime. It is also society at large. Our system recognizes that when a person commits a crime, that person hurts our society. Criminal laws are directed at protecting our society. Although an individual victim, like a rape victim, may not want to participate in a case against a defendant, that doesn't mean the prosecutor will drop the case. She may have enough evidence against the defendant and choose to prosecute him in the interest of protecting our society, with or without the victim. Think about murder cases, where the victim is never available. Thankfully, this doesn't stop the prosecutor.

## The Judge

Everyone knows the judge is the person in the black robe. What you may not know is what role the judge plays in the criminal system. Her main function is to oversee the criminal proceedings. In my discussion of the role of the prosecutor I referred to our system as adversarial, with two sides fighting each other. You can think of the judge as a referee. She decides whether the criminal case is proceeding as required by our laws. She makes decisions like whether certain evidence is admissible. These determinations are considered "legal" questions. The judge does not make credibility determinations, like whether the defendant is telling the truth, unless it is a bench trial and the judge is serving in a capacity of "fact-finder," the role reserved for the jury in jury trials.

The best recent example of the role of the judge in a criminal case is Judge Ito in the trial against O. J. Simpson. Judge Ito oversaw the "fight" between the Dream Team led by Johnnie Cochran, and prosecutors Christopher Darden and Marcia Clark. He made legal determinations about whether certain evidence was admissible based on his understanding of the requirements of the law. But he did not decide if Simpson was guilty. That task, as we know, was left to the jury.

## The Jury

The jury is the group of individuals selected from society to serve the court in different roles depending on the situation. A prosecutor may rely on the decision of a grand jury when deciding whether to prosecute a person for a crime. In these circumstances, the grand jury may issue an indictment, which is a declaration that there are enough facts to warrant a trial. In the Simpson case, the jury only had the task of determining whether the prosecutors had introduced enough evidence on behalf of the State of California to prove that Simpson was guilty beyond all reasonable doubt. In some states, the jury can also play a part in the sentencing phase, where it decides the kind of retribution the defendant must pay society.

## The Witnesses

During any criminal proceeding, there will be witnesses. The witnesses for the state are typically law enforcement officers. These can include the arresting officers, those who witnessed the crime, those who helped interrogate the defendant, and detectives who may have investigated the crime scene. If you are the criminal defendant, then you will have your own witnesses. These could include what is referred to as "alibi witnesses," who are people who can testify that you were not at the scene of the crime because you were somewhere else.

## The Court Reporter

This is the person responsible for recording what is said in court. She usually sits in front of the courtroom and off to one side. It is important that you speak loudly enough to permit the reporter to accurately transcribe what you are saying, and that you speak only when it is your turn to speak. If you would like to order a transcript of the proceeding, which is a typewritten version of what was said in court, then you should speak with the reporter (or ask your attorney to obtain it for you). It is especially important to consider investing in a transcript if you have represented yourself and the proceeding went in your favor. If you don't and you need to prove what was said at a later date, it may be impossible if you did not request the transcript within a certain time after your proceeding.

## The Judge's Clerk

This person serves as an assistant to the judge. She is like the judge's secretary. If you telephone the judge regarding your case, you will likely speak with the clerk. During the court proceedings, she makes sure the judge has the right files and so forth to render a decision on the case at hand.

## The Bailiff or Court Officer

The job of this person goes far beyond saying "all rise," as you have seen on television. The bailiff, who is like the court's security guard, can usually provide a lot of important information. She usually knows all of the players. She probably knows who the prosecutor is and what she looks like; she knows who the court-appointed attorneys are for that day; and she usually knows what time you can expect the judge to take the bench.

As soon as you get inside the courtroom, you should approach the bailiff and ask if you need to do anything like sign in. Different courts operate differently and sometimes there may be someone else handling these matters. But the bailiff or court officer should be able to make sure you're in the right place and can direct you to the right person. I overheard one poor guy saying he sat in a courtroom all day and his case was never called. Once he got in the courtroom, he never approached anyone to make certain he was in the right place; he relied only on what one of the court clerks told him at the counter in the court's lobby. After everyone else's case had been called, he discovered he was in the wrong place. By that time, his case had already been called hours before in a different courtroom, and the judge had entered a "default" judgment against him for failing to appear. Now he had to have his matter rescheduled, ask that this default be set aside, and then handle the original matter. One question to the bailiff or court officer could have saved this poor guy a huge hassle.

## Criminal Proceedings

The process of dealing with the criminal system can be intimidating and confusing. Whoever said "ignorance is bliss" definitely wasn't considering how painful it is to not understand criminal proceedings. This pain is a great deal worse than the initial pain of understanding the steps and legal terms of the process. And as you will soon discover, a little bit of information may be just what you need to save yourself or a loved one from unnecessary suffering.

A recent study by the Human Rights Watch reported that one out of every twenty black men over eighteen is in either a state or federal prison. In some states, this figure is as high as one out of every thirteen. This same study reported that most people are imprisoned for drug offenses and noted that whites, who are less likely to be prosecuted for these offenses, are five times more likely than blacks to use drugs. These statistics alone suggest that many of us will at some point benefit from understanding the criminal process.

By now you may be wondering just what exactly is a "criminal proceeding." It's the process the government uses to bring a case against a person for violating a law. The steps in the process vary from state to state. Sometimes the name one state uses for one of the steps is different from the name another state uses for the same step. The same is true for the crimes themselves. Although there are federal crimes, like assaulting a postal worker, most crimes are state crimes.

## Distinguishing Civil Actions from Criminal Actions

There are a few major differences between civil and criminal actions. First, civil actions usually involve a dispute between private individuals

or organizations. The focus of civil actions is to compensate the plaintiff, the person bringing the action, for the alleged wrongdoing. These
types of disputes are usually resolved with monetary settlements or jury
verdicts. The purpose is not to punish the defendant, the person or organization charged with the wrongdoing. Although a monetary award in
a civil case may include punitive damages, which is a large fine imposed
on the defendant for the wrongdoing, the primary purpose of these
cases is to make the person bringing the suit "whole"—as if the wrongdoing had never occurred.

Criminal actions, however, always involve the government against
a person. The government is viewed as being responsible for suing on
behalf of our society to punish those who have violated our laws. These
types of actions are resolved by the alleged offender paying a fine, serving time in jail or prison, or a combination of both. A person has certain constitutional rights in many of these cases due to the threat of
imprisonment.

## A Few Defipnitions

In criminal actions, there are basically three levels of offenses. The main
difference between the levels is the amount of time a person could
potentially spend in jail or prison.

### Citations, Infractions, and Violations

These are minor offenses like jaywalking or speeding. You may receive
a piece of paper with words like "citation," "summons," or "citation
for civil violation," depending on your jurisdiction. These infractions
force you to pay a fine; they should not result in incarceration. (I say
"should not" because I had to rescue a client who was inappropriately
incarcerated for having garbage in his yard. Sometimes, what should
happen under the law is not what actually happens at the police station.)

## Misdemeanors

These are offenses that can result in a person being incarcerated for up to one year. They may be serious offenses like DUI. But I recently handled a misdemeanor case for someone who had been charged for operating a motorcycle without the right type of license.

## Felonies

These are major offenses that can result in a person being incarcerated for more than one year. Felonies are serious charges such as rape, murder, robbery, and kidnapping.

## Felonies vs. misdemeanors

The line between felonies and misdemeanors can vary depending on the degree of the offense. For example, you can be charged with petty theft (a misdemeanor) or grand larceny (a felony) depending on the value of the alleged stolen property.

## A Word About Traffic Tickets and Minor "Criminal" Proceedings

Some proceedings are not necessarily "criminal" proceedings, like those involving traffic tickets. Most, if not all, states have separate proceedings and sometimes separate courts for these types of offenses. Even so, these proceedings, like criminal proceedings, involve a government against an individual.

When you receive a traffic ticket, or if you're under suspicion of a similar minor violation, you have likely received a traffic citation or summons, which is the piece of paper that should list your alleged infractions, or the reason you received the ticket. It should spell out exactly what you need to do to handle the ticket. Depending on your circumstances, you may want to retain an attorney for these types of violations. If you have been cited for any crime involving alcohol or drugs, you should really consider hiring an attorney that specializes in such offenses. Because criminal laws vary from state to state and can change within a state over the course of a few years, a person who practices regularly in this area will be able to advise you of ramifications you may not have considered.

## THE CRIMINAL PROCESS: STEP-BY-STEP

The criminal process begins with initial contact from law enforcement and ends with a person being released from the criminal system, perhaps after serving time on probation or in jail or prison. The steps in the process and the names used for the different steps vary from state to state and also depend on whether the crime is a federal or state crime. Generally, the steps proceed in the manner shown in the corresponding flow charts and as described below.

### Step One: Initial Contact with Law Enforcement

This can occur while driving or riding down the highway, while walking down the street, or while sitting at home listening to music or watching the box. This initial contact is one of the most crucial steps in the process. That's because what you say, and what you do, can and will have significant consequences.

#### If You Are Stopped by the Police While in a Vehicle

Calmly stop and pull over. If it is dark and you are not in a well-lit area when the police initially signal you to stop, then calmly proceed to a well-lit area to pull over.

If stopped at night, turn on your interior lights so the police will be able to easily see into your vehicle. Remain in your vehicle unless the police ask you to get out of your vehicle.

Do not reach for anything unless the police officer gives you this order. In other words, wait until the police officer is at your window requesting your driver's license and registration before you reach for

# ■ THE PROSECUTION OF CRIMINAL OFFENSES

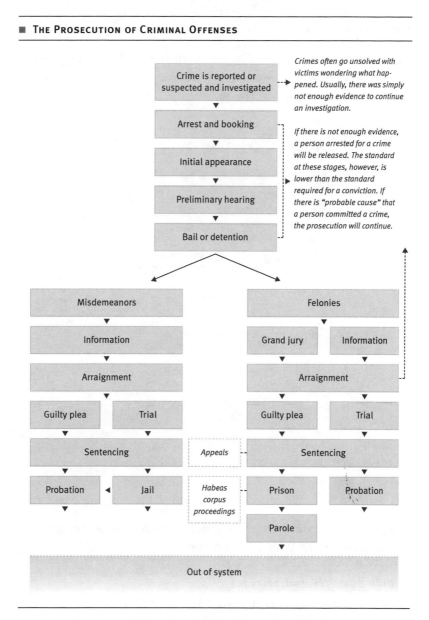

---

### ■ Juvenile Offenses

---

The age of the alleged offender and the nature of the crime will determine if a minor is prosecuted as a juvenile. The process is quite similar to adult offenders, with the exception of the length and type of penalty.

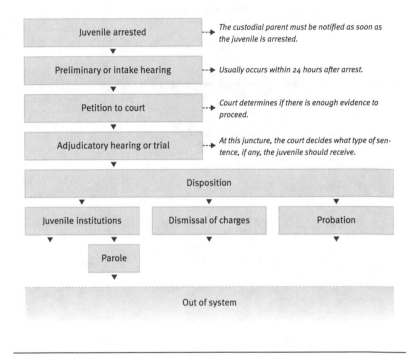

Juvenile arrested → *The custodial parent must be notified as soon as the juvenile is arrested.*

Preliminary or intake hearing → *Usually occurs within 24 hours after arrest.*

Petition to court → *Court determines if there is enough evidence to proceed.*

Adjudicatory hearing or trial → *At this juncture, the court decides what type of sentence, if any, the juvenile should receive.*

Disposition

Juvenile institutions    Dismissal of charges    Probation

Parole

Out of system

---

these items. This could serve to squash any suspicions the officer might have that you are reaching for a weapon.

### *Vehicle Searches and Seizures*

A police officer cannot search your vehicle if you are stopped for a minor traffic offense. The police officer should tell you why you are being stopped. If this does not occur, politely ask the officer why you have been stopped. Generally, a police officer can search your vehicle only in these few limited circumstances: (1) if you are being arrested for a crime that will require the officer to take you into custody, (2) if the area being searched is within the so-called wingspan of the driver, which is any area a driver could easily reach, like the glove compartment of the vehicle, and (3) if the officer has "probable cause," defined as a reasonable basis to believe the vehicle contains illegal contraband.

The police can seize any evidence that a crime has been committed. Say, for example, you are pulled over for a minor traffic offense and the officer spots a little plastic bag of chronic (or Mary Jane for you old-schoolers) on your front seat. The officer can legally seize the bag of marijuana. This seizure is considered a lawful "plain-view" seizure.

Never consent to a search of your vehicle. The police officers may give you the old "if you had nothing to hide then you would let me do a search . . . " line. If this happens, try to maintain your composure and explain that you would rather the officer proceed with a search only after a search warrant has been obtained.

If the police decide to search your vehicle anyway, do not interfere. Just tell the officers that you are still not consenting to the search. Do not help them search your vehicle. (Helping an officer search your vehicle could later be used against you as a means of showing that you impliedly consented to the search.)

### If You Are Stopped by the Police While in a Public Place

Police officers may stop you in a public place for several reasons. Maybe they believe you witnessed a crime and could provide valuable information. Or maybe they think you are the person who has just committed a crime. If a police officer stops you, politely ask the officer why. You can answer the officer's questions, but you do not have to if you do not want to. Wherever you are, you're probably there for a reason. Maybe you're at your favorite club and the officer is interrupting your fun. Inform the police officer that you and your attorney will agree to meet her and the investigating detective at the police station at a later date. The police officer may persist. If so, ask her if you are free to leave. If she says "yes," end the conversation and walk away. If the officer says "no," then she has basically placed you in custody and you are under arrest. Either way, unless the questions are insignificant, like "What is your name?" do not answer them.

Obviously, the general rule about answering police questions should not be applied in all cases. Crimes are solved by a community effort. The police might want to ask you questions like "Have you seen this little girl who disappeared last night?" Before answering any specific questions, you may want to ask the officer what the questions are about. If the police are trying to solve something like a missing persons crime, you should do everything you can to help them.

### Searches and Seizures of Your Person

**Stop and frisks.** If you are walking down the street, the police can stop and frisk you, even prior to asking you any questions, if they *reasonably* suspect that you are engaging in criminal activity and are armed and dangerous. Say it is ninety degrees outside and you have on a heavy winter coat and are walking up and down the street in front of a pawnshop. The officer may reasonably suspect that you're sizing up the place to commit a burglary. The officer can order you to stop, and then conduct a frisk or "pat-down search" for weapons even before asking you questions like "What are you doing here?"

**Seizures.** The police can seize any evidence or illegal contraband it discovers while conducting a lawful search. Consider the example above. If the officer noticed a hard rectangular object that felt like a wrench, she could seize it from your coat pocket. If it turns out to be a container to hold illegal drugs, this evidence could later be used against you.

### If You Are Confronted by the Police in a Private Place

You could be sitting in your living room watching a ball game when confronted by the police. In most instances, if the police are knocking on your front door, it is because they have some serious business with you. The first thing you should pin down is the purpose of the visit.

Once you know why the police are there, decide how to proceed. The police officer might say he has a few questions. Remember, you do not have to answer any questions. Whether you should answer questions will depend on the circumstances. Again, if the officer is asking questions about a missing child in your neighborhood who you happened to see last week, you should seriously consider answering the questions. More than likely, though, the police are at your door to gather incriminating evidence to use against you or someone you know.

### Searches and Seizures in Your Home

The police can only lawfully conduct a search and seizure of your home if they have obtained a search warrant. The search warrant must specifically state the address of your home and list the items the police are searching for. If the police officer wants to arrest someone from your home, both an arrest warrant and a search warrant are required. An arrest warrant authorizes the police to arrest the person named on the warrant. A search warrant authorizes the police to search a place for anything, including people, listed on the warrant.

If, for example, the police suspect that your adult daughter has committed a serious crime and want to arrest her from your home, they will need two warrants. They will need a search warrant that includes your address and states that the police are authorized to seize your daughter from your home. They will also need an arrest warrant that authorizes them to arrest her. Without both, unless you consent, the police cannot lawfully enter your home to look for your daughter.

Always ask to see the warrant. Make sure that the address on the search warrant corresponds to your address. Make sure the person named in the arrest warrant is the right name.

Never consent to the police conducting a warrantless search of your home (or the home of someone else for that matter). If the police insist, and they will, refuse. Police officers do not want you to know that you can say "no" to their so-called requests, but you can. If the

---

---

Many people mistakenly believe that the police must read people their Miranda rights whenever they make an arrest. This is simply not true. Of course, people probably got this idea after seeing countless television shows where police officers hurriedly read these rights to offenders while executing an arrest. Miranda rights, though, are really warnings. The first lines of the rights—"You have a right to remain silent . . . anything you say can and will be used against you . . ."—warn you about speaking to the police. The police are only required to read you these rights, or "Mirandize" you, if they intend to interrogate you *after they have arrested you*. This is precisely why they first tell you you have a right to remain silent. You are then warned that anything you say can and will be used against you. If a police officer is only arresting you, or only asking you questions, he or she doesn't need to read you anything.

---

police ask if it would be OK if they went ahead and searched your home, just say "no."

Do not interfere with any type of search and seizure. This applies both when the police have a search warrant and when they do not. If the police officer has obtained what appears to be a valid search warrant, step aside and permit the officer to execute the warrant by conducting his or her search. If the police officer has insisted on conducting a search even after you have refused to consent, step aside in the interest of your own safety. As soon as you can, contact the officer's police department and report the officer for conducting an unlawful search without your consent.

## Step Two: Police Detainment

During this step, a person is arrested, taken to the police station for booking, and then detained until further proceedings. If you have been arrested, you will be fingerprinted and may be required to provide handwriting samples. You may also be required to appear in a lineup. If formal charges have been filed, you have the right to have your attorney present during the lineup.

The police may lawfully detain a person for a short period of time when they have probable cause for believing the person has committed a crime. A short period of time, however, can be up to forty-eight hours. I don't know about you, but I think two days in the local jail is an awfully long time. Usually, though, this is the maximum amount of time a police department will keep someone without filing formal charges. In most cases, a person is arrested and detained just long enough for the paperwork formally charging that person with a crime to be completed so that the process can continue. (Detroit has criminal arraignments 365 days a year to keep this initial detainment period as short as possible.)

## Step Three: Pre-Trial Hearings

### Initial Appearance

A person charged with a crime may have what is referred to as an "initial appearance." This is a routine proceeding during which the judge

---

### ■ You Have the Right to an Attorney

---

Throughout the criminal process you have the right to have an attorney represent you. If you have waived your right during one step of the process, this does not mean you cannot have an attorney represent you during a later step in the process. Sometimes, a police officer will acknowledge your right to an attorney but will ask you questions even after you have requested one. Police officers might even seek to delay your attorney while trying a second or third time to get a confession from you before your attorney arrives. This may occur minutes or hours after you have made your initial request. Do not cooperate and answer the officers' questions. Police officers know that once your attorney arrives, their show is over. Have a friend or relative immediately contact an attorney for you. If you can't do this, wait until your first court hearing and ask the judge to appoint an attorney to represent you.

---

## ■ THE ROLE OF BAIL AND BONDSMEN

Bail is the amount of money a judge will order you to pay as a condition for releasing you prior to the completion of the criminal process. The amount set for bail will depend on the nature of the crime (e.g., whether it is a misdemeanor or felony) and other factors (e.g., your ties to the community). Recently, I represented someone whose bail was set for $1,000 after he was charged with driving with a suspended license, a misdemeanor. This is a fairly high bail for this type of charge, but he was issued the ticket in Florida, miles away from his home in Michigan, and the Florida court therefore set the high bail to compel him to return and answer the charges against him.

You do not have the right to be released on bail. The judge could decide that your particular circumstances do not warrant releasing you for any amount of money. If, for example, you pulled an O. J. and attempted to flee the police prior to your arrest, the judge may decide that you should be detained until the entire process has been completed.

In some states, you are only required to pay a portion of the amount of money set for your bail. If your state requires you to pay 10 percent of the amount set for bail and the judge ordered your bail to be set at $10,000, you would only need to raise $1,000 to be released. This amount is paid directly to the bond department at the court.

Other states allow criminal defendants to use the services of bond companies (although in some states, like Illinois, bail bondsmen are illegal). These companies usually require the defendant to raise a portion of the bond and guarantee the remainder. The bond company will then guarantee the court the defendant's appearance at the next scheduled court date. If the defendant fails to appear, the company is liable to the court, and the defendant is liable to the company.

Whatever method is used to procure your release, you must abide by its terms. This means that you must appear in court at the time designated for your next hearing. Even if you have an attorney and your attorney cannot appear with you at this time, you must appear. If this occurs, just inform the judge that you have retained an attorney but that your attorney could not appear with you. The judge will adjourn your hearing until a later date. If you do not appear, you will forfeit the amount of money you have posted for bail—even if you can claim it is your attorney's fault.

advises the defendant of the charges, explains to the defendant his or her rights, sets an amount for bail, and sets the date for the preliminary hearing.

The initial appearance is a fairly quick hearing: it could easily last less than five minutes. It is essentially used to address preliminary matters like choosing a suitable date for the preliminary hearing. If you want an attorney and have been unable to obtain one, or your attorney is not present at the initial appearance, explain this to the judge. The judge will make sure an attorney is appointed to represent your interests.

### Preliminary Hearing

The preliminary hearing can be considered an initial screening of the charges to determine if the person charged should be held, or "bound over," for trial. During this hearing, the government is required to produce enough evidence to establish that there is probable cause that the person being charged with the crime committed the crime. Because of this standard, it is sometimes referred to as a "probable cause" hearing. Quite unlike the other pre-trial hearings, preliminary hearings can last a few hours.

### Information

An information is a written accusation made by the government through the prosecutor that is directed to the criminal defendant. It outlines the nature of the charges so the defendant can prepare for trial. An information is similar to an indictment, which is issued after a grand jury has determined that there is probable cause that the defendant has committed the alleged crime.

Many states also use the information to formally bring charges against a defendant. As in a federal information, these are written documents signed by the prosecuting attorney. The prosecuting attorney uses information contained in the criminal complaint as a basis for executing the information. (The criminal complaint is the document prepared by the arresting police officers or investigating detectives.)

### Grand Jury

Formal charges are not always brought by the prosecutor issuing an information. Sometimes, a grand jury will be convened to determine if a person should be "bound over" for trial. Several states and the federal system use grand juries, which typically consist of anywhere from twelve to twenty-three jurors. If you are summoned to be on a grand jury, your task will be to determine whether there is enough evidence against a person to justify a trial. If so, the grand jury will issue what is referred to as a "bill of indictment." If it fails to do so, then the prosecution will end.

### Arraignment

If you are a defendant, this could be your first pre-trial hearing, depending on the nature of your offense and, if it is a state crime, the laws of the particular state. During an arraignment the judge reads the defendant her rights and the nature of the charge. Sometimes, prior to your case being called, you will be asked to read and sign a document that describes your rights. Courts do this to make sure people understand their rights. After you have been read your rights, you will be asked how you plead to the charges. This is a critical question, and your answer will have a significant impact on the remainder of the process—including the appeals process.

### Pleas

Pleas are statements given by the criminal defendant indicating whether she did or did not commit a crime. In most states, a person charged with a misdemeanor will be asked to enter a plea at the first appearance, which is usually the arraignment. At this step, you may: (1) plead guilty to the crime, (2) plead not guilty to the crime, or (3) plead neither guilty nor not guilty but "stand mute" until a later proceeding. A criminal defendant may also offer a plea of nolo contendere if the prosecutor and judge agree to accept such a plea.

You must be aware that a plea could have extremely serious ramifications. I currently have a client who was subjected to an unlawful search, seizure, and arrest. He was driving home and noticed that the police were behind him. They did not signal him to pull over so he continued to his house. He got out and went inside. One of the police officers noticed that he had not completely closed the door to his truck. This officer proceeded to search his entire vehicle, finding a plastic bag with a little marijuana in it and an old gun in his console. The officers then proceeded to his back door and demanded that he exit his home. This was all done without a search warrant or an arrest warrant. Furthermore, the only reason the police officers were at his house in the first place was because they thought he was speeding (they later alleged that they thought he was in a stolen vehicle, but the tape recording to the precinct during this incident suggested that they knew this was not true).

Nevertheless, he was charged with carrying a concealed weapon without a permit—a felony in Michigan. My client's first attorney raised the issue that my client had been subjected to an unlawful search and seizure, but the judge denied the attorney's motion to suppress the evidence. Within a couple of minutes, my client was asked to enter a plea and agreed to plead guilty. Because his record was clean, he and his attorney thought he'd only be sentenced to probation. They were wrong. The judge sentenced him to six months in jail and two years of probation.

Of course my client can appeal his conviction based on the use of evidence found during the course of this unlawful search and seizure. But it will be much more difficult to do so because he pled guilty. As his appellate attorney, I have explained to him that the appellate court would probably agree that he was subjected to an unlawful search and seizure. However, I also explained that getting the court to address this issue after his guilty plea will be quite difficult.

Now, you might just be wondering why the trial court refused to grant his trial attorney's motion to suppress the evidence. I mean, if it is so clear that this was an illegal search and seizure, why would the judge refuse to grant the motion? There are numerous possibilities. One, though, is that the thought of getting another case off his docket sounded much more appealing than granting the motion. I don't know. But I do know that you should not let anyone coerce you into entering a plea. Especially in felony cases, a plea of guilty can have consequences that affect you for a lifetime (in Florida, for example, convicted felons cannot vote). Below are descriptions of the most common pleas.

- **Guilty:** It was me. It's that simple.
- **Not guilty:** This type of plea is slightly more complicated than "it wasn't me." You might think you are guilty of a crime, but guilt is actually a legal determination. To be guilty of a crime each element of the crime must be met. The statute defining the crime may be complex, with several exceptions for various circumstances. After speaking with your attorney, you may learn that under your particular circumstances, you are in fact "not guilty."
- **Nolo contendere:** This phrase literally means "I do not contest the charge." This type of plea is treated almost identically to a guilty plea, but it serves an important function and differs from a guilty plea in at least one material effect. First, people are sometimes inappropriately charged with a crime. Who wants to plead guilty to a crime, even a minor offense, if they know they did not commit the crime? No one. The nolo contendere plea is a way of saying to the government, "My time is too valuable to argue about this. I didn't do it, but I won't contest the charge if y'all just back up off me." Because a nolo contendere plea is treated like a guilty plea, you should be especially cautious about entering such a plea if the charges are serious. Both a guilty and nolo contendere plea can have serious collateral consequences, such as affecting your ability to qualify for government benefits or subjecting you to deportation proceedings.

Only if you enter a not guilty plea will your case then be scheduled for a trial. In all other instances, the next step will be the sentencing phase. This phase can occur immediately. Especially in misdemeanor cases, the judge, after giving you an opportunity to plead for mercy, may sentence you only minutes after accepting your plea.

## Step Four: The Anatomy of a Criminal Trial

If you have pled not guilty, you will be afforded the opportunity to have a jury decide if you are guilty. A criminal trial follows the basic steps outlined in the corresponding flowchart. The trial begins with opening statements. The prosecutor informs the jury what the charges are and what evidence it will use to show that the defendant committed the crime. The defense tries to show why the prosecutor will not be able to meet its burden of proving the defendant committed the crime beyond a reasonable doubt, and what evidence it expects to introduce to that effect.

Perhaps the most important stage of the trial occurs when evidence is introduced. Both the prosecution and the defense can rely on various sources to prove their case. The prosecution may rely on physical evidence like the murder weapon. The defense may rely on testimonial evidence, like testimony made by an alibi witness who says the defendant could not have committed the crime because he was with her when the crime was committed. In most cases, both sides rely on a combination of physical evidence, testimonial evidence, and circumstantial evidence, which is evidence that indirectly, rather than directly, establishes a point.

The prosecution puts on its case first. Using any admissible evidence available to it, the prosecution will try to prove beyond a reasonable doubt that the defendant committed the crime. During this stage, the defense is permitted to rebut the prosecution's evidence through cross-examination. Typically, the defense attorney cross-examines the prosecutor's witnesses and shows why the prosecution's physical evidence should not be trusted. The prosecution will rest after it has introduced its evidence and made its case.

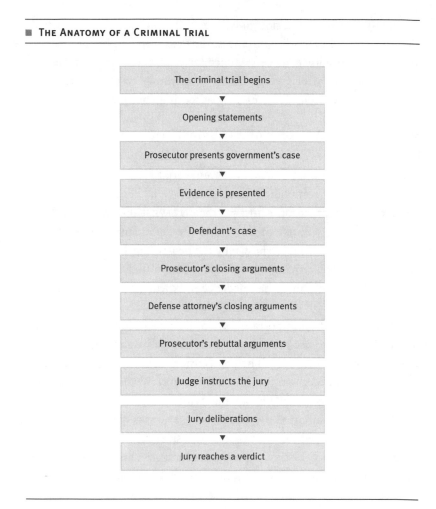

Because the burden is on the prosecution to establish its case beyond all reasonable doubt, the defense does not have to introduce any evidence at all. If you are a defendant, work with your attorney to help defend yourself. You do not have to testify if you do not want to. Listen to your attorney's advice when deciding whether to take the stand.

If the defense does introduce its own evidence, then the prosecution, like the defense, will also have a chance to rebut this evidence through cross-examination.

Incidentally, if you are a witness you can be forced to testify. This can be done by serving you with a "subpoena," a court order executed by an officer of the court, such as a criminal defense attorney, commanding your appearance at a court proceeding. Do not ignore a subpoena. If you do, you can be held in contempt of court. If you have any questions about the subpoena, contact the court or the person who signed it.

Once both sides have had an opportunity to put on their case, the closing arguments begin. The prosecutor makes a closing argument that highlights the evidence that has been presented against the defendant. During this argument, the prosecutor explains why this evidence proves that the defendant committed the crime beyond a reasonable doubt. The prosecutor may also explain that "beyond all reasonable doubt" does not mean beyond *any* doubt. Naturally, what follows is the closing argument of the defense. If the defendant is lucky, the defense attorney will make an effective closing argument, like the "if it doesn't fit, you must acquit" Johnnie Cochran argument, that shows why the defendant is innocent and how the prosecution has failed to meet its burden of proof.

During the final steps, the jury is in the hot seat, so to speak. The judge will instruct the jury on the elements of the crime and inform the jury what it must find to return various kinds of verdicts. Jury deliberations then begin. During the deliberation process, the jury may ask to review evidence submitted during the trial. For example, the jury in the Rodney King case asked to review the videotape of the police officers "subduing" King. As most people know, jury deliberations can take anywhere from a half hour to days. If the jury cannot reach a decision, it is a "hung jury," which is a jury that simply cannot agree on a verdict. Hung juries result in a mistrial.

Hopefully, though, the jury will reach a decision. When this occurs, the jury will instruct the judge that is has reached a verdict and the foreperson will then read the verdict during open court.

## Step Five: The Sentencing Phase

The sentencing phase is the step that follows a conviction, whether it is a conviction based on a guilty plea or a jury's verdict. This phase can occur weeks or months after the conviction. If the defendant has been convicted of a felony, the date for the sentencing is usually delayed long enough for the probation authorities to complete a pre-sentencing investigation report. This investigation serves to evaluate the defendant. The report usually addresses issues like the defendant's employment situation and whether she has a prior criminal record.

Once the pre-sentencing report has been completed, it is submitted to the court for the judge to review. Usually, though not always, the judge alone determines the sentence. In the federal system and in some states like Michigan, judges must follow sentencing guidelines when determining a sentence. These guidelines provide the judge with some discretion by providing maximum and minimum sentences. Typically, a judge will use the pre-sentencing report to determine where along this range the person should be sentenced. The judge may also consider aggravating circumstances, such as whether the crime directly injured someone else. He or she may also consider mitigating circumstances, like whether the person is supporting a family with regular income from a stable and lawful job.

Sometimes a jury will determine the sentence. In some states, if the jury returns a guilty verdict in a murder case, the sentencing phase begins almost immediately. In cases like these, this phase is like another trial.

If you are the defendant, the judge should permit you to make a statement prior to sentencing you. The judge may also permit family members to speak on your behalf as well. In some states, victims and their families also have an opportunity to speak during this phase.

## Step Six: Probation and Incarceration

After the sentencing phase, you begin serving your sentence by either being placed on probation or being incarcerated. If you are placed on probation, you will be required to go to the probation department for further processing. The probation officers will explain the terms of your probation. If you have any questions, do not hesitate to ask the officers at this time. It is in your best interest to get to know your probation officer, so you might as well start at this first meeting.

If you have been sentenced to serve time in jail or prison, you may request the court to give you a few more days of freedom so you can handle personal matters. Prior to your incarceration, try to get as much information as you can about where you will serve your time. You can then provide this information to your relatives and friends. Although you will not have the same constitutional rights as a prisoner that you have as a free person, you still have some constitutional rights. These rights are described in Chapter 1. If you believe your rights are being violated, you should inform your relatives and file a formal complaint.

## Step Seven: Post-Conviction Proceedings

### Criminal Appeals

Only the defendant in a criminal case has the right to appeal. Marcia Clark and Christopher Darden probably wanted to appeal the O. J. case so they could get the court to reconsider that glove that just wouldn't fit. But the government cannot appeal a not guilty verdict. To do so would violate the constitutional prohibition against double jeopardy, which prohibits the government from prosecuting a person more than once for the same crime.

A criminal defendant who has been found guilty has a few options, which include: (1) making a motion to the trial court to request that the trial court overturn the jury's verdict and return a verdict of not guilty, (2) making a motion to the trial court to request that the trial court declare a mistrial and start all over, and (3) appealing the decision to a higher court.

A criminal defendant has the right to appeal a guilty verdict or sentencing to a higher court. However, appellate courts are required to review these cases for "reversible error." This is a high standard to meet: it requires that the court find the error so significant it would have changed the outcome of the case. Therefore, most cases that are appealed do not lead to the conviction being reversed. Rather, the appellate court will review the trial court's proceedings and typically find that if any error did occur, it was a "harmless error" that does not justify a reversal of the conviction.

Consider carefully whether and when to file an appeal. In most states, you can only file one appeal. There are strict time limits—sometimes only days after a final order of conviction has been entered—for doing so. Therefore, seriously consider hiring an attorney who specializes in criminal appeals. Just as in the original case, if you cannot afford an attorney, you can apply to the court to have an attorney appointed to you to process your appeal.

### Habeas Corpus Actions

Habeas corpus, which literally means "you have the body," is a post-conviction proceeding that criminal defendants use to challenge their incarceration (as opposed to their conviction). As with appeals, there are strict time limits for seeking habeas corpus relief. Habeas corpus actions are not criminal actions but civil actions that challenge the defendant's incarceration on constitutional grounds. Criminal defendants often file habeas corpus writs attacking their incarceration by arguing that they received "ineffective assistance of counsel" because their trial attorney was incompetent. These actions are rarely successful, especially in light of recent decisions from our conservative United States Supreme Court making it even more difficult for criminal defendants to use this procedure. And with the passage of the Anti-Terrorism and Effective Death Penalty Act (AEDPA) in 1996, which specifies that relief should only be granted if certain criteria have been met, these actions have become even more restricted.

If you are a criminal defendant and want to begin a habeas corpus proceeding, you must pay close attention to the strict time limits for filing these actions. I strongly recommend that you retain the services of an attorney. Some criminal defendants make the mistake of filing actions without any assistance. This can be harmful since a court could hold against you the number of habeas corpus writs that have been filed on your behalf. As in all stages of the criminal process, you have the right to an attorney. If you are indigent, you have the right to have the court appoint an attorney to represent you. If you are being held for a state crime, closely adhere to the habeas corpus rules for your particular state; they vary greatly from state to state.

For more information on federal habeas corpus actions, you may want to contact the American Civil Liberties Union at the following address:

ACLU National Prison Project
733 15th Street, NW, Suite 620
Washington, DC 20005
(202) 393-4930

## VICTIMS HAVE RIGHTS, TOO

Technically speaking, as part of our adversarial system, the criminal system pits the government on one side against the criminal defendant on the other. The government is tasked with prosecuting the defendant with the interest of the public in mind. In this type of system, the obvious interest victims have in the process can go virtually unrecognized.

The growing victim's rights movement has changed our system to provide victims with more rights. As a victim, you are entitled to have the authorities expend some effort in solving the crime. However, and especially if you live in a large city like Chicago, what might be reasonable for the authorities in light of their other cases may not appear reasonable to you as a victim. If you believe the authorities are not spending enough time investigating your case, contact the police department and find out which detective has been assigned to the case. Try to remain in contact with the detective and provide him or her with as much information as possible. Solving crimes in this country has long been a community effort. If you want the authorities to find the person responsible for the crime, you may need to hire your own private investigators and/or enlist the help of neighbors and others to make the job of the authorities that much easier.

If the authorities locate the people responsible for the crime and convict them, as the victim you have additional rights. In many states, victims are permitted to make "victim impact statements." During these statements, which typically are made during the sentencing phase, victims explain how they have been affected by the crime. Most states notify the victims during subsequent proceedings like parole hearings. In some states, a victim is permitted to speak during these hearings and can make statements to help keep a person in prison. Beyond victim impact statements and notification procedures, there is little else a victim can do.

Remember the family members of the victims in the O. J. Simpson trial, no doubt victims as well? All they could do was be present during the jury trial. Because the jury found that Simpson was not guilty, their only recourse then was to file a civil suit for monetary damages. Because the burden of proof is lower in civil trials, they were able to establish that Simpson was civilly liable for the wrongful death of their loved ones. They were therefore awarded monetary damages for their pain and suffering.

In this respect, they were fortunate. Many criminal defendants are judgment-proof because they do not have any money. If you are a victim of a serious crime, your best bet may be to contact an organization that addresses the rights of victims. This nation's oldest organization advocating the rights of victims is the National Organization for Victims (NOVA), which can be contacted at:

**National Organization for Victim Assistance (NOVA)**
1730 Park Road, NW
Washington, DC 20010
(800) TRY-NOVA
www.try-nova.org

## CLEANING UP YOUR CRIMINAL RECORD

Criminal charges, even those resulting in an acquittal, can affect your life long after the initial arrest. Ask O.J.; people are still trying to squeeze "the Juice." For example, say you were convicted of a misdemeanor for possessing a little chronic back in the day. You are now thinking about applying for a new job but you don't want to have to disclose your criminal conviction during the application process. You might have never even been convicted but you know there is a record of your arrest. No matter how long it has been since the initial arrest or conviction, the government is not going to automatically expunge or seal your records. You are responsible for making sure your record is cleaned up. The steps you need to take depend on whether you are seeking to clean up a criminal conviction or a record of an arrest on criminal charges.

If you were arrested and charged with a crime but then acquitted, you can apply to the court to have the records of the arrest and the charge sealed immediately following the acquittal. If you have retained an attorney, this is something that an attorney may handle for you. However, since attorneys in criminal cases typically charge an hourly fee, you may want to handle this yourself. You can usually get any necessary forms from the clerk's office. You may want to wait about a week so you can be sure the paperwork showing you were acquitted has been recorded. After that, you should be able to submit your application and promptly have it processed as a routine matter.

The more involved scenario involves cleaning up a criminal record after a conviction. In most cases, although not all, you will be able to apply to the court to have records of old criminal convictions expunged after a year or so. I say most because many states will not expunge records of serious crimes like felonies, especially those involving sex offenses. The process of getting a record expunged depends on the court where you were convicted. Generally, however, as long as you've finished your sentence, including any probation, and you've stayed out of trouble for a significant amount of time, you'll be able to have your record expunged.

## A WORD ABOUT THE BLACK RAGE DEFENSE: WHAT IT IS AND WHAT IT ISN'T

> This is a crazy country
> They use terms like
> Psychosis and paranoid
> With us
> But we can't be Black
> And not be crazy
> How the hell would anyone
> feel
> With a mechanical dick
> in his ass
> lightening the way
> for whitey . . .
>
> —excerpt from Nikki Giovanni's poem, *A Short Essay of Affirmation
>     Explaining Why (With Apologies to the Federal Bureau of Investigation)*

The black rage defense recognizes what all of us who are completely honest with ourselves know: To be black in this country can be so painful and frustrating sometimes that we literally have to do all we can to contain ourselves.

Most white people cannot even conceive of being pulled over and stopped by the police eight times in less than two weeks. That's probably more times than many of them get pulled over in a lifetime. And a white person, especially a young white female driving alone, probably never would have been slung onto her car and handcuffed and detained for more than an hour for absolutely no apparent reason. But when this happened to me, I was frustrated for sure but recognized that this was just par for the course when you're black and in America.

But what if I had snapped? That's what Colin Ferguson, the black man who killed and injured several people on a Long Island subway, did. To save his life, his attorneys proposed to use the black rage defense to explain why this man pulled a gun out and randomly began killing people. Ferguson, who was probably suffering from both black rage and mental insanity, fired his attorneys and represented himself all the way to hundreds of years in prison.

The black rage defense, though, when used in the right kind of cases, can be a successful strategy for blacks facing serious criminal charges. An example of a case where the defense was successful is the murder trial of Stephen Beverly. His attorney, Jorge Godoy (a public defender, I should add), along with co-counsel Mark Catanzaro, were able to save Beverly from the death penalty with their skillful use of this defense.

Beverly was a black prisoner at the Bayside State Prison in New Jersey. He was engaged in a relationship with his cellmate and had been informed that the two of them were about to be split up because the relationship was against the rules. One of the guards, Corrections Officer Fred Baker, came into Beverly's cell and told both him and his lover to pack up their belongings because they were being separated. When Beverly, who was obviously upset, asked Officer Baker for some boxes to pack up his belongings, Officer Baker replied, "No, I don't give boxes to niggers."

Beverly went out to the prison yard and dug up a shank to use as a weapon. He then went back inside, found Officer Baker, and stabbed him one time in the back. The officer died from the single wound.

The prosecutor decided to charge Beverly with first-degree murder. Incidentally, prosecutors frequently decide to charge black defendants with the most serious crimes possible, mostly because they are more confident—and with good reason, I should add—that they can get a conviction. In this case, a black prisoner killed a white guard, so the decision to charge Beverly with first-degree murder, even though the circumstances suggested the crime was done in the heat of the moment, was probably a "no-brainer."

During the trial, Beverly's attorneys were able to show a pattern of behavior that had likely contributed to the incident. Officer Baker constantly harassed Beverly, who had become a quiet, model prisoner. Baker regularly used terms like "homos" and "faggots," and encouraged other guards to join with him in degrading these men, which sometimes led them to conduct searches of their cells to harass them. Beverly had complained to the administration on several occasions but his complaints were never addressed. Notably, his attorneys were able to show that the Bayside Prison was poisoned with guards sympathetic to the Ku Klux Klan.

The jury convicted Beverly of first-degree murder. It recognized that Beverly was not legally justified or excused from killing Baker even if he was a bigot. But during the sentencing phase, the jury refused to sentence him to death. Thus, the defense was considered as an extenuating circumstance that served to mitigate Beverly's punishment.

The black rage defense cannot be used as an excuse for committing a crime. I have heard critics of this defense claim that this is precisely what it is—a chance for blacks to get away with murder. This criticism is completely unfounded. Were this true, Beverly would not have been convicted at all. Rather, the black rage defense is a tool that savvy criminal defense attorneys use to explore what may have led a person to commit a crime.

If you or someone you love is a criminal defendant or even in jail or prison now, it is crucial that you have an attorney who is willing to listen and to understand your circumstances. Beverly was lucky. He had a public defender who was willing to try to understand why he did what he did. In the section on choosing an attorney in Chapter 8, I discuss whether or not you should hire a black attorney. As most of us know, skin color alone will not indicate a willingness to engage in this type of understanding. There might be a time when you could benefit from the use of this defense. Should this occur, take this advice: forget about race and just find an attorney you can talk with and be real—and I mean really real.

For more information on the various aspects of the federal criminal justice system, you can contact the National Criminal Justice Reference Service at (800) 851-3420. This service is sponsored by the United States Department of Justice.

## Frequently Asked Questions

**Q:** *What can I do as a criminal defendant if I expect misconduct on the part of the prosecutors or judges?*

**A:** The unfortunate answer to this question is that there is not much you can do. If you are incarcerated, you can file a habeas corpus action challenging your incarceration on this basis. You can also file a grievance against the prosecutor or judge with your state bar association's grievance commission.

**Q:** *I was stopped for driving while under the influence. Can they make me take those drug and alcohol tests?*

**A:** They can't "make" you, but they can coerce you. Most, if not all, states have laws permitting the use of a driver's refusal to take such a test against him or her. Additionally, many states will automatically suspend or revoke your driver's license if you refuse to take such a test.

**Q:** *I was arrested and the police officer failed to read me my Miranda rights. Is that legal?*

**A:** Yes. A police officer only needs to read you Miranda rights if she or he intends to question you. Oftentimes, a police officer will arrest a person based on his or her determination that there is probable cause that the person committed a crime. Say, for example, the person is arrested for driving on a suspended license. Because the officer is fairly certain the person has committed this crime because she or he has probably retrieved the driver's information from the online computer in the squad car, the officer will make an arrest without questioning the driver. The officer therefore would not need to read the driver Miranda rights.

**Q:** *What can I do to help a person who has been incarcerated for a crime she did not commit?*

**A:** Try to obtain as much information as you possibly can to prove this person's innocence. One way to help is by submitting a Freedom of Information Act (FOIA) request to the law enforcement department asking for information regarding the crime (see the Resource Guide for an example). If you are dealing with a federal crime, submit the request under the federal Freedom of Information Act (FOIA). If you are dealing with a state crime, submit the request under the state's freedom of information act. Any information you can obtain to prove the person's innocence can be used in various post-conviction proceedings like a habeas corpus writ challenging the constitutionality of the imprisonment.

**Q:** *What can I do if the proper procedures are not followed during my criminal trial?*

**A:** You can challenge the trial during an appeal or by filing a habeas corpus writ. Whether you will be successful will depend on the type of error that has occurred. If it is a minor error, the court will determine that it is a "harmless error" and refuse to change the status quo. If the error is significant, like the jurors were impaneled improperly because the trial court permitted the prosecutor to strike all black jurors from the jury, it should be considered a "harmful" and "prejudicial error." This type of error can serve as a basis for setting aside your criminal conviction or seeking a new trial.

**Q:** *I told the police what happened after they arrested me, but I didn't sign anything. Is this a confession?*

**A:** Yes. A confession does not have to be a signed written statement. You can orally give a confession that can later be used against you.

**Q:** *What can I do if law enforcement officials have not followed the proper procedures during any step in the process?*

**A:** There is a thing called "power," and there is a thing called "right." Law enforcement officials, because of their position, have the power to do just about anything. But they might not have the right. If you suspect that a law enforcement official has failed to follow proper procedures, say, for example, when you are being subjected to an illegal warrantless search of your home, during this illegal search there is really not much you can do. Later, though, you can challenge their right to conduct the search on the basis that you have a constitutional right to not be subjected to illegal searches and seizures. This is done by challenging the improper procedure in court by filing an independent civil action for damages on the basis that they have violated your rights, and/or challenging the improper procedure during your criminal prosecution.

# 3

# FROM YOU'RE HIRED
# TO YOU'RE FIRED

## Understanding Your Rights as an Employee

■

MALCOLM IS A SINGLE father of two young kids. He is in his mid-thirties, has a high school diploma, and has attended some community college classes. He is bright and energetic and for the past six years he has worked at an automotive parts supplier. Because the mother of his two children—or "babies' momma" if you're new school—had insurance, he decided to opt out of his company's insurance plan, which would have cost him an extra twenty dollars per week. He figured he was a healthy black man who wouldn't need health insurance.

Then one spring, within three weeks, his mother was murdered and his brother was killed in a car accident. He took time off from the job for both funerals but afterward realized that he was having a hard time coping with these losses and needed a few weeks to deal. Malcolm was smart; he got counseling. He also asked his employer for time off under the Family and Medical Leave Act (FMLA).

When Malcolm was ready to go back to work, his employer asked for a fitness for duty statement from his doctor. Malcolm didn't have insurance; he wasn't seeing a medical doctor but a free social worker.

The employer was adamant that Malcolm needed to provide a statement from an "MD—a medical doctor," or risk being terminated. Malcolm was fired when he failed to provide this doctor's statement.

Malcolm went downtown to the unemployment office to apply for benefits, but when the employer was informed about his application, it argued that Malcolm had fired himself because he did not provide a doctor's note. The employer won and Malcolm was out of a job and unemployment benefits.

What Malcolm and many others do not know is that the employer and the unemployment office were wrong. We often think that "the establishment" is right. We figure they know the law better than we do and they wouldn't tell us it was required by law if it wasn't. When Malcolm's employer demanded a doctor's note and said that it was required by law, Malcolm didn't question his employer. And when the unemployment compensation officer refused to give him benefits based on his employer's statements, Malcolm didn't question him. Like most of us, he probably figured that both the employer and the unemployment office must have been telling the truth about the law and must have been following the law.

Malcolm was wrong. And let me say this: it's not that the employer and the unemployment compensation office are "the man" trying to "hold another brother down." It's simply that neither cared enough to do the research. The Family and Medical Leave Act states that Malcolm could have given his employer a statement from the social worker who was counseling him about his losses. Had Malcolm done a little research, such as consulting a book like this one or going to the FMLA Internet site hosted by the U.S. Department of Labor, Malcolm may have discovered this. He could have then informed his employer that it was mistaken, perhaps by giving his employer a printout from the Department of Labor Web site. Had he done this, his employer, who hopefully would have then done its own research, would not have fired Malcolm.

Ideally, Malcolm's employer would have checked its information before making a blanket statement about what the law required and taking action based on its presumptions about the law. In reality, though, employers quite frequently fail to first research an issue.

Don't be a Malcolm. Don't rely on your employer to inform you of your rights. If you do, you may be without a job and benefits required to be provided to you by the law. More than 80 percent of all black adults of working age are employed. Unless your daddy is a former president, you probably had to work to get wherever you are. You should understand the law on employment relationships to protect your job. Many black people on the job have expressed frustration over not knowing the basics of how this relationship works. And, quite frankly, many black people may find that their employer is not going to be too forthcoming in providing them with the information they will need to protect themselves. The following sections briefly outline the most relevant areas of employment law.

## Defining the Employment Relationship

The employment relationship is frequently described in legalese as a "principal–agent" or, in older terms, as a "master–servant" relationship. Either way, the law recognizes that the relationship, even if it is a private relationship, is too significant to be left to private agreements. Therefore, there are some quite extensive laws, both federal and state, governing the employment relationship.

### At-Will Employment
Most of us are what attorneys and human resources personnel refer to as "at-will" employees. As you might suspect, this means that your employment is "at the will" of both you and your employer. If you wake up one morning and on a whim decide that you no longer want to work for an employer, you can quit at your will without penalty. Likewise, if your employer decides that it no longer wishes to retain you, it may, at its will, terminate the employment relationship. As long as it has not based its decision on an illegal consideration, for example, your race or a disability, it can legally decide to terminate you for no reason at all.

There are some limits to at-will terminations. In fact, two states—South Dakota and Montana—actually do not permit private-sector employees to be terminated unless there is just cause for the termination. Even if you are an at-will employee and your employer terminates your employment at its will, this termination may be illegal if:

- You were terminated because you complained about racial discrimination, sexual harassment, or some other issue. Terminations like these are forbidden by anti-retaliation clauses in both state and federal anti-discrimination or harassment laws.
- You were terminated because you reported your company to an agency for violating a law. These types of terminations are prohibited by "whistle-blowers' protection" laws. Whistle-blowers are employees who have reason to suspect their employer of wrongdoing and report them to a federal or state agency for suspected illegal conduct. A person who is terminated without actually making a report may be protected under a state's whistle-blower protection laws if the employer terminated the employee because it suspected that she or he had made a report or was getting ready to make a report.
- Your employee handbook or manual provides for a performance review prior to terminations and you were terminated without such a review. The employer arguably violated this policy by terminating you without such a review. (To guard against this argument, you will find that many employee handbooks include language stating that they should not be interpreted as "contracts." Whether this type of language makes any difference depends on the law in your state.)

## Just Cause Employment

"Just cause" employment relationships require that an employer have some "cause" for your termination. Public employees are, in most instances, just cause employees since a public employer must have cause for firing or disciplining them. Some employers create just cause relationships by placing in their employee handbooks statements indicating that the relationship is a just cause relationship and that you will only be terminated for certain reasons. These reasons may include factors related to you as an employee, such as poor work performance or attitude, or they may include reasons not related to you, such as lack of work. If an employer terminates you for no reason when you are a just cause employee who is only subject to termination based on specified reasons, then you may file an action against your employer based on its breach of this agreement.

### Union Employees and Other Contract Employees

Most union workers—but not all—are just cause employees. These employees, through their union, have entered into what is referred to as a collective bargaining agreement (CBA). If you are a unionized employee, all of the conditions of your employment are subject to collective bargaining. Please be aware that the discussion above may not accurately reflect your situation if you are a unionized employee covered by a collective bargaining agreement or a contract employee covered by other explicit terms. Under your agreement, you may have greater rights than those I've outlined. Under no circumstances should you have less than these rights, because these rights have been provided in statutes for the protection of the employer–employee relationship.

## WRONGFUL DISCHARGE ACTIONS

If you are terminated improperly, you will be able to file a "wrongful discharge" action against your former employer. These types of cases can be difficult to establish, especially if the employer did in fact have some legitimate basis for your termination. Also, an employee has the duty to mitigate her damages. This means that after you are discharged, you must at least go out and attempt to find another comparable job. If you successfully find a job that pays more than your previous job, then practically speaking you will no longer have a case against your former employer. The discharge may have been wrongful. But it will be difficult to establish that you suffered any damages from this wrong. You could still be awarded nominal damages, like one dollar for your worries, but it may be wiser to resist the temptation to file an action if you are better off financially because of your termination.

## FEDERAL LABOR LAWS

Some people are surprised to discover that labor laws apply to both unionized and non-unionized work forces. One person even confided in me that he thought he, an at-will employee at a non-union shop, could be terminated because he was involved in the union. His supervisor had told him that there would be "no union stuff around here."

Federal labor laws, however, regulate both unionized and non-unionized employers, and all employers are expressly prohibited from engaging in this type of conduct. The three main federal labor law statutes are the National Labor Relations Act (NLRA), the Labor-Management Relations Act (also known as the Taft-Hartley Act), and the Labor-Management Reporting and Disclosure Act (LMRDA). These statutes were enacted to protect the ability of employees to organize and become affiliated with a union, to regulate how employers treat employees and unions regarding union activity, and to regulate how employees and unions treat employers regarding union activity.

The National Labor Relations Board (NLRB) is the federal agency responsible for enforcing rights under these acts. It has regional offices in several major cities that process charges over certain geographic areas. This agency plays an active role in certifying a union as the exclusive representative of the employee, addressing issues regarding representation, and resolving disputes concerning unfair labor practices (ULPs).

Employees often have disputes that could be the basis for filing a charge with the NLRB against the employer, the union, or both. In the example above, the employee could file a petition against his employer with the NLRB for committing an unfair labor practice because of his employer's "no union stuff around here" statement. Although an individual like this employee could file a charge with the NLRB, federal labor laws usually protect an employee only if he is engaged in what is referred to as "concerted activity," which is conduct engaged in as part of a group or performed on behalf of the group as its representative. The NLRA does not protect an employee acting as an individual on his own behalf.

Imagine an employer, a local car parts factory, has just become unionized. The lead organizer, Bernard, is a fairly new janitor. After the NLRB has certified his union as the exclusive bargaining representative of the employees, Bernard approaches his supervisor and demands a raise. The supervisor says, "Yeah, right. Not with the union in here." Does Bernard have a basis for filing a charge against the employer for an ULP?

As in most of these types of cases, the answer to this question depends on other circumstances. If the supervisor made this statement because he knew that he was no longer able to negotiate with individual union employees over raises, then Bernard would not have an ULP against his employer. But if the supervisor made the statement to indicate that the employer would not be giving raises because the employees had elected to have a union, then Bernard could file a charge with the NLRB against his employer. This comment, which arguably reflects an anti-union animus, could reasonably be viewed as an attempt to discourage union activity and support. Discouraging union activity and support violates federal labor laws.

## ANTI-DISCRIMINATION AND HARASSMENT LAWS

Employers are prohibited from discriminating against employees. This applies not just to hiring and firing, but to all aspects of the employment process. An employer who is discriminating in promoting or training can also be sued for unlawful discrimination.

Anti-discrimination and harassment laws apply not only to race, but also to age, religion, sex, nationality, ethnicity, pregnancy, and disability. Title VII of the Civil Rights Act of 1964 is the main federal law that prohibits discrimination in employment. Several states have fair employment practices statutes that provide even more protection than Title VII.

## Title VII of the Civil Rights Act

Affectionately known simply as "Title VII," this Act is the most comprehensive federal statute banning discrimination in employment. Title VII, 29 USC § 2000e, was enacted as part of the Civil Rights Act of 1964. It has been amended since 1964 and now is even broader—for example, it now prohibits discrimination based on pregnancy. It expressly makes it illegal for an employer with fifteen or more employees to engage in any type of discrimination based on race, color, religion, sex, national origin, or pregnancy.

Discrimination is interpreted broadly to include "harassment." Therefore, sexual harassment actions against an employer are frequently brought under this statute. An employee can also sue an employer for racial harassment under Title VII.

## Civil Rights Act of 1991

The Civil Rights Act of 1991 gave employees the right to sue their employers under Section 1981 (42 USC § 1981) for post-hiring conduct. You're probably asking, "Doesn't Title VII protect against this?" Yes, it does. But I suppose it goes without saying that what the law says about how an employer should behave and how employers actually behave can be completely different. I know y'all can testify to this one.

At any rate, Title VII was enacted with the rest of the Civil Rights Act of 1964. Blacks did begin to see some benefit from the Act in terms of access to better jobs. But, as we soon found out, being hired was not the end of the story. On-the-job treatment like job loss forced by seniority rights or outright discrimination continued.

By 1991, it became obvious that even though Title VII prohibits this type of conduct, it was not successful enough to prohibit discriminatory treatment after an employee had been hired. First of all, it didn't apply to all employers. Only private employers with more than fifteen employees were covered. The Civil Rights Act of 1991 was enacted to solve this problem.

Unlike Title VII, the Civil Rights Act of 1991 applies to all employers, both public and private, regardless of the number of its employees. It prohibits discrimination based on race and ethnicity. The EEOC does not process complaints based on the Civil Rights Act of 1991. How do you determine which Act is involved? The best way to think about it is to count the number of your employer's employees. If there are fewer than fifteen employees, you will not be able to sue under Title VII because it does not apply. If there are fifteen or more employees, you could have a cause of action under both Title VII and the Civil Rights Act of 1991. You would then want to file with the EEOC.

## Filing a Complaint with the EEOC

The Equal Employment Opportunity Commission (EEOC) is the federal agency that processes complaints alleging violations of these statutes, like a Title VII action for race-based discrimination. So, for example, if you think a company has refused to hire you because you are black, you can file a complaint with the EEOC. Because it is difficult to know whether a company has refused to hire someone because of race, it is particularly important to file a complaint with the EEOC if you think this may have occurred. If a company really failed to hire you because of your race, you might just find that several others have filed complaints as well. Or you may be the first of many who will eventually file such a complaint. In either instance, the EEOC can investigate these complaints and issue what is referred to as a "right-to-sue" letter so you can file a complaint against the company in court. If the EEOC learns that several individuals are alleging a company discriminated against them because of race, it may also institute a class action suit on behalf of all black applicants who have applied to work with the company.

To file a complaint with the EEOC, which is referred to as a "charge," you will need to file within 180 days following the incident. The EEOC will provide you with the proper forms and will also offer assistance in completing the forms. You have the right to have an attorney represent you during the EEOC proceeding, but you do not have to have an attorney. You may want to contact an attorney to assist you with completing your "charge." Some attorneys provide representation at a reduced rate during these types of proceedings. Merely having an attorney present may cause the employer, who may appear without representation, to take you seriously and offer to settle the dispute. It is absolutely crucial that you file within the 180-day deadline. If you think you missed the deadline, though, you should still file your complaint. Before you can file your complaint in a federal or state court, you must file your complaint with the EEOC or the agency in your state that handles EEOC complaints. For more information on the EEOC, including information on the laws it enforces, contact it at:

> **Equal Employment Opportunity Commission (EEOC)**
> 1801 L Street, NW
> Washington, DC 20507
> (202) 663-4900
> (800) 669-4000 (to file charges or locate the telephone
>    number for your field office)
> (800) 669-3362 (information and publication hotline)
> www.eeoc.gov

## THE FAMILY AND MEDICAL LEAVE ACT: FREQUENTLY ASKED QUESTIONS

Malcolm, his employer, other employers like his, and, incidentally, I—until I looked at the law—have all misunderstood the requirements of the FMLA. This Act can be a bit complicated. During a NAACP-sponsored workshop while I was conducting a seminar on the FMLA, I found that most people have a few important questions about this Act.

**Q:** *Which employers are covered by the FMLA?*

**A:** Private employers with fifty or more employees and public employers are covered.

**Q:** *Which employees are eligible for family medical leave under the FMLA?*

**A:** To be an eligible employee under the FMLA:
- You must have been employed for twelve months.
- You must have worked at least 1,250 hours during the preceding twelve months.

**Q:** *What are eligible employees entitled to under the FMLA?*

**A:** Eligible employees are entitled to twelve workweeks of leave during any twelve-month period.

**Q:** *Why would an eligible employee be entitled to FMLA leave under the Act?*

**A:** Eligible employees are entitled to family medical leave for the following reasons:
- The birth of a child, up to the first twelve months of that child's life;
- The placement of a child or parent with the employee for adoption or foster care;
- Care of a spouse, child, or parent who has a serious health condition; or
- The employee's own serious health condition, which makes him or her unable to perform the functions of the job.

**Q:** *Is leave under the FMLA paid or unpaid?*

**A:** It depends. The FMLA does not require employers to provide paid leave. However, if an employer chooses to, it may provide paid leave to an employee. Furthermore, an employer may require an employee to use all of her or his vacation time and sick time before receiving FMLA leave.

**Q:** *What is a serious health condition under the FMLA?*

**A:** A serious health condition must involve (1) inpatient care in a hospital or medical care facility, or (2) continuing treatment by a healthcare provider.

Examples of serious health conditions are:

- Most cancers
- Heart attacks or heart conditions requiring bypass surgery
- Spinal injuries
- Appendicitis
- Severe nervous disorders
- Miscarriages, complications, or illness related to pregnancy and need for prenatal care
- Childbirth and recovery from childbirth
- Alzheimer's disease, clinical depression, and schizophrenia

**Q:** *Can an employer require an employee to provide information on her or his serious health condition?*

**A:** Yes. An employer may require an employee seeking FMLA leave to provide medical verification of the serious health condition. The employer may require the employee to see a second physician for a second opinion as long as the employer pays for the second opinion. If the second opinion conflicts with the first opinion, the employer and the employee may choose a third physician, and the employer must pay for the third opinion.

**Q:** *Does an employee have to take the entire twelve workweeks at one time?*

**A:** No. An employee may take FMLA leave on an intermittent basis. If the leave is for the birth or placement of a child, the employer must first agree to the employee taking FMLA leave on an intermittent basis. If the leave is for the employee's serious medical condition, or the serious medical condition of the employee's spouse, child, or parent, leave may be taken on an intermittent or reduced schedule basis, but the leave must be medically necessary.

## EMPLOYEE RIGHTS PROTECTED BY OTHER LAWS

All states have statutes that protect the rights of employees. In some instances, these statutes may provide greater protection than federal laws. (I say "some" because other state statutes provide *the same* protection as do federal statutes. For example, a state may enact a law providing certain protections and the federal government later enacts a law making sure people in all states receive the same protection. A state cannot provide less protection than federal law.) Several states provide greater protection against discrimination and harassment. Some even provide greater protection than federal wage laws. For example, some states require employers to pay its employees at a rate higher than the federal minimum wage standards. States also have statutes to protect employees from job loss, like unemployment compensation laws, and to protect employees from being injured on the job, like workers' compensation laws.

There are many sources for more information about employee rights in a particular state. You may contact your local bar association. Sometimes, bar associations provide individuals with pamphlets outlining these types of state laws. They may also sponsor workshops for nonlawyers that will answer many of your questions.

You may also contact your state's attorney general office, which can typically steer you in the right direction. One of the best sources is the Internet. Most states sponsor Internet sites geared toward answering these types of questions. To find the Internet site you need, you can access www.findlaw.com and go to the state you are looking for; from there you will be able to find a number of sources to assist you.

## LET'S GET REAL

OK, let's get real. Raise your hand if an employer has ever discriminated against you because of your race. Raise your hand if you're not sure, but you think you may have been discriminated against because of your race. If you're like most of us, you can probably at least raise your hand to the second question.

Recently I told my father a story my cousin Victoria shared with me. A proud graduate of Tuskegee University, Victoria is now a practicing nurse in Mobile, Alabama. After a few years on the job, her supervisor asked her to train a new employee. As requested, she trained the person, and to reward her for her efforts her supervisor promoted her trainee. And yes, you guessed it—the supervisor is white, the trainee is white, and, well, my cousin is not.

In relaying this story to my father, he chuckled and said something like, "the old train and promote scheme. . . . Her supervisor probably thinks she should be proud that she promoted her trainee." Yeah, right. Not Vickie, not these days. She promptly filed a grievance over the issue for racial discrimination. She believes that her supervisor would have never treated her that way had she not been black. Would her white supervisor have asked a white woman to train a less experienced black woman, and then promote the black woman? Never. Not in the Deep South. And probably not anywhere.

This was probably the best way for Vickie to handle this situation. She was working at one of the best hospitals in the area and it would be difficult for her to find a job at another hospital like that. The hospital had a grievance procedure and she would likely have her concerns addressed.

Before you get frustrated about working with a bigot, consider what you want to do with your frustration. Do you want to spend a couple of years fighting over the problem (and I am not at all suggesting that you should not), or do you want to just up and find another job? Or you can quit, sue, *and* find another job. Train-and-promote practices still exist, as do other racially discriminatory practices.

But I want to be real. Right now, at least, it is extremely difficult to prove a case against an employer, especially a racial discrimination case. The plaintiff, thanks to our conservative judges, must provide clear and convincing evidence that the employer subjected him or her to unlawful discrimination. An employer will then have an opportunity to provide evidence that it had some legitimate reason for the action. So, according to the law as it is currently interpreted, an employer who refuses to promote you because of your race, but who could have refused to promote you for some other reason, is protected. The law also questions whether the employer intended to discriminate against a person. I have always wondered about this one. I mean, I could never imagine saying to Sgt. Smith, my NCO at Ft. Bragg while I was an Army cadet, "You know, I didn't intend to not have polished my boots, so therefore I am not liable to you for twenty push-ups." It wouldn't work with Sgt. Smith, but it works for employers in our courts. Under most circumstances, as long as they can show they didn't *intend* to discriminate, they are fairly well protected.

Times have not changed so much that racial discrimination does not exist in the workplace, but there are definitely more options out there for us. You may just want to hop and roll. I left Chattanooga, Tennessee, for the "D" because of the racial discrimination there. I'm not saying you should pack up and leave a state, but you may just want to pack up and leave an employer. It may not solve the problem of racial discrimination, but it may just save your sanity.

## FREQUENTLY ASKED QUESTIONS

Q: *I think an employer refused to hire me just because I am black. What should I do?*

A: File a complaint with your EEOC office. It could be difficult to establish that a company refused to hire you because of your race if the company has several other black employees. But if you are applying for a management position and the company does not have any black managers, it will be easier to establish. When you are just a prospective employee, it can be difficult to know, as an outsider, if you were refused a position because of your race. This is where the EEOC can help. It permits you to file a charge and conducts an investigation.

**Q:** *I was taking a package to the post office for my company on my way home from work and got in an accident. Can my employer be held responsible?*

**A:** Yes. The precise answer to this question will depend on your state's workers' compensation laws. If you were injured before you arrived at the post office, it will likely be concluded that you are entitled to workers' compensation benefits because you were still working at the time of the injury. If, however, you were driving away from the post office when the accident occurred, some states may find that you were no longer at work. You would then be prevented from receiving workers' compensation benefits.

**Q:** *Can my employer fire me just because it finds out I have a second job?*

**A:** Yes. Several companies actually prohibit what is referred to as "moonlighting," which is considered working for another employer. Even if your employer does not expressly prohibit moonlighting, as long as you are an at-will employee you can be fired for any reason at all— as long as it is not for some illegal reason like because you are black. If, however, the company fires only black people for moonlighting, then you should be able to establish that you were subjected to unlawful discrimination.

**Q:** *I didn't receive a promotion I applied for and I think it was because I am black. How do I know for sure?*

**A:** You don't. But one clue could be the number of black people the company has hired for the position you would be assuming. If you applied for a promotion to a position that has several other black people, it will be difficult for you to show how you were discriminated against because of your race. If, however, you think you've hit that all-too-common glass ceiling because the only other people who have held the position you applied for look like our past presidents, then, if you were qualified for the position, it will be fairly easy to show that you were discriminated against because of your race.

**Q:** *How do I know if I have a "good case" for racial discrimination against my employer?*

**A:** Would a white man think you were discriminated against? If so, you've probably got a pretty good case. If not, you may have a serious problem. Race discrimination cases are difficult to prove. A plaintiff has the burden of proving that she or he was treated differently than other "similarly situated" people. A special tactic of employers is to say the black applicant was not qualified because of a lack of experience. If the company hired a white applicant, it could try to use the white applicant's resume to show how he or she was in some way superior to the black applicant. If, for some reason, the white applicant appears less qualified on paper, the employer may then say it didn't hire the black applicant because he or she was overqualified. Unless you have evidence of fairly blatant discrimination, like the "black jelly bean" statement made by a top Texaco official, you could have a difficult time proving your case.

# 4

# BUYING AND BORROWING

## Your Rights as a Consumer

■

Mo MONEY, MO MONEY, mo money. Companies are in business to make that money. And we as consumers—people who purchase products or services—help them stay in business by making these purchases. I know this is simple stuff, but you must keep this in mind when confronting any legal issue as a consumer. Know that the driving motive is money—making money, saving money. If you remember this, you will be able to address almost any consumer issue.

The phrase "consumer issue" refers to a number of things, from basic purchases of products or services like tennis shoes and health club memberships, to credit history reporting practices, debt collection practices, telemarketing, mail order catalogs, Internet transactions, and warranties and guarantees. What they all have in common is that they involve a consumer. A consumer is defined by law as a "natural" person, or an individual rather than a company or organization. Commercial laws protect you as a business owner engaging in transactions with another business. But when transacting personal business, the law considers you a consumer. You are therefore entitled to protection under several consumer protection laws.

## Why a Company Would Rip Off Consumers

Clients have actually asked me: "Why would a company rip me off?" My response is: "It's big business." It's that simple. If a company sells you a product for $19.95, it is banking on the fact that you will not sue the company to recover your damages if the product doesn't work. Plus, the company knows you'd probably have to take some time away from work to go after it for its faulty product. You won't be able to recover the money you may have lost by spending time away from work. So when your dispute is over, you may get your $19.95 back but you will have lost a lot of time.

The company, on the other hand, has much more to gain, at least in the short term, from marketing a faulty product and selling it for this same $19.95. If only a thousand or so people buy the product in each state, the company could stand to make a million dollars on nationwide sales. Assuming that the product is completely worthless, the company may again be counting on the fact that most consumers will not bother with trying to remedy the situation. Unfortunately, a company that rips off consumers may still profit. Many people believe that companies, especially big successful companies, do not engage in certain conduct because the conduct is illegal. Companies are in many ways like people, and they sometimes engage in illegal conduct because the risk of getting caught is slim.

## What You Can Do to Protect Yourself

The old saying "an ounce of prevention is worth a pound of cure" certainly applies in consumer protection cases. There are certain ways you can protect yourself to limit the chances of falling prey to an unscrupulous company.

Use a major credit card to make purchases. If you have a problem with an item, you will be in a better position to contest the charge. You can return the item and notify your credit card company that you would like to dispute the charge. Remember that money motivates. Your credit card company will remove the charge and the company will be forced to go after you for the $19.95. Twenty dollars may not be worth a lawsuit, but it's certainly worth a phone call to your credit card company. Just as you probably won't sue the company for $19.95, it won't sue you for $19.95 either.

Read the fine print—if you can. I'm not going to suggest that you go blind trying to read all of the fine print contained in various consumer agreements. But skim all of these types of documents for items like warranties, guarantees, and refund and exchange policies. A company that has expressed that there are no warranties, no guarantees, and the consumer cannot receive a refund or exchange might not be worth any further consideration.

Do a little research. Get on that chicken wire, folks, and ask people about that product or service you are considering. This is especially important when considering entering into a long-term relationship for services like cellular telephones. A company with good service in one part of the country may not have good service in another. You should also use the Internet to do your research. Often other consumers, individuals just like you and me, use the Internet to publish their bad experiences with a company. Consult *Consumer Reports* and your local Better Business Bureau (BBB) as well. A few minutes on the telephone or Internet can help make you a more informed consumer. I know it's a hassle, but it's less of a hassle than having to sue a company. Trust me.

Even when you have taken all of the right steps, if you live long enough you will have problems with a company. And unfortunately this is especially true for black people, who are sometimes viewed as easy targets for consumer scams. Everyone should know at least the basics of consumer protection laws. Remember the scam directed at elderly people in our community? People received pamphlets directing them to apply for "Newly Approved Slave Reparations!" These so-called applications were used by identity thieves to get elderly people's personal information so the thieves could open credit card accounts and the like in their names. There are certain transactions you should carefully consider.

## Warranties and "Extended Warranties"

Warranties can be "expressed" or "implied." If they are expressed, the person or company extending the warranty has expressed in writing the nature of the warranty. If it is implied, the law automatically provides the consumer with a warranty.

Expressed warranties usually warrant against defects in the product and usually last for a limited amount of time, like a few years. Depending on your state, implied warranties last either for the length of time the express warranty lasts or forever. There are two types of implied warranties.

One is the implied warranty of merchantability. This warranty provides a consumer with assurance that the product purchased will work for all reasonably expected uses. For example, say you just purchased a new dining room set for your brand-new crib. Instead of going to get a ladder, you use one of the chairs that came with the set to clean your chandelier. The chair breaks and you bust your behind. You would be able to rely on the implied warranty of merchantability because you were using the chair for a reasonably expected purpose. Sure, chairs are for sitting and not for standing. But since it could be reasonably expected that a person would use a chair as a sort of makeshift ladder, the manufacturer of the chair could be liable to you for damages under this implied warranty.

Another type is the implied warranty of fitness for a particular purpose. This applies when you make the seller aware of your needs and the seller then warrants that the product will fit your needs. If it doesn't, you can sue for breach of the implied warranty of fitness for a particular purpose. Maybe you're shopping for some brand-new kicks at the local Foot Locker. You inform the salesperson that you are looking for something you can ball in and also wear around town. Instead of selling you a pair of basketball sneakers or a pair of cross trainers, Foot Locker sells you a pair of walking shoes. A week later, when playing in a pick-up game, you twist your ankle so severely that you'll be on crutches all summer. You could sue Foot Locker for breach of the implied warranty of fitness for a particular purpose if you discover that the shoes you thought were suitable for playing basketball caused your injury.

Even though all products come with an implied warranty and most with an express warranty, you may have noticed more and more companies selling "extended warranties." You might be at Best Buy ready to purchase an eighty-dollar cordless telephone. Before completing the purchase, the cashier asks if you would like to pay ten dollars for an "extended service warranty." You can't really understand all the details of the offer, but you figure it's only ten dollars so you might as well go ahead and purchase it—just in case.

Companies capitalize on these extended warranties by asking you to consider them right before you make a big-ticket purchase. Especially if purchasing electronic equipment for a couple of hundred dollars, many consumers would find the added ten, twenty, or thirty dollars for the extended warranty a reasonable purchase.

The problem with these so-called extended warranties is that they rarely cover anything and everything that could possibly go wrong with the product and most times they cover exactly what you receive by implied warranties. Moreover, often these so-called extended warranties are actually service contracts. Federal law requires that the terms of service contracts be made available to you before you purchase the warranty. But who wants to be the person who holds up a cashier's line reading the warranty even if it is available? These circumstances cause a person to go ahead and purchase the warranty without having a realistic time to review its terms. You would be better off using a credit card that offers an extended warranty with products purchased with the card. Instead of purchasing an additional warranty, you can review your credit card's warranty and rely on both this and your implied warranties.

## PREDATORY LENDING OR REDLINING

Both the Equal Credit Opportunity Act (ECOA) and the Fair Housing Act (FHA) make it illegal for companies to discriminate against potential borrowers based on race. But, as you probably know, that doesn't mean it doesn't happen. It happens, it's illegal, and it's called "redlining" or "reverse redlining."

Redlining is when lenders refuse to make financing available or provide insurance policies based on the nonwhite racial composition of an area. A bank that refuses to finance the purchase of a home located in Detroit is engaged in redlining. An insurance company that refuses to make car insurance available to residents of Detroit would be engaged in redlining. Some fairly substantiated claims indicate that companies will actually use a map to draw red lines around areas it will not consider. Historically, these areas are predominantly black.

Reverse redlining is when a lender extends credit, or an insurance company writes a policy, but only on terms that are "unfair." A New Jersey appellate court just recently recognized that this practice is illegal under both federal and state consumer protection laws. In this case, an African American woman in her seventies and her son applied for a home repair loan. After two years, the holder of the loan instituted foreclosure proceedings against them to take the home. Apparently, the company had engaged in a practice of financing loans to minority consumers at a higher interest rate and with higher fees than on average. This pair had good credit and had a favorable debt-to-income ratio, yet they were still not offered a fair interest rate. In fact, it seemed as if the loan may have been granted with the intent of making it difficult to repay so the company could foreclose on their home.

Both redlining and reverse redlining occur in the insurance industry as well. I had to confront the horrors and frustrations of this practice when I purchased a condo in Detroit. When I attempted to get insurance for my car, one of the customer service representatives of my then current insurance company told me she "wasn't sure they serviced that area." That would have been redlining and expressly illegal under consumer protection laws. I was then informed that they did in fact serve the area, but that my insurance would increase by more than 300 percent. No wonder this woman thought her company didn't serve Detroit.

We can only fight redlining and reverse redlining by taking action against these companies and complaining to the necessary government agencies. If you suspect a violation of the Equal Credit Opportunity Act by a consumer finance company like a mortgage company, report the violation to your state's attorney general office and the Federal Trade Commission (FTC) at:

**Federal Trade Commission**
Consumer Response Center
Washington, DC 20580
(202) 326-2222

## DOOR-TO-DOOR TRANSACTIONS: YOU HAVE THE RIGHT TO COOL OFF

Someone rings your doorbell and, without even thinking, you answer. This time, it's not the Jehovah's Witnesses but a nicely dressed young person selling magazines to put himself through college. You let him in. Before it's all over, you've ordered hundreds of dollars' worth of magazines and an encyclopedia of African American history. None of this was in your budget and, on second thought, you realize you can't afford this purchase. What can you do?

### The Cooling-Off Rule

Under the Federal Trade Commission's cooling-off rule, you have the absolute right to cancel certain door-to-door transactions and other transactions. This rule applies to:

- door-to-door transactions for more than twenty-five dollars
- purchases for over twenty-five dollars at the seller's other than normal place of business, like a sales presentation at a hotel

You can cancel any of these types of purchases until midnight of the third business day after an agreement was signed or after the original transaction occurred.

## PAYDAY LOANS, CASH ADVANCES

"Get CASH Fast, No Credit, Bad Credit . . ."

You've probably seen the ads. Today, unfortunately, there are several companies out there pitching small short-term loans to people who are already desperate enough to need them. I've seen several of these companies in my community, and they've almost become as predictable as liquor stores on every corner—at least in the "D."

Sure, they sound tempting. Maybe you're sick and tired of borrowing money from friends or relatives and only need a little bit of cash to get to that next payday. But what is really sick is the true cost of these loans.

Here's how they work. You write a check for the amount of money you want to borrow, plus the company's fee. The company will hold your check until your next payday. The cost of borrowing this way can be expensive, and I've heard of companies charging $25 for every $100 you want to borrow. If you need $500 to cover an emergency medical expense and you'll only need it until payday, you'd pay $125 just to borrow the $500. Even though $500 is not a lot of money these days, I bet when payday finally rolls around you'll find it hard to fork over that entire $625. You might just find yourself refinancing this expensive loan and paying another $25 fee. You'd be better off being late on a couple of your other payments and suffering the consequences of late payments than to take out this type of loan.

The Truth in Lending Act does apply to these loans just like other consumer loans. I've never seen the companies put in their advertisements things like 400 percent APR. Before you enter into an arrangement like this you must be given certain information in writing. This includes the finance charge and the annual percentage rate (APR), which is what it costs for you to owe the money on a yearly basis. If you or a loved one has fallen prey to such a scheme and you did not receive this information, you should report the company to the FTC and consider filing an action against it in court.

# USING CONSUMER PROTECTION LAWS TO YOUR ADVANTAGE (YOU BEST PAY, SAY THE DEBT COLLECTORS EVERY DAY)

### Your Rights Under the Fair Debt Collection Practices Act

If you are like most Americans, you owe somebody. You may have a few credit cards, owe on a home mortgage, or perhaps have a car loan. You might even owe on all three. No matter what you owe, you are a "debtor." The person or company you owe the money to is your "creditor." If you've ever fallen behind on your bills, then you might have received a few telephone calls and/or letters from creditors trying to get their money.

Calls and other communications from third parties that the creditor has contracted with to collect your debt are covered by the Fair Debt Collection Practices Act (FDCPA). While the debt collector is right—you best pay—it cannot use certain means, like making harassing telephone calls to you at home or at your place of employment, to make you pay. Here is what you should know about the FDCPA.

This Act covers all personal debts. These include debts for family or household items like purchases you may have made on a credit card. It applies to all debt collectors, who are people or companies who regularly collect the debts of others. It does not apply to creditors. So, if you purchase a computer on lease from an office store and you fall behind in your payments, it will not apply to communications made by the office store. It specifically prohibits certain conduct, including:

1. Telephone calls before 8:00 A.M. or after 9:00 P.M. your time.
2. Threats that you will be faced with legal action when it does not intend to take such action.
3. The use of profane or obscene language.
4. Misrepresenting that it is an attorney when it is not.
5. Stating that you could go to jail for not paying your debts.

Debt collectors absolutely cannot give false information to credit bureaus. If you respond to a debt collector that a debt is not yours, especially if you provide legitimate proof, the debt collector should not then threaten you with statements that the information is going to "go on your credit report" and "ruin your credit." Some debt collectors threaten negative information on a credit report to coerce you into paying a debt that you do not in fact owe. This type of conduct is illegal and a person or company can be found liable to you for damages under the FDCPA.

## Enforcing the FDCPA

You can take a couple of actions if you believe you have been subjected to treatment that violates the FDCPA. You can contact the Federal Trade Commission (FTC) and your state's attorney general office and report the suspected violation. You can also file an action against the company in state or federal court for actual damages, plus up to $1,000, plus your costs and attorneys' fees. You can even file a small claims action against the debt collector if you want. (Small claims courts are especially suited for individuals who want to represent themselves. If you decide to take this route, refer to Chapter 9.)

## You Have a Right to a Fair and Accurate Credit Report

In my estimation, the Fair Credit Reporting Act (FCRA) is probably the single most important consumer protection law. Credit bureaus maintain extremely private information about all of us. This information is then shared with companies who make decisions that can affect almost every aspect of our lives. The information contained in your credit report can make a difference in receiving a school loan for your child's college education. It can mean not receiving a job or health insurance. It can also mean not being able to finance the house of your dreams or even changing that old hoopty for a nicer ride.

The cost of making sure the information contained in your credit report is accurate is a lot less than the cost of bad credit. Negative information means you will be borrowing money as a subprime borrower, a person with a tainted credit history who will not qualify for the best rates. You could pay more than thousands of dollars per year on the average car loan because you will be forced to borrow at a higher interest rate. If this negative information is inaccurate, you should not be penalized by being forced to pay higher rates. It may take a little time to take the steps I outline below. But the time will be well spent. You could easily stand to save yourself thousands of dollars within only years by making sure only accurate information is contained in your credit report.

First, obtain a copy of your credit report by contacting the credit bureaus. As many of you probably know, if you are denied credit you will be entitled to receive a copy of the credit bureau report that was used to deny your application if you make your request within sixty days after the denial. The three major credit bureaus are Equifax, Trans Union, and Experian. They can be reached at:

- Equifax, P.O. Box 740241, Atlanta, GA 30374, (800) 685-1111
- Experian, 701 Experian Parkway, Allen, TX 75013, (888) EXPERIAN (397-3742)
- Trans Union, 2 Baldwin Place, P.O. Box 1000, Chester, PA 19022, (800) 916-8800

Then, carefully review your credit report for inaccuracies. Get out that highlighter and mark any negative information, and pay close attention to items that might be listed more than once. For example, maybe you had a credit card account that was closed for nonpayment. If the company used more than one debt collector to collect the debt, this same item could be listed more than once.

Also pay close attention to the status of your loans. Many people find that they have paid a loan off and yet it continues to appear on their credit report as an open loan. That is because once the company has been paid, it has no incentive to spend its money—remember money motivates—by making sure it has reported that the loan has been paid off. You must therefore be the one who makes sure that your loans are reported properly.

Also make sure that your late payments are reported correctly. Companies are notorious for inappropriately reporting consumers for making late payments to credit bureaus even when these payments are not past thirty days overdue. If you made a payment twenty or so days after its original due date but the status of the account was reported as past thirty days late, then you have a legitimate basis for asking that this negative information be deleted.

If you find inaccurate information in your credit report, write each of the credit bureaus and inform them. Provide them with enough information and documents to permit them to also conclude that the information is inaccurate. You can do this in the form of a FCRA demand letter. In the letter, inform the bureau that, if it fails to report your information properly as required by law, you will consider filing a civil action against it for damages. (See the Resource Guide for sample FCRA demand letter and see Chapter 9 if you decide to file an action against the bureau or information provider.)

You should also send this same letter and information to the company providing the bureau with the information. The FCRA also covers those who provide credit information, so if a company has wrongly indicated that you owe it money when in fact you do not, it can be held responsible for providing this inaccurate information.

The Federal Trade Commission (FTC) enforces the FCRA. If a credit bureau refuses to investigate your claims on the basis that they are frivolous, contact the FTC to inform them of this fact. Even though the FTC cannot act as your personal lawyer, when it comes to consumer issues, one consumer is never alone. If it has happened to you, it has happened to a hundred and two of you. The more reports the FTC receives from consumers about a particular company, the more likely it will take action and investigate the problem. Direct any complaints or experiences to:

Consumer Response Center/FCRA
Federal Trade Commission
Washington, DC 20580
(877) 382-4357
www.ftc.gov

## WHAT TO DO IF YOU'VE BEEN RIPPED OFF

If you've been ripped off, first, refuse to pay for the products or services. If you've paid for them using a credit card, try contacting the credit card company and disputing the item. Even if you've paid cash, you can still take action against the person or company.

Write a letter demanding the person take certain action (see the Resource Guide for a sample demand letter). It should be short, to the point, and include:

- The date or dates of the alleged transaction
- The place the transaction occurred
- The specific amount in dispute
- A statement of which law or laws you believe have been violated (if you know)
- An offer to settle your dispute, which can be higher than the disputed amount since you've been forced to deal with this problem
- A statement as to when you expect a response from the company; e.g., "Failure to either contact me or submit payment to me at my address within ten (10) calendar days will cause me to proceed against you in court."
- Your complete contact information, including telephone number

## IDENTITY THEFT

Advances in technology have come with a cost to consumers. In minutes, an identity thief can use the Internet or telephone to charge thousands of dollars on credit cards you still have in your wallet. In fact, identity theft has become such a problem that Congress recently passed the Identity Theft and Assumption Deterrence Act, 918 USC § 1028, which makes using another person's identity with the intent to commit any unlawful activity a federal crime.

Protect yourself by guarding your personal information. This means refusing to provide your social security number to companies that ask for it as a condition of service. It also means guarding your credit card receipts, which sometimes have all the information necessary for a person to make Internet purchases with your information. You might even consider investing in a reasonably affordable paper shredder from your local office supply store to destroy personal information on documents you no longer need.

However, you can do everything right and still be victimized. It happens, and not only to people with good credit or who have mad bank. Identity thieves do not discriminate. They might take your baby's social security number and try to establish credit in a different name.

So, what do you do if it happens to you? There are a number of steps you should take.

### File a Report with the Police

Contact the police and file a police report. If one of the officers says something like, "we don't do stuff like that," ask to speak to a supervisor and explain your need to file a police report. Filing a police report can be helpful in many respects. Some credit card companies require you to file a report and send it to them before they will remove charges from your cards. You can also send this report to credit bureaus as a way of supporting your claim that you are a victim of identity theft.

### Contact the Credit Bureaus

At the very least, contact the three major credit bureaus, listed on page 99. You can ask that a "fraud alert" be placed on your credit history file to make it difficult for someone to use your identity to open additional accounts in your name. The credit bureaus may ask that you provide a written statement, in which case you can write each of them a brief letter and simply enclose a copy of your police report.

### Contact Check Verification Services

Not only should you report your stolen checks to your bank, but you should also contact the national check verification services to report your checks have been stolen. Check verification services are those companies that help companies decide if they should accept your check. As soon as you discover your checks have been stolen, contact at least these companies: Equifax (800) 437-5120, International Check Service (ICS) (800) 631-9656, Telecheck (800) 710-9898, SCAN (800) 262-7771.

### Change Your Information

You may be eligible to change information like your driver's license number if you have been the victim of identity theft. You would need to contact your state's licensing agency to apply to change your driver's license. In certain limited circumstances, you can contact the Social Security Administration and apply to have your Social Security Number changed. I, however, do not recommend doing so since having a new social security number can cause a whole new set of additional problems.

### Keep a Record of Each Phone Call and a Copy of Each Letter

There's no need to be elaborate. Just make sure you record all of your phone calls and keep all of your letters. This can be helpful in clearing your credit history and possibly showing a bank or other lender that it really should consider you for a loan.

## FILING COMPLAINTS WITH ORGANIZATIONS

The federal agency that investigates consumer complaints is the Federal Trade Commission (FTC). Each state also has a consumer organization that processes consumer complaints. Filing these types of complaints is not the same as filing a complaint in court directly against a company. These are reporting agencies that will maintain complaints filed against a company. If the agency notices a practice of defrauding consumers, it may then investigate the company further. To file a complaint with the FTC, call its toll-free telephone number, (877) FTC-HELP [(877) 382-4357]. You can also file a complaint on its Internet site, www.ftc.gov, or at this address:

**Federal Trade Commission**
CRC-240
Washington, DC 20580

The federal government also sponsors the Federal Consumer Information Center, which can be reached at (800) FED-INFO. More information is available at these federally sponsored Web sites: www.consumer.gov and www.pueblo.gsa.gov. You can also get assistance from the National Fraud Information Center, an organization that assists victims of fraud. It can be reached at:

**National Fraud Information Center**
P.O. Box 65868
Washington, DC 20035
(800) 876-7060
www.fraud.org

## OBTAINING MORE INFORMATION

I have not even attempted to address all consumer issues in this chapter. However, this general information should highlight some of the more important consumer transactions affecting the black community and provide you with a basis for using the extremely important consumer protection laws like the ECOA, FHA, FDCPA, and FCRA. I have not covered some common transactions, like automobile purchases, which are regulated mostly by state laws. For more information on the laws in your state, contact your state's attorney general office.

# 5

# THE LANDLORD SAYS THE RENT IS LATE

## The Truth About Landlord–Tenant Law

■

Some things are unavoidable—including the legal issues that go along with renting a living space. In fact, even if you do everything right, you may still need to address certain legal issues. One legal issue all renters must consider is the terms of lease or rental agreements. Your agreement with your landlord and the law, including federal and state statutes and any city or municipal codes or regulations, will largely influence the basic aspects of the all-important landlord–tenant relationship.

Although this chapter does not consider all of the laws that may influence this relationship, it does consider the most important legal aspects of rental agreements and provide you with a frame of reference for navigating the legal issues you will likely confront as a renter.

## LEASE OR RENTAL AGREEMENTS

Many landlords lead you to believe that everything in a lease or rental agreement is enforceable and "the law." Your landlord has probably given you a piece of paper with type so small you'd need a magnifying glass to read it. This document is referred to as a lease or rental agreement, which, incidentally, are the same thing. The landlord's attorneys usually draft these documents. You probably won't be given the agreement until you're all excited and set to move into your brand-new crib. And it may be just one of several documents you will be asked to sign. Later, when you have a maintenance, repair, or other problem, you might be told to refer to this document, the all-important lease agreement, which probably provides you with very limited rights.

Landlords often trot out the lease agreement like it is The Word, saying they don't have to do anything about your problems, and they may even circle certain parts in their defense. They may say things like "Well, you signed it" and "That's what the agreement says." What most landlords do not want you to know is that even if you did in fact sign the agreement, you have certain rights. Sometimes it does not matter what the agreement says. You have these rights regardless of what the agreement says and you will still be able to take certain actions to protect your interests.

But you don't want to find yourself in the position of having to argue that a clause in a document you signed is illegal or unfair and therefore should not be enforced. These arguments are usually better left to attorneys. What you want to do is make sure that either you have a favorable agreement, which is one that at least provides you with certain protections, or you have received certain concessions, like a reduced rental rate, for an unfavorable agreement. Also, an agreement that is completely slanted toward the landlord could be a reflection of the landlord's unwillingness to take responsibility for anything—including things like ordinary maintenance and repair work. You should certainly be wary of these and may even want to find another crib. By reviewing the agreement, you will be better able to gauge what type of landlord you are considering. If it is a company whose agreement indicates it lacks a basic respect for the rights of its renters, seriously consider looking elsewhere.

## Negotiating a Lease or Rental Agreement

Everything is negotiable. This even includes the fine print in a standard lease agreement. Terms you disagree with in the lease agreement are more important than that phat new dishwasher that may come with the crib. If the lease agreement includes a really bad term and you cannot get the landlord to either change it or reduce your rent, think twice about renting from this landlord. Look for the following in the lease agreement before you sign.

### *Termination Clauses*

Maybe the reason this is such a great apartment is its location. Say you live in Washington, D.C., and it's walking distance from where you work. But what if you are informed that your company is relocating to New York and you can either go with the company or be fired, thereby forcing you to relocate or find another gig? Your once great apartment will no longer seem that great.

What you need is a flexible termination clause. This type of clause protects you from having to pay an exorbitant amount of money if you need to break your lease. It is usually contained in the agreement under the heading "termination," "premature termination," or "early termination." One of the better clauses is one that will permit a renter to leave without penalty with a thirty-day notice if the renter has been transferred, either voluntarily or involuntarily, to a job at least fifty miles from the apartment. Another, although less favorable to renters, permits you to transfer with a thirty-day notice and payment of one month's rent. Both are better than the clauses contained in many standard lease agreements, which state something like: "If you vacate the apartment prior to the expiration of this lease, your liability to pay rent shall continue until the expiration of your lease term or until the apartment is re-rented. . . ." These threaten to force you to pay rent for months when you can no longer live in the apartment, even due to circumstances beyond your control.

## Maintenance and Repair Clauses

Before agreeing to rent an apartment, you should first thoroughly inspect the apartment for problems. This includes checking to see if the water faucets are functioning properly and making sure there is no visible damage to the ceiling and floors. Sometimes, landlords will show you a model unit without showing you the exact unit you will be renting until much later—sometimes not until your proposed move-in date. If this happens, make sure that you will have at least some time to check out the property before actually taking possession of your unit. Or, in the alternative, make sure that the landlord agrees, either orally or in writing, to make any repairs you believe necessary once you have had a chance to see the place.

A lease sometimes fails to mention that the landlord has an express duty to maintain the premises. Again, leases without these types of clauses suggest that the landlord may not be willing to maintain the premises, which it is legally required to do. Think twice about renting from a landlord who has not included such a clause in the lease.

More often than not, lease agreements include clauses on maintenance and repair. Unfortunately, though, they specify that the tenant bears the responsibility of maintaining the property and making repairs caused by the renter's actions. What these agreements fail to state is that the landlord has the absolute duty to maintain the premises. A favorable clause for renters includes a statement that the landlord has the duty to maintain the premises. It may even provide that if a renter has given notice to the landlord and the landlord has not taken action to maintain the property, then the renter may make the necessary repairs and deduct any amount it has paid from the next month's rent. These are called repair-and-deduct clauses. If your agreement does not have such a clause, do not despair. As discussed below, you may still be able to make necessary repairs and deduct them from your rent. A statement to this effect in your lease, however, makes it easier for you to rely on this provision. Then, you can be the one who trots out the lease agreement and demands maintenance or repair work based on its content.

### Security Deposits

Typically, state laws govern how a landlord must treat the security deposits of its renters. This does not mean all lease agreements are written to conform to these laws. For example, you may live in a state that requires all security deposits to be held in an interest-bearing escrow account. If you are aware of this requirement and the agreement you are asked to sign states that the security deposit is a non-refundable deposit that is the property of the landlord, you may want to think twice about renting from this landlord. The inclusion of such a clause may show a predisposition to disregard the law. It is a good idea to contact your local renters' association to pinpoint your state's security deposit requirements.

### Late Payments

Checking out the late payment language in the agreement is one of the best ways to determine how humane your landlord truly is. Does the agreement have "zero tolerance" language and impose heavy fines if you are a single day late? Or does the landlord grant a grace period of a few days? In some states, landlords are required to provide a grace period. Even in these states, though, landlords sometimes inform the renter, either in the lease agreement or through other means, that there is absolutely no grace period. A lease with a grace period can suggest that the landlord respects the law on this issue, if this is a matter prescribed by your state's laws, or that the landlord is humane enough to provide you with this small window of time to make your rental payments. Either way, it suggests that you are dealing with a fairly reasonable landlord.

### Clauses You Should Avoid

There are certain clauses or provisions you should try to avoid, either by striking them out and initialing the strikeouts, by asking the landlord or its representative to have them changed, or by finding another place to live. These include:

- Clauses that provide that, by signing the lease, you are "acknowledging that the premises are in good repair except as noted in the lease," when the lease fails to provide a place to note problems with the premises. The same type of clause, if it includes a place for the tenant to write down any problems with the premises, is acceptable.
- Clauses that state the tenant is liable for the entire amount payable under the lease if the tenant breaches the lease agreement for any reason, including terminating the lease by moving out of the premises.
- Clauses that state the tenant cannot sublet the premises under any circumstances. These are especially harmful if the agreement does not have an early termination or transfer clause that permits the renter to vacate the premises with notice.
- Clauses that state the landlord may enter the premises at any time, with or without notice. This type of provision allows a landlord to permit law enforcement officials to search your place without your consent or obtaining a search warrant. A more favorable clause permits the landlord to enter the premises only in emergency situations or with your prior notice and approval.
- Clauses that state the tenant's security deposit will be returned only if the tenant has satisfied *all* obligations under the lease. Such a provision makes it easy for the landlord to withhold your security deposit, since it could be difficult to establish that you have satisfied *all* of your obligations. If you were late paying your rent one month, such a provision would entitle the landlord to withhold your security deposit.

## Tactics for Negotiating Your Agreement

As I stated before, everything is negotiable. A few years ago I met a woman at a meeting and learned that we were both living in the same apartment complex. After speaking with her for a while, she explained that she loved the spacious floor plans but felt that the rent was too high since it had increased so dramatically over the last couple of years. I must have given her a puzzled look because she then asked me how much I was paying for rent. She was not happy with my response. Apparently, she had just accepted all of the rent increases without so much as making a fuss. I, on the other hand, always asked that the rent remain unchanged since the complex had not been improved. As the Book says, ask and you shall receive. This simple step, which is one of the most important and easy steps to take in negotiating, is frequently overlooked.

Prepare a wish list, either a mental or written list of things that are important to you. You may have decided to live in a particular apartment complex, and pay a higher rent, because of the fitness room and its hours. Include the fitness room and any other amenities, like on-site laundry facilities, on your wish list. Also include terms of the lease agreement, like a flexible termination clause, that you have considered when deciding that this is the place for you. Now, you're ready to negotiate.

Go ahead and negotiate changes to the agreement right before you plan to move in. The landlord may not provide you with the agreement until right before you are scheduled to move in, a time when you may find it difficult to change your plans. You may even feel like you are in a bad position to bargain with the landlord by this time. But remember that the landlord is counting on you to tender your rent check and security deposit, usually a good sum of money. Don't discount the fact that the landlord loses money if the agreement falls through at the last minute just because the lease contains a few clauses that you find unacceptable. Even if the landlord can find another tenant, it will not happen overnight. In fact, that could take months, after the landlord has lost hundreds or thousands of dollars. The best time to bargain is right after the landlord has incurred the costs of readying the apartment for you, but before you have tendered a significant amount of money to the landlord, usually in the form of your rent and security deposit. At this time, review the lease for the clauses addressed above and ask for certain changes to be made.

Use your wish list. When you finally have the lease in your hand, look for the sections addressed above and for sections that address your wish list, and make changes that favor you. If the landlord has not stated it has a duty to make necessary repairs upon notice of the tenant, simply write in something like, "landlord will make all necessary repairs upon notice by tenant." If the landlord has not even mentioned the fitness room, write in something like, "landlord agrees to maintain fitness room in its current condition." Chances are, to seal the deal, so to speak, the landlord's representative will accept your requests.

## Renting Without a Written Lease Agreement in a Month-to-Month Tenancy

Sometimes landlords rent premises without asking the renter to sign a written agreement. If you are renting a house from a less formal landlord and you are not required to sign a lease agreement, should you be alarmed? Not necessarily. These arrangements can be beneficial to both parties due to their flexibility. Typically, these oral lease agreements will be treated as a month-to-month tenancy. A month-to-month tenancy permits either the landlord or the tenant to terminate the relationship by giving the other party only days—usually thirty—of notice. Tenants uncertain about their housing needs can benefit from these leases. Unlike written agreements, which are usually for a year and which impose severe penalties for early termination, month-to-month leases permit tenants to decide whether to remain in a situation on a month-to-month basis without penalty. Of course, what's good for the tenant is also good for the landlord. Like the tenant, the landlord can determine, on a month-to-month basis, to continue renting to you. And with thirty days' notice and with no reason at all, you can be forced to find another place to live.

## LEGAL WAYS TO WITHHOLD RENT IF YOUR LANDLORD DOESN'T MAKE NECESSARY REPAIRS

Your landlord is responsible for maintaining the premises. The premises include your particular apartment unit and the common areas like parking areas and laundry facilities. Your landlord's duty to maintain the premises may stem from the lease agreement. However, the landlord usually just obligates itself in an agreement to mimic what is required by the law. This obligation exists regardless of whether there is a formal written lease or rental agreement. This is because with every rental agreement, the law imposes on the landlord what is referred to as a "warranty of habitability."

The warranty of habitability is exactly what it sounds like—a guarantee by the landlord that the premises are safe and fit for a person to inhabit or use. This duty is imposed on landlords by the law, through decisions rendered by courts and health statutes, municipal codes, and local housing ordinances.

If your landlord fails to maintain the premises in a safe and sanitary manner, first contact your landlord. If this does not resolve the problem, notify your landlord in writing of the problems you are experiencing and indicate that you will withhold your rent, or a portion of your rent, until the problem is fixed. If the problem is still not resolved, you have a number of options depending on the state in which you reside. Your options likely include being able to repair the problem and reduce your rent by the amount of repairs, or reduce your rent based on the problem. You can also sue your landlord in court for breaching the warranty of habitability.

### Repair and Deduct Clauses

Several areas, either by state statutes or local ordinances, permit a tenant to make repairs that are essential, like repairs to your heating system during cold winter months, then deduct the amount of the repairs from your rent. Before taking this course of action, find out what the law is in your area by contacting your local renters' association or your state attorney general's office, housing department. The telephone numbers for these agencies are usually listed in the white or blue pages of your local telephone book and may be found on the Internet.

If you live in a repair-and-deduct area, inform your landlord in writing that you need certain repairs to be made. If the repairs are truly essential, they will likely need to be made quickly. Assert that the repairs are essential and that you need them to be made within a certain amount of time, like twenty-four hours. Also state in this notification that if the repairs are not made within this period of time, you will have the repairs made and deduct the cost from your next month's rent. Naturally, keep your receipts for any work you have done and then only deduct the exact amount from your rent.

## Reduction in Rent

Even if you do not live in a repair-and-deduct area, you can reduce your rent when your landlord has failed to properly maintain the premises. Housing codes and regulations require a landlord to keep rental premises in a certain condition. If the landlord has failed to do this, you can reduce your rent based on this failure.

For example, say the housing code states that the landlord must provide sanitary living conditions. You live in an apartment complex and the sewage from the bathroom of the apartment above you leaks into your second bedroom so that you cannot use the bedroom. If you are paying $850 per month for your two-bedroom apartment, you could reasonably reduce your rent by $400 based on the fact that you cannot use the second bedroom. There is no specific formula for determining how much you can reduce your rent; arguably, you could reduce your rent by more. But any reduction should have some sort of sound basis and be proportionate to the harm the landlord has caused by not maintaining the premises.

In case you are wondering, yes, you can withhold the total amount of rent based on the landlord's failure to maintain the premises. If you do this, though, the landlord might serve you with eviction papers. If this happens, you can go to court and explain to the judge that you withheld rent because the landlord failed to maintain the premises. If you still live in the apartment, the judge should rule that the premises were at least somewhat habitable and force you to pay at least a portion of the rent. If this occurs, at least you do not have to worry about the headache of starting your own lawsuit against the landlord, and you probably will succeed in forcing the landlord to make the necessary repairs.

## TERMINATING THE RELATIONSHIP

To successfully terminate the relationship with your landlord, make sure you do the following.

### Notify the Landlord in Writing

When you have decided to move out of your apartment, notify your landlord in the manner specified in your agreement. Because there is what is called a "legal presumption" that something mailed has been received, mail your notification letter to your landlord even if your agreement states that oral or hand-delivered notices will be accepted. Doing this protects you in the event your landlord later claims it never received notice that you were terminating your lease.

### Approximate a Specific Date for Your Move Out

You may not have a definite move-out date when you first decide you will be moving out of your apartment. Instead of waiting until you do, notify your landlord in writing of your approximate move-out date. Also inform your landlord that the date is approximate and that you will notify the landlord when you solidify your plans. Of course, if you cannot move out on your chosen date, your landlord will hold you liable for rent payments at least on a prorated basis. But by the time you do move out, your landlord will have had ample notice that you were intending to relinquish possession of your unit.

Give the landlord all the keys to the unit and your forwarding address. Most states require renters to provide landlords with a forwarding address when they move out and completely relinquish possession of the premises. This is good practice because it prevents the landlord from saying it was forced to keep your security deposit because "I didn't know where he was." Don't let the landlord get away with this common excuse. Write a letter that says something like: "My forwarding address is [*insert your address*]. Since the premises were relinquished, wear and tear excepted, in good condition, please forward my security deposit to me at this address."

## EVICTION

A landlord cannot evict a tenant. Only a court can evict a tenant, and only after several steps have been taken. In most cases, if the tenant has been sued for nonpayment of rent, the tenant need only tender the full amount of any rent owing prior to the eviction to stop the eviction. Consequently, most landlords will work with a tenant who may have fallen behind on paying rent. If you are served with eviction papers and know you will be able to pay your rent within a matter of weeks, contact your landlord and its attorney and inform them of this. You should know that landlords will often add attorneys' fees to the amount they claim you owe. Most states do not permit the nonpayment of attorneys' fees to serve as a basis for an eviction. If you can pay what you owe for rent, but not attorneys' fees, then you should try to tender the landlord this amount (I say "try" because the landlord might refuse to take an amount less than what it believes it is owed).

If you are served with eviction papers, you have also been ordered to appear in court. Whatever you do, show up. If for some reason you cannot personally appear, perhaps due to a medical emergency, call the court. Ask to speak to the clerk of the judge who will be handling your case. Explain your situation and ask that your hearing be adjourned until a later date.

If you do not appear in court for these types of proceedings, the court can order a default judgment to be entered against you. A default judgment is an order that is entered when a party fails to defend a claim brought by another party. If a default judgment is entered against you, still contact the landlord. The landlord might still be willing to work out some sort of arrangement. If this is unsuccessful, consider retaining an attorney since you will have to ask the court to set aside your default judgment and ask the court to address the eviction action. Your local court can provide you with more assistance and may even publish a pamphlet on landlord–tenant rights in evictions.

## A Few Words on Discrimination in Renting and Subsidized Housing

It is illegal for a landlord to discriminate against you because of your race. It is also illegal for a landlord to discriminate against you for certain other reasons, like your sex, religion, physical or mental disability, or family status. This means that a landlord cannot refuse to rent to a single mother. While a landlord cannot discriminate against you for these reasons, a landlord can discriminate against you because of your credit history, criminal record, occupation, or employment. If a landlord wanted to refuse to rent to a lawyer because of her occupation, the landlord can. Discrimination based on factors like race, sex, and religion is considered "unlawful discrimination." Discrimination based on other factors, like a tenant's occupation, is considered "lawful discrimination."

Both federal and state laws protect tenants from unlawful discrimination. The Fair Housing Act (FHA) is the federal statute that protects renters from being discriminated against in renting apartment units. The Department of Housing and Urban Development (HUD) enforces the FHA by processing discrimination complaints. Although this agency cannot act as your personal attorney against a landlord, it can provide you with assistance in pursuing your own legal action. HUD also sponsors many subsidized housing programs. If you suspect that you have been subjected to unlawful discrimination, file a complaint with HUD by visiting its Web site at www.hud.gov. You can also call (800) 669-9777 or write them at your area's HUD office or at this address:

**Office of Fair Housing and Equal Opportunity**
U.S. Department of Housing and Urban Development
   (HUD), Room 5204
Washington, DC 20410-2000
(800) 424-8590
TDD: (800) 543-8294

Your letter should be as specific as possible and should include:

- Your complete name
- Your current address
- The date of the suspected discrimination
- The name and address of the person and/or company your complaint is about
- The address of the place you were trying to rent or buy
- A short description of what occurred

HUD can also answer questions about your rights under certain subsidized housing programs like Section 8. These rights vary greatly depending on the type of program associated with your housing situation. Rules for these programs also frequently change. Although your landlord may be capable of answering some of your questions, don't rely on your landlord to provide you with answers about your rights. Your landlord might be more interested in getting as much money in rent from you as it can. HUD can provide you with an unbiased response.

### Retaliation for Exercising Your Rights

Just as it is illegal for a landlord to discriminate against you because of your race, it is also illegal for a landlord to discriminate by retaliating against you for exercising rights as a tenant. If you have exercised any of the rights mentioned in this chapter, like withholding rent or filing a complaint against your landlord for refusing to make necessary repairs, your landlord cannot raise your rent to retaliate against you. If this occurs, you can sue the landlord in court, or file a complaint with your state's housing agency and possibly even HUD depending on the reasons for the retaliation.

## FREQUENTLY ASKED QUESTIONS

**Q:** *I am renting an apartment in a commercial-use-only building. The roof leaks and I do not have enough heat. My landlord has refused to repair the building. Is this legal?*

**A:** No. Just because you live in what is classified as a "commercial-use-only" building does not mean you give up your rights under landlord–tenant laws. A landlord who rents residential space in a building that is not zoned for residential use is violating your area's zoning laws. That is your landlord's problem, not yours. As long as you are renting space to use as a resident and your landlord is aware that you will be living in the space, the landlord must make sure the premises meet the standard warranties, including the standard warranty of habitability.

**Q:** *If I complain to the housing authorities about my building, can my landlord evict me?*

**A:** No—at least not legally. A landlord cannot retaliate against a tenant for complaining to a housing board. If the landlord does institute eviction proceedings because you have made such a complaint, you can sue the landlord for retaliation. In some states, the landlord could face actual damages and what is referred to as "treble" damages, which is three times the actual damages.

**Q:** *The place I live in is kept in such bad shape it's a crime. What can I do?*

**A:** Call your police and fire departments. It may actually be a crime for your landlord to keep the building in such poor shape. These departments may have a department specifically assigned to what is referred to as "environmental" crimes. They will investigate the situation and issue a citation if appropriate. Some of these crimes are punishable by serious fines and jail time. Being faced with the threat of spending time in the local jail could cause your landlord to quickly resolve these types of problems. You should also contact the local housing authorities in your area.

**Q:** *I have been served with a Notice of Eviction. What can I do?*

**A:** Pay any outstanding amount owed. If you cannot pay this amount before your court date, do not just skip the court date. Whatever you do, go to court. You may be able to work out a plan to catch up on your rent.

**Q:** *My girl's landlord called her and told her she had two days to get her stuff out because she was being evicted. Is that legal?*

**A:** No. States have banned what is referred to as "self-help" evictions, so a landlord should not threaten her with action it cannot legally take. A landlord cannot evict anyone. All a landlord can do is file paperwork with the court to begin the eviction process. Only a court has the authority to evict a person. A court does this by issuing what is typically referred to as an "Order to Evict." It will only issue this type of order after several steps have been completed.

# 6

# BLOOD IS THICKER
# THAN WATER

## An Introduction to Family Law

■

JUST WHAT IS this thing we call "family law"? Those who watch the television show *Family Law* of this name may think that the term covers just about anything. That's actually not too far-fetched an assumption. Family law does cover a number of issues, but what the television show doesn't tell you is that family law is essentially the law of personal relationships. Marriage, separation, divorce, child custody, and child support issues are all family law matters.

Your family law issue may be as simple as figuring out how to procure a birth, marriage, divorce, or death record. Or you may have an issue as serious and complex as getting separated and divorced. This chapter will not address all issues that can be considered family law issues, but it will answer many questions people frequently have about this area of the law. It will also provide you with the type of information you will need to handle more serious issues.

# Jumping the Broom or Getting Married

Marriage is a three ring circus:
engagement ring
wedding ring
and
suffer-ring

—Unknown

Back in the day when the law did not recognize the marriages of black people, black couples held their own ceremonies and jumped the broom to publicly declare their commitment to one another. Now that the law recognizes our right to get married, it takes a little bit more than a hop over a broom. Marriage is not only a social institution but a legal institution as well. Once two people jump the broom or tie the knot, their relationship acquires a legal status that gives them certain privileges and responsibilities. Today, to get married both you and your fiancée need to meet the legal requirements of being married. This entails obtaining a marriage license, having a marriage ceremony, and having your completed license recorded at the court. The marriage license, the "piece of paper" signifying this status, is the first example of how the law regulates the relationship.

## Obtaining a Marriage License

You must obtain a marriage license in the state where you intend to be married. The license can usually be obtained from the county clerk. There is a nominal fee for the license and you might be required to submit to a test for sexually transmitted diseases. Most states also require a waiting period of a few days before they will issue a license. Once your marriage ceremony has taken place, you need to make sure the license is completed by the official marrying you and your fiancée and then recorded with the clerk at the local courthouse.

## Legal Requirements for Marriage

In order to enter into any type of agreement, both parties must have what is referred to as the "capacity" to enter into an agreement. This typically means that each person is an adult of sound mind and understanding at the time the agreement is entered into. In the context of marriage, "capacity" means that both parties are at least eighteen years old, not close blood relatives, of different sexes, and are not mentally ill or incapacitated due to drugs or alcohol. If all of the requirements in accordance with the place where the marriage will take place have been met, then the marriage will be considered valid.

## Domestic Partners

Today, it is not uncommon for people to live together before, or in lieu of, getting married. Most states, however, have outlawed common-law marriages, where a couple would be considered married if they lived together as husband and wife for a certain number of years. The privileges and responsibilities of marriage are typically reserved for married couples.

You may be asking, "What privileges?" Well, there are a number of them, which is precisely why the gay and lesbian community is pushing for the legal recognition of same-sex marriages. For example, if your long-term domestic partner becomes seriously ill and you wish to take time off from work to care for her or him under the Family and Medical Leave Act (FMLA), in most places you will not be able to do so unless your employer has chosen to extend this privilege to domestic partners. Family and medical leave, bereavement leave, health care benefits, and retirement benefits all depend on a partner's status as a married person.

Some places will accord couples "domestic partnership" status if the couple properly registers the relationship. This can be one way of formalizing and protecting your relationship. However, even a couple acquiring "domestic partnership" status will not be afforded many of the rights (such as the right to federal benefits) that married couples receive. Nevertheless, if you are in a long-term relationship, explore this as a means of protecting both you and your partner. Another way to protect yourself is by entering into a written agreement with your committed partner. You will find it helpful to contact a lawyer in your state who specializes in this area of the law because the laws concerning domestic partners vary greatly from state to state.

## DIVORCE AND SEPARATION

Maybe you wish you'd never jumped that broom or tied the knot and are considering divorcing your spouse. Or maybe you've been served with divorce papers and are wondering what a divorce will entail. If you don't know this already, it will be a bit more costly than obtaining a marriage license. A simple uncontested divorce where there are no children and little property involved could cost a couple of thousand dollars if you hire an attorney. However, in these types of cases you may very well be better off handling the divorce yourself. Many states provide divorce forms on their court's Internet site or at the clerk's office. By completing these forms, you will be proceeding "pro se," which means you are representing yourself. First, remember you obtained your license from the place where the ceremony was held. This will not be the place to file your divorce. Choosing the right court to file for a divorce is the first important step. Here are the basic factors you must consider when deciding how to proceed.

### Residency Requirements

Your divorce papers should be filed where you and your spouse reside. Most states require at least one spouse to have resided in the state for a certain number of months before accepting a divorce complaint. But what if you have left your spouse and moved somewhere else, maybe to a different city or state? Legally, you will be able to file your complaint where you reside after meeting the residency requirements. If there are children involved, or if you will be seeking alimony, I recommend filing your complaint in the place where your spouse resides unless it would be extremely inconvenient for you to do so. This is because, although the court where you reside can legally grant a divorce, it may not have what is termed "personal jurisdiction" over your spouse. In family law cases, courts are less liberal with this requirement and regularly refuse to hear cases if a person has no connection to the geographic location of the court. Without personal jurisdiction, the court will not be able to hold your spouse in contempt of court if he or she fails to follow through on the terms of the divorce decree. If, for example, your spouse is a deadbeat mom or dad and hasn't paid child support or permitted you to visit your children, only courts who have personal jurisdiction over the spouse will be able to have her or him arrested and held in contempt of court on these charges. Especially if your spouse has no connection with the place where you now reside, file where your spouse continues to reside. Likewise, if you have been served with divorce papers and the court is in a place you have never even been to, you may consider asking the court to have the complaint transferred to a court in your area.

## No-Fault Divorces

Presently, all states recognize no-fault divorces. Some states require the parties to live apart for twelve to eighteen consecutive months before obtaining this type of divorce.

In New York, for example, a couple can obtain a no-fault divorce if they continuously live separately for one year under a separation agreement granted by the court or signed by both parties. Other states permit a couple to allege "irreconcilable differences" or an "irretrievable breakdown in the marriage" to obtain a no-fault divorce. You may be wondering whether "no-fault" divorces are better than "fault" divorces. The answer to this question depends on the state and other circumstances. No-fault divorces are relatively new. It used to be that couples had to prove they were entitled to a divorce based on the fault of the other party. Generally, no-fault divorces are considered favorably because neither party is forced to use the courtroom to air that old dirty laundry and engage in finger-pointing. Emotionally, at least, going the no-fault route could make for an easier divorce. However, agreeing to a no-fault divorce may be harmful if a court will also be asked to address issues like spousal support, child custody, and significant property and debt divisions. These are complex issues and a court sometimes considers the fault of the party when resolving them. If you need to address such issues you will be better off if you hire a divorce attorney.

## Fault Divorces

States provide several different grounds for fault divorce. Although the list differs from state to state, it usually includes habitual drunkenness or use of addictive drugs, insanity, impotence, adultery, physical cruelty, infection with a sexually transmitted disease, and desertion or abandonment. In most states, imprisonment is treated as abandonment. If there are clear grounds for obtaining a fault divorce—for example, if your spouse has been declared legally insane or has been sentenced to a life-long prison term—you would be advised to obtain this type of divorce.

## Alimony, Spousal Support, or Maintenance

States use various names like these when referring to the financial support one spouse may be required to provide to the less economically well-off spouse. Courts consider a number of factors when deciding whether to award alimony, such as the length of time the couple was married, the fault of the parties, the finances of the parties, and whether the parties are capable of supporting themselves.

## Marital Property

There are basically two legal systems that deal with the division of marital property and debt. One is the community property system, which is in effect in western states like Arizona, California, Wisconsin, New Mexico, Nevada, and Idaho. Community property states consider everything earned during the marriage—all income, earnings, and property—as belonging to both husband and wife as community property. Most states are not community property states, but "common-law" states. These states permit spouses to keep property belonging to them prior to the marriage as separate property as long as they truly keep the property separate during the marriage.

Most states, both community property and common-law states, generally adhere to an "equal is equitable" concept, meaning all property of the marriage (defined by what type of state you are in) will be divided equally between the parties. Remember Eddie Murphy's skit on divorce? "I want half-Eddie! I want half." This is that half.

## Using the Services of a Divorce Attorney

Because obtaining a divorce can be complex and the rules vary from state to state, I highly recommend that couples obtaining a divorce hire an attorney. You may be thinking you can't afford an attorney, or maybe you want to at least try to handle it yourself. Many people may think this is an all-or-nothing proposition, but the truth is that if you hire an attorney after you have done your preliminary research and obtained all the information your attorney will likely require, you can save yourself the cost of having your attorney do this research. Since family law cases are usually taken on an hourly basis, you can save yourself hundreds of dollars by making sure your attorney doesn't spend time asking you basic questions and doing preliminary research you could have done yourself.

You should gather the following information:

- Copy of the marriage license
- Tax returns for the duration of the marriage and as far back as possible
- Insurance policies like health and life insurance policies
- Real estate papers
- Titles to automobiles

- Credit card statements
- Banking, savings, and stock account statements
- Pension and retirement statements
- Information and statements on all loans, including personal loans

You should provide a written statement about the following:

- All addresses where you and your spouse have ever lived
- Description of the type of place where you and your spouse lived (e.g., studio apartment or five-bedroom house)
- Names, ages, and sexes of all children
- Description of the way each spouse supports each child (e.g., takes daughter to basketball practice each day, pays for son's violin lessons)
- List of all relatives in the area and all relatives in your and your spouse's immediate family (mother, father, sisters, and brothers)

## CHILD CUSTODY AND CHILD SUPPORT

Traditionally, courts decide how child custody issues should be resolved during a divorce. Because many children in our society are born to unmarried parents, this can be a problem. I've heard several fathers complain in child support cases that they don't want to pay child support because the mother never lets them see the child. Almost always the mother complains that the father never wants to see the child and that he should at least be forced to help support his child.

When children are born out of wedlock, the law does not automatically require the parents to settle issues of child custody. Although the law automatically requires the parents to provide child support, you need to file certain paperwork with the court to address child custody issues. A father who uses the old "the-mother-never-lets-me-see-my-child" line won't stand a fighting chance against a mother suing for child support. If you have a child and are not married to the child's other parent, you need to resolve both the issues of child custody and child support. You must file a separate action to address these issues, and you will not be able to defend a child support suit on the basis that you do not have custody or visitation rights.

## Child Custody: The Best Interests of the Child Prevails

In the early 1800s, while southern blacks were still slaves, white fathers separated from the mothers automatically received custody of their children. Since white females were almost completely banned from the workplace, it was presumed that fathers had the responsibility and duty to financially support their children. In many respects children were considered property.

From approximately the mid-1800s to the 1980s, most courts followed the "tender years" philosophy. The underlying presumption of this philosophy was that all children are better off being raised by their mother, at least during their "tender" or early childhood years. Courts would use this doctrine to almost automatically grant the mother custody of the child.

Now, courts have rejected the "tender years" doctrine. Men can have complete custody of their children. Today, courts look at the "best interests of the child" and award custody on this basis. Courts usually defer to the wishes of the parents. There are at least four types of custody a court may award—sole custody, joint custody, legal custody, and physical custody.

- Legal custody: custody over the major decisions of the child, like education and health care.
- Physical custody: daily caretaking of the child. The child lives, eats, and sleeps with the parent who has physical custody.

- Sole custody: given to one parent.
- Joint custody: means both parents share equally.

Most custody orders use a combination of these terms. A mother can be awarded joint legal custody and sole physical custody. The father would then be awarded joint legal custody and have visitation rights since he was not awarded physical custody. This type of custody order, which is quite common, requires the mother to ensure the child's daily needs are met but also requires that the father have input in major decisions like those involving the child's health care and education.

### Visitation Rights

The parent who is not awarded physical custody will have a right to visitation. Most states have recommended minimum requirements sometimes referred to as visitation guidelines. Parents should contact the court for these guidelines and should try to reach an agreement to follow them. If these guidelines are unacceptable, or if one parent refuses to follow at least the state's minimum requirements or the agreed upon visitation rights, then you should contact the family law court for more information on how to proceed. Because these are common issues, many courts offer free instructional forms and classes on how to contest an improper denial of visitation rights.

## Child Support

Courts are becoming extremely strict about forcing parents to support their children. Furthermore, the law imposes on all parents the duty to support their children. This means that all children, regardless of whether their parents were ever married, are entitled by law to be supported by both parents.

If you don't pay, you won't be able to play—you'll be subject to a nice fine and maybe even some jail time. A few months ago I saw about five men handcuffed to each other being escorted into the courtroom in those quite unattractive bright orange jumpsuits. One of these men told the judge he had a good construction job making decent money. Based on this, he asked the judge to not jail him so he could work to pay his child support. He also tried to support his argument by saying that the child's mother never let him see the child. The judge took an "interesting, but irrelevant" posture and sentenced him to ninety days in jail. The judge told him that the fact that he had a good construction job making decent money made it all the more contemptible that he had failed to pay child support.

Another man, who looked like a teenager, told this same judge that he couldn't pay child support because he didn't have a job. The judge told him that his child had to eat every day, just like he did, and that not having a job was not an acceptable excuse. He too was sentenced to jail time to "think about his situation."

If you have a child and cannot pay support for some reason, contact the court to make arrangements. Whatever you do, don't make them have to come after you. The explanations these men gave may have

---

### ■ Now About "Domestic Violence"

---

The phrase "domestic violence" is used to refer to violence in marriages and other intimate relationships. Over the years, this phrase has come to include violence in relationships involving children, siblings, and the elderly. Domestic violence is not something that just happens to other people. The National Center for Injury Prevention and Control estimates that 12 in every 1,000 black women are victims of domestic violence (compared to 8 out of every 1,000 white women). The sobering story of Cherica Adams, the young pregnant girlfriend of NFL player Rae Curruth, who was murdered in 1999 when she was six and a half months pregnant, is one of the worst instances of domestic violence in our community. If you are a victim of domestic violence, call your local police and the National Domestic Violence Hotline at (800) 799-SAFE (7233). Also consider calling your local battered women's shelter. Depending on the circumstances, like whether your assailant is likely to retaliate, you may want to apply for a restraining order or personal protection order (PPO).

---

kept them out of jail if they kept the court informed about their circumstances. And the young man who was unemployed probably would
have been entitled to some sort of temporary abatement had he voluntarily gone to the court to inform it of his job situation.

Today, courts seem to have lost any tolerance they may have once
had for people not paying child support. In fact, a federal law has now

---

### ■ Protecting Yourself with Personal Protection Orders (PPO) or Other Restraining Orders

---

Personal Protection Orders (PPO) or restraining orders protect people from violent relationships. You can apply for this kind of order if you have been the victim of domestic
abuse, stalking, or other types of abuse. In fact, people dealing with abusive neighbors or coworkers have been able to obtain these orders.

The order is granted after the court has had a hearing on an application or petition, which is usually a fairly short form filed with the court seeking such an order. The
person filing the petition is a complaining party and may be referred to as the "complainant." The person who must respond to the petition is typically referred to as the
"respondent."

The order is a document issued by the court. It directs a person to not engage
in certain conduct and sometimes orders a person to engage in certain other kinds of
conduct. It may require a person to not have any contact with the complainant. Frequently, it specifically prohibits a person from visiting the complainant at her or his
place of employment or home, and it might prohibit the person from coming within a
certain distance of the complainant as well. In some states, the order can prohibit a
person from purchasing or possessing a firearm. If the order is violated, you can then
contact the police for assistance. (The order empowers the police to arrest a person
without having to wait until a problem, like another violent incident, occurs.)

Usually you can obtain these orders within a short period of time, possibly within
a day if your situation is extremely urgent. If you need this kind of order, contact your
local state court. The court clerk can provide you with more information, including any
application forms. Typically, these forms come with a detailed instruction sheet you
should follow to obtain your order.

---

been passed requiring all states to set up procedures to enforce child support orders. States now cooperate on sharing child support information and will assist parents in locating and obtaining orders against out-of-state parents. Some courts will automatically deduct payments from the parent's paycheck to ensure prompt and regular payment. Wages can be garnished and bank accounts seized if payments are not made. Licenses, like professional and driving licenses, can also be suspended for failing to pay support.

Both parents should be proactive when it comes to paying child support. I don't recommend handing your baby's mother cash to support your child. She may later claim you never paid any amount and sue you for years of child support. If you have a child and the baby's mother hasn't taken any steps to require you to pay, that doesn't mean you should sit around and do nothing. You are better off protecting yourself by making arrangements to have a portion of your paycheck go to the family law court to be disbursed to your baby's mother, or you should at least pay something to support the child by personal check and remember to keep a record of these payments. If you are owed child support payments and have not received anything, don't wait indefinitely for payments. Take legal action to compel support payments if you haven't received a payment in over a year. Also consider contacting your state's child support enforcement office for assistance.

## Modifying a Divorce Decree or Support or Custody Order

After going through the process of getting separated and divorced, you may find that the divorce decree you agreed to is just not working out as planned. Or maybe circumstances have changed and the support or custody order is no longer feasible. You are not alone. This happens so frequently that there is a simple process to modify your divorce decree or order. You will be required to complete a form and file it with the family law clerk. By filing this form you are asking the court to have a hearing to determine if any of these items should be changed.

The most common reason for modification is "changed circumstances." For example, you may have agreed to support your spouse and now he or she is making mad bank at this great job. Of course you're going to feel like you shouldn't have to support this person, and if anything, she or he should be supporting you.

All you need to do is go to the court and ask for the form to "motion" or "petition" the court to have your divorce decree or support or custody order changed. You will then be scheduled for a hearing to have your issue decided. Since state courts are practically overrun with people who have family law issues, most states require a hearing before someone other than a judge. This person is usually an attorney experienced in family law issues who may be referred to as a "magistrate," "facilitator," or "referee."

Although these hearings are informal, this person will issue a recommendation and a decision, the latter implementing the former. The decision will become final unless you file a timely appeal. The steps you need to take to appeal usually are found in the form you use to file your motion or petition, or in other informational documents from the family law court, local law library, or local public library.

Depending on your circumstances, you may wish to handle this type of issue without hiring an attorney. If it is as simple as the above example where you will be asking the court to modify support payments, you can probably handle it yourself. If it is more complex, say for example you are seeking custody of your child because you believe your spouse is no longer a fit parent, you should at least consult an attorney, and you may wish to hire an attorney to handle the entire process.

## Steps for Modifying a Divorce Decree or Support or Custody Order

1. Go to or contact the court that issued the decree to get the right forms.

2. Complete the forms by stating specifically why you believe the decree or order should be modified. Reference the exact section and page number(s) of the portion you believe should be revised. Also attach a copy of the decree or order as an exhibit.

3. Make at least four copies of the forms, including your decree or order as the exhibit.

4. File the forms with the court by either taking them to the family law clerk or mailing them to the clerk. Include the necessary filing fee, which is usually a nominal amount.

5. Have the forms "served" on the ex-spouse or the other party in the case. You can serve the forms by mailing them via certified mail. You can also ask the court if it will handle service of process for you.

6. After you are certain the forms have been served, which means you have received a return receipt in the mail if you served them via certified mail, ask the court to schedule your motion for a hearing.

7. Attend the hearing and present your reasons for requesting a modification of your decree.

8. If you disagree with the decision, file an appeal to the decision.

Remember, your right to modify a divorce decree may depend on what the decree says about modification. A number of states have enacted statutes authorizing parties to enter into nonmodification clauses pertaining to alimony. Consequently, most attorneys preparing divorce decrees now include a general nonmodification clause. Be wary of signing a decree that has such a clause, especially since divorce decrees frequently contain support and custody orders. Nevertheless, even if there is such a clause in your divorce decree or order, use the above steps to seek a modification. Especially if your circumstances have changed dramatically, a judge may decide to disregard a nonmodification clause and instead modify your decree or order.

## OBTAINING RECORDS OF VITAL STATISTICS: BIRTH CERTIFICATES, MARRIAGE, DIVORCE, AND DEATH RECORDS

Many people have questions on how to obtain records of vital statistics. The process differs from state to state and depends on when the event occurred. Even so, in most states you can obtain these records by contacting the clerk of the county courthouse in the county where the event occurred or where the record was likely filed.

For example, say your parents were married in Detroit, Michigan. You were born there, in Wayne County, and you later moved with your parents to Berkeley, California. There, in Anaheim County, they were divorced and your mother later died. You need to obtain your birth certificate, your parents' marriage certificate and divorce records, and your mother's death record. You may think that this is a complex legal issue and that you need to hire an attorney to obtain these legal records, but in this instance, at least, that is not the case. It is quite simple to obtain these types of records.

First, you locate the telephone number and address for the county clerks, both Wayne County and Anaheim County in the example above, by either looking in the telephone book, calling directory assistance, or researching on the Internet. The Internet may be the best approach because many courts now have frequently requested forms like the ones you need on their Internet sites. Contact the clerks and tell them you want a certified copy of these records. Certified copies are usually more expensive but well worth the few extra dollars since you may later find that you need a certified copy instead of just a copy of the record.

You will then likely be directed to go to the courthouse or, if this is not possible, be asked to send a letter to the court along with the fee for each of the requested records. Yes, the fee. We might call this a "free" country, but that just means you're free to pay for the records you are entitled to receive. If you don't provide the right fee, your request will not be processed. If you do, you will receive your records anywhere from a few hours to a couple of weeks after making a request. No attorney is necessary.

## FREQUENTLY ASKED QUESTIONS

**Q:** *My baby's daddy wants to amend his child support obligation to me because he now has another child from another woman. Can he?*

**A:** Yes. An order for child support can be amended due to a change in circumstances. Certainly, having another child could be considered a change in circumstances. As in most family law cases, the law in your state will control the outcome of an issue like this. But generally speaking, in this situation your baby's daddy would be able to seek to have the order modified so he could also meet his obligations to support any additional children.

**Q:** *Who must pay child support?*

**A:** The parent who does not have physical custody of the child, referred to as the "noncustodial" parent, must pay child support. This obligation does not depend on the marital status of the parents. So, brothers, you could get stuck paying child support for eighteen years if you father a child, even if the child is the result of a one-night stand. Think about this the next time you rely on only a woman's birth control precautions. If you're not ready for some serious obligations, financial and otherwise, you should also use birth control.

**Q:** *My baby's momma resides in another state. She has an order for support filed in her state where she and our child reside. But what about my visitation rights?*

**A:** Contact the county court where your child resides and ask for the family law court. Then ask the family law clerk which forms you need to file to petition the court for visitation rights. (Remember not to ask something like, "How should I go about getting visitation rights?" A clerk could refuse to answer the question since it may seem like you're seeking legal advice. Just ask for information on obtaining the forms.) Usually, these forms come with complete instructions. Although you can file the forms by simply mailing them to the court, you may be forced to travel from your state to the state where your child resides to complete the process. By the way, once you have obtained an order for visitation rights, courts in other states will be obligated to enforce the order.

# 7

# IT'S MY BUSINESS

## Legal Basics for the Entrepreneur

■

THE INCREASE IN the number of small business owners has been staggering over the past few decades. Technological advances have made it easier for smaller businesses to compete with larger organizations. The failure rate for new businesses, however, remains high. One of the most difficult aspects of owning and operating a new business is dealing with the legalities. But as the examples below demonstrate, it'll cost you a great deal more if you get caught *not* dealing with them.

This chapter does not cover everything you need to know about operating your particular business; for example, it will not discuss the advantages and disadvantages of the various forms of businesses. Information like whether you should form a corporation, partnership, "S" corporation, or sole proprietorship is beyond the scope of this book and can be found in almost any book dealing with the basics of business ownership. You can find other important information on operating a business at www.employers.gov, an Internet site sponsored by a partnership of federal agencies, including the IRS, the Department of Labor, and the Small Business Administration. This chapter explains the basic legalities of business ownership. Although geared toward the small business owner, this chapter provides a checklist of the most crucial legal issues associated with owning and operating any type of business.

## Licensing and Permit Requirements

If you want to own and operate your own business, you've gotta first handle your business. To do this, one of the first questions you must ask yourself is: "Am I 'legally qualified' to run this business?" Do this before you begin to paint your first house as a handyman, fix your first car as a mechanic, wrap your first head as a hairstylist, or whatever business you have in mind.

Being "legally qualified" doesn't have anything to do with your ability. What it really means is making sure you have complied with your state's licensing and permit requirements. Lawyers and doctors are not the only people who need to have licenses. Barbers, hairstylists, mechanics, and child care centers, to name a few, usually have to have licenses as well.

To learn more about the licensing and permit requirements of the type of business you are interested in starting, contact your local library, urban league, and county courthouse, which usually have pamphlets on state licensing requirements. Focus on your business rather than businesses as a general matter. If you plan to open up your own nightclub, consider the requirements for these types of establishments—like obtaining a liquor license. If you are planning to be a handyman and fix up houses for a living, determine if your state has any specific licensing requirements for residential contractors. Trying to run a business without the right license or permit can be devastating.

### ■ Case Study: Damon's Do-It-All

Damon is an intelligent brother who has decided to fix up houses for a living. He doesn't have a college degree; in fact, he didn't even finish the tenth grade and doesn't have his GED yet. He is smart, articulate, and has a good reputation in the community for doing a good job.

All of his business comes from referrals. This past year, he got a pretty big job to fix up a man's house because he had done work for the man's sister, who really liked the work Damon had done. This man saw Damon's work for himself and thought he had done a good job. Damon is confident about his ability and has been operating a somewhat successful business for over a year. Damon and this man agreed that the work on the house would cost about $8,000. Damon didn't have him sign a formal agreement, but he was smart enough to have him sign his standard proposal form, which describes the project and its cost.

Now, this man was another brother and Damon didn't expect a brother would try to take advantage of him. But when Damon was almost finished with the job, brother man decided to "fire" him and refused to pay him. When Damon insisted that he be paid, this man dared Damon to sue him and told him he couldn't because he didn't have the right license.

Damon contacted me and naturally I've already sued the man. But Damon does not have a license to fix up houses. The laws on these types of licenses vary from state to state. Under the Michigan consumer protection laws, a handyman without a license technically cannot sue for a breach of an agreement. So even though Damon is "qualified" to do this type of work in the sense that he's very good at fixing up houses, he is not "legally qualified" without the right license. Because he didn't have the right license, Damon may lose this case and all the money the man owes him.

Think of these licenses as another way states tax businesses. In many instances, if you have failed to fulfill a state's requirements, you will not be able to enjoy certain benefits. This particular licensing requirement is no different. It's just another way of Michigan saying, "you've gotta pay to play." Unless you want to see countless hours go to waste, make sure you're legally qualified to operate your business and get all the necessary licenses and permits.

### "Doing Business As" or "Assumed Name" Certificates

If you want to do business under a name that is not yours, you need to file an "assumed name" or "doing business as" certificate. Most states require you to file these types of certificates in all of the counties where you will be engaging in business. Usually, you can obtain the necessary forms by visiting your local county courthouse or public library. These forms will also inform you how often the certificate needs to be updated. Sometimes, you only need to update the form if you've moved your business to another location or you are no longer in business.

Don't think that this is just another technicality and skip this step until you're "really in business." You can take this risk, but you'll suffer the consequences. In some states, you will not be able to sue to recover money a person or company owes you if you haven't filed the right certificate, just like the Michigan licensing requirement described above. You may also be assessed fines for unlawfully engaging in a business without having filed the proper certificate. It doesn't cost much to file these types of certificates. The highest fee I've ever heard of is twenty dollars, and many places charge only five or ten dollars. Trust me. The cost of not filing this certificate can be far greater than twenty dollars.

## TAXES AND OTHER FINANCIAL MATTERS

One important issue you need to address is how you will pay your business's taxes, local, state, and federal, and how you will handle your other accounting affairs. This will depend largely on how you choose to structure your business. The IRS and the SBA offer free instructions that explain the tax consequences of various business structures and activities. You can obtain this information by contacting your local IRS or SBA office, visiting your local library, or visiting the IRS and SBA Web sites at www.irs.gov and www.sba.gov or the www.employer.gov site.

As a first step, I advise all business owners to complete the paperwork to obtain an EIN (employer identification number). An EIN is like a SSN (social security number) for businesses. You can request an EIN via telephone, fax, mail, or the IRS Web site by completing form SS-4, which is a short form asking for basic information. For more information, call the IRS at (800) 829-1040. There is no fee associated with obtaining an EIN.

Federal law requires most businesses to have an EIN. Presently, only sole proprietorships with no employees are excluded from this requirement. However, when you want to do almost anything in the name of your business, like opening up a business checking account, you will be asked to provide your EIN.

You will probably begin your business as a sole proprietorship with you as its only employee. Many businesses that begin like this eventually expand by adding at least one other employee or independent contractor. Confusion occurs when the SSN of the sole owner has been used in place of the EIN until it is legally necessary to obtain an EIN. This is why I recommend you obtain an EIN from the get-go. By doing so, you start a healthy practice of keeping all your personal stuff separate from your business. This will make it easier for you to deal with legal issues that may arise in the future, like proving that your personal assets are not assets of a failing business, for example.

## Addressing Your Insurance Needs

I'm a huge Chris Rock fan. In Rockology, insurance is called "In Case Shit Happens." In one sense, that's really what it is. But when you're operating your own business, it's definitely a CYA (cover your ass) proposition as well. Sometimes, insurance is technically an option, while other times it is a legal requirement. In most, if not all cases, even the smallest of small businesses need insurance. Evaluate your business's needs for at least these types of insurance.

## Liability Insurance

This insurance is just like its name suggests—it protects a business from most claims that the company is liable to someone for some reason or another. Liability insurance can cover claims if a person injures herself on your premises, at one of your functions, or by using one of your products. Say you've finally realized your dream of owning your own nightclub and one of your patrons slips on the dance floor and is injured. If she sues you, you'd be covered by your liability insurance. And remember, owners of premises are not the only business owners that should consider getting this type of coverage. You may be a professional party organizer and the person may have been attending one of your parties at the local club. The dancer who slipped could still sue you and your company. In fact, she would probably sue you, your company, and the local club. Liability coverage protects you from these types of claims.

## Business Interruption Insurance or Business Continuation Insurance

This type of coverage protects a business when it cannot continue to operate, usually due to a catastrophe like a major flood or other act of God. You may recall that many insurance carriers sought protection for claims that would be brought by businesses forced to close as a result of the September 11, 2001, World Trade Center and Pentagon attacks. As you can imagine, insurance agreements specify either what will, or will not, be covered. There were likely businesses who had exclusions for "acts of war" but not "acts of God" or "acts allegedly for God by evil misguided terrorists." At any rate, this is the type of insurance that covers a business if it is forced to close its doors. While you may think this kind of coverage is unnecessary for small businesses, this is simply not true. Small businesses are exactly the type of businesses that need this coverage. Usually they cannot easily absorb these types of losses and will find it difficult to raise capital to continue their operations. Furthermore, small businesses, because of their size, can get this coverage for a fraction of what it costs larger businesses. While you're not legally required to have this type of insurance, it makes a lot of sense, especially for small businesses.

## Malpractice Insurance

Don't think that malpractice insurance is only for lawyers and doctors. Other professionals, like accountants who prepare tax returns, may be required to obtain malpractice insurance. In some states, if you fail to get this type of insurance you can lose your professional license and the privilege of providing those types of professional services.

## Disability Insurance

Disability coverage protects the business owner when she or he cannot work because of a medical disability. It pays a portion of the salary of the covered person. Self-employed people can qualify for disability insurance by providing proof of income like old tax returns to the insurance company. Disability insurance is especially important if your company is run exclusively by you. If you become disabled and are not covered, you could lose the business and risk the financial security of both your business and yourself.

## Unemployment Insurance

To date, all states have an unemployment compensation system that provides unemployment compensation to long-term employees who become unemployed. If you hire anyone other than yourself, you will need to determine whether you are required to have this type of coverage. If you wait until a former employee files for unemployment, you could face fines for failing to properly maintain this coverage.

## Workers' Compensation Insurance

Referred to as "workers' comp" and sometimes just "comp," this type of insurance protects workers and employers from work-related injuries. The size and type of your business will determine whether you are required to maintain this type of insurance. You shouldn't, however, assume that just because you have a small business you will not be needing this type of coverage. Again, this is a type of insurance that most businesses are required to maintain. You must therefore determine whether your business is required to have this coverage.

## Homeowners' Insurance

If you are a homeowner, you should also check your homeowners' insurance to see how this insurance may affect any additional coverage. You may be able to add a type of insurance if you intend to own and operate your business from your home. You may also be able to add a type of insurance to protect you from losing your home if you are a business owner. Owners of small businesses, especially when they are not yet profitable, run a real risk of being personally sued for liabilities associated with the business. In these cases, the business owner can risk losing the equity in a home, or the home itself, when not properly insured.

## ■ Case Study: T. J. Construction Company

Terry Johnson had done most things right. He filed his "doing business as" certificate with the right county courthouse since he was operating a construction business under the name of T. J. Construction Company. He had taken care of his taxes and had the right business license. What he hadn't fully considered was his need for insurance. In fact, he grossly underestimated this necessity and almost ended up paying for it with his family's house.

Terry owned and operated a small construction business that usually got business from larger construction companies. One of these larger construction companies used him as a subcontractor. To get the job, Terry was required to sign a standard subcontractor agreement that stated he had complied with all of the state's requirements to operate his business. The size of Terry's workforce depended on his needs and varied greatly from month to month. Sometimes, he did all of the work himself. When he got larger projects, he paid friends of his to help with the work. When he received this particular contract, he paid one of his friends to help with the work. Terry didn't have his friend sign an agreement.

The friend was injured at the work site. He then filed a workers' compensation claim to pay his medical bills and compensate him for his injuries. Terry did not have workers' compensation insurance but the larger company did. Instead of Terry being forced to pay his friends' claims, the larger company's insurance carrier was forced to pay.

Unfortunately for Terry, this was not the end of the matter. The insurance carrier, based on the agreement its construction company had with Terry, or T. J. Construction Company, sued him individually and his company. It insisted that T. J. Construction company had agreed it had all the necessary insurance. Because it in fact did not, the insurance company claimed it was entitled to be "indemnified," meaning that it should be reimbursed for all of its payments to Terry's friend.

Generally, the law presumes that a person is an employee. This is to ensure a person is taken care of when injured at work. Terry and the larger construction company therefore had the burden of proving his friend was not an employee but an independent contractor. Because Terry did not have his friend sign an independent contractor agreement like the larger company forced Terry to sign, he knew he would have a hard time proving the friend was an independent contractor. And, because Terry was not organized as a corporation or other entity that protected him from being sued individually, the insurance company went after him personally and even threatened to take his home. After paying a substantial amount of money in attorneys' fees, which his firm really couldn't afford to pay, Terry took his attorneys' advice and agreed to settle the claim with the insurance carrier. He also closed his business.

Terry probably didn't think he needed workers' compensation insurance. He could have protected himself, though, by having his friend sign the type of agreement he signed with the larger company. If it's good enough for a large company, it's certainly worth considering if you own a small company. Use agreements presented to you by larger companies to learn strategies for protecting your own company.

Some small business owners tend to have friends perform work for them without ever completing any paperwork. However, this is really not worth the risk. Although he may be one of your brothers from back in the day, if this brother gets injured on the job and faces serious medical bills, don't be surprised if he sues you and your company. Consider that most cases are between parties who at one point had a good relationship, parties who at one time were friends or business partners. Getting things in writing between friends doing business together isn't unfriendly. Not getting things in writing between friends doing business is, however, dangerous—for both your friendship and your business.

## MANAGING RELATIONSHIPS: GET IT IN WRITING

Whoever said an oral agreement isn't worth the paper it's written on was right on time. Maybe this person had been burned one too many times by agreeing informally with someone and not bothering to formalize the agreement by putting it in writing. Small business owners have a number of reasons for not wanting to ask people to agree to terms in writing. The reasons range from, "I'm just trying to keep it on the 'd'-'l', you know," to "why can't we just all get along, I ain't trying to complicate things," to what seems to be the all-time favorite, "just keepin' it real." That's just keepin' it real dumb. I don't care if it's between you and your cousin, your baby's daddy, your momma's pastor, or all y'all—get it in writing. And if anyone questions you, just tell them that you're a visual person and that unless you see something in writing, you might not fully understand all the details. The truth is that most of us are better at comprehending things in writing. We all know two completely honest and well-meaning people can hear the same thing but interpret it differently. Because this is true, you must be especially certain that you formalize your business agreements in writing.

That said, do not think that you need to make your agreements ultra-formal. Agreements that have been pieced together by statements found on restaurant napkins have been used in court as evidence of the agreement and have served the same purpose as more sophisticated agreements. Any agreement that tells who, what, when, how, and how much will likely suffice and be far better than the "he said, she said" you get when there is only an oral agreement. Forget about "keepin' it real" and try "keepin' it business." Business is business, and in the business world the written word is worth far more than the spoken word.

## Protecting Your Business Relationships with Written Agreements

Businesses regularly ask other businesses and individual consumers to formalize their business relationships by entering into written agreements. These written agreements are often standard agreements, and many people think they're nonnegotiable. One of my clients told me he was shopping for cell phone service for his business. He needed to keep his business line separate from his personal line. When he asked the salesperson if he could take the agreement home to review it, the salesperson refused. The salesperson said that this was the standard agreement and that the company never changed its terms.

I instructed my client to contact the business or corporate sales department of the company. The salespeople in this department, who regularly deal with other businesses, faxed him a copy of the company's standard agreement. He was also given the name of a person he could contact and was able to negotiate the "nonnegotiable" terms of the agreement, like asking the company to give him forty-five days to pay its invoice.

Small business owners often think the same as they would if they were individual consumers. This client had not considered how other businesses purchased cell phone service. But by thinking this way, he was able to negotiate terms suitable for his business, which the company apparently was not willing to offer its nonbusiness consumers.

I have heard some successful business owners even suggest that an entrepreneur, when purchasing products or entering into agreements, act as if he or she will have to report back to the boss on all the particulars. This means that when a salesperson refuses to provide you with an agreement, say something like, "Well, I'm sure your business doesn't just enter into agreements without having someone in your management or legal team review its terms. I need to have this agreement to have this thing reviewed." After receiving the agreement, you can go back to the person to negotiate over the terms of the agreement, saying something like: "My company really wants to work with you on this project and we think we can have a long-term relationship, but in order to do this we need X, Y, and Z, or a longer time period to pay our bills." The company may not negotiate its terms. But most successful companies are forever mindful of their bottom line and would rather give in a little than see you skip off to one of their competitors. Try it. You might just be surprised. If you approach a company in a business-to-business manner, which you no doubt should, you will be forced to take yourself seriously and others in turn will take you seriously. Part of taking yourself seriously is carefully considering any and all terms of a written agreement.

There may be times when you deal with people who aren't in business for themselves. Take the above example of Terry Johnson and his T. J. Construction Company. He finally landed a sizable project and thought he'd help a jobless friend by sharing the wealth and giving him some of the work. He didn't think he needed to have his friend enter into any type of legal agreement. But under the circumstances, Terry should at least have had him enter into a basic independent contractor agreement that would have stated he was not an employee of T. J. Construction. This could have protected him from the sizable lawsuit that resulted when he got sued for not having workers' compensation insurance. As a business owner, consider at least the following agreements.

### Independent Contractor Agreements

An independent contractor, unlike an employee, is a person who provides services for the business, usually on a project basis. It is almost always more economically feasible to have independent contractors than to have employees. This is because of the way federal and state laws are drafted. Most of these laws, like discrimination, pension, and health insurance (COBRA) laws, only cover employer–employee relationships. If you hire an employee, you will be faced with unemployment compensation insurance, workers' compensation, and possibly unpaid disability leave. If instead you have only independent contractors, you will be spared the legal headaches often associated with employer–employee relationships.

Remember, though, that because the presumption is that there is an employer–employee relationship, you should protect yourself when you pay someone for services by having him or her sign an independent contractor agreement. Microsoft used these types of agreements with several of its computer specialists. Some of them, who were seeking the Microsoft employee benefit package, sued the company and argued that the agreement should not be enforced since they were really Microsoft employees. The agreement doesn't guarantee that a court will find your business has an independent contractor relationship with the person, but it will be much harder for the person to prove he or she was an employee instead of an independent contractor. These types of agreements also spell out all of the terms of the relationship and typically indicate that the person will be receiving an IRS Form 1099 at the end of the year. (See the Resource Guide for a sample agreement.) They can go a long way toward protecting your business from employer–employee relationship liability.

### Confidentiality Agreements

Confidentiality agreements can protect your business from employees or independent contractors who are intent on using your business's confidential information. Confidential information includes customer lists or business know-how, often referred to as the trade secrets of your business (discussed in further detail later in this chapter). You don't need to have an entire agreement dedicated to protecting the confidentiality of your business. I recommend a basic confidentiality clause that can be as simple as one or two sentences included in either an employment or independent contractor agreement (see the Resource Guide for a sample agreement).

### Noncompete Agreements

Noncompete agreements or clauses are just that—they protect your business from competition. But because our society promotes fair competition, these agreements can be hard to enforce. To be enforceable, they must be drafted narrowly enough to protect only your business from unfair competition. Good noncompete clauses usually state that the intent of the clause is only to protect the business from unfair competition and go on to limit the clause to a small geographic location and length of time. For example, a small accounting firm had all of its employees execute noncompete agreements to protect the firm. The agreements stated that if the employment relationship were ended for any reason, the employee would not work for a competitor or start his or her own practice within a thirty (30) mile radius of the firm for at least two (2) years. This particular agreement has been enforced and many courts would likely find that it was a reasonable agreement since it only covers a thirty-mile radius and only lasts for two years.

### Lease Agreements and Noncompete Clauses

If you are entering into a lease agreement for your business, depending on the type of property you are leasing, you should consider insisting on a noncompete clause. If, for example, you agreed to lease space from a shopping mall, you would want a clause that protects you from competitors being able to lease space in the same shopping mall. Who would want to enter into a three-year agreement to rent space for a beauty salon if one year later that meant facing competition from other beauty salons in the same shopping mall?

Maybe you're thinking that agreements like these are only for large companies. Smaller companies, however, are the ones that are most vulnerable to people divulging trade secrets and using confidences for their own gain. Most small businesses that use these agreements find that they are no worse off from insisting that they are signed. It's one of the cheaper ways to protect your business. Other than a little time in research, your only real cost will be what it costs to reproduce the agreements (see the Resource Guide for sample agreements).

### ■ Case Study: Soccer Waza

Soccer Waza was founded by two young men, Dominic and Mario Scicluna, who have a passion for soccer. The company is dedicated to not only producing talented soccer players who could potentially play on the collegiate and professional level, but also to providing young girls and boys with a healthy way to interact and grow physically. Both of its founders have played college and professional soccer. The company was founded on principles they developed after years of playing the game and has at its center what has come to be called the Waza technique.

The business is run by both the co-owners, at least one employee, and several other soccer players who serve as coaches and trainers. All costs of developing the business, like the costs of advertising, have naturally been incurred by the business. The business recruits its trainers, solicits young people to play, and ensures that its trainers and players will have adequate fields and games. In other words, the business handles all of the administrative matters.

The business is well run, but unfortunately it did not address its need for noncompete and confidentiality clauses from the start. And at least one of the company's trainers, who was introduced to a team of players and the Waza technique, ended up offering his services to the players on his own. Waza ended up losing a valuable client to one of its very own trainers. A simple noncompete clause in an independent contractor agreement could have protected the business from this type of behavior.

## Copyrights, Trademarks, Patents, and Trade Secrets

You may think you know all you need to know about copyrights, trademarks, patents, and trade secrets. Maybe you're a new business owner and think that these are issues you can address later. However, you could buy yourself a lawsuit by starting your business without addressing these issues.

Maybe you have a great idea for a coffee shop and want to name it Starbacks. Or you want to open a chain of fast-food restaurants that sell hamburgers and fries and call it Mickey D's. You might not have intended to infringe on another company's "intellectual property" rights, which is what copyrights, trademarks, patents, and trade secrets are considered, but for the most part this will not matter. You shouldn't at all be surprised if you get served with a complaint by Starbucks and McDonald's for infringing on their intellectual property rights. To guard against this, you need at least a general understanding of intellectual property law. You should also understand how to protect the intellectual property rights of your business while not infringing on the rights of other businesses.

### Federal Laws and International Treaties Protect Intellectual Property Rights

The United States Constitution in its original form gave Congress the right to protect the intellectual property rights of people. But remember that blacks were not people under the original Constitution. It was not until the post-slavery Amendments were passed that blacks began their road to personhood under the law. Before that, black inventors were not able to protect their inventions with intellectual property rights since they were not people as defined by the law.

But now, blacks can seek the same type of protection for intellectual property rights as whites. Many of us have been frustrated by what some have referred to as cultural theft—when time and time again something develops in the black community but then is taken by a white-owned business, trademarked, and becomes off-limits to everyone but the business. Take, for example, the phrase "It's All Good." That's been black slang since way back in the day. Recently, Burger King started using this phrase. Because Burger King now uses the phrase in its course of business, it can claim it as its own trademark even though it didn't develop the phrase. You too can obtain valuable intellectual property rights by using the law to your advantage.

## Copyrights

Copyright law protects a broad class of works, usually artistic in nature, from others copying and appropriating the works for their own use. The broad class of works includes:

- Literary works like Maya Angelou's *I Know Why the Caged Bird Sings*
- Musical works like Lauryn Hill's "Doo Wop"
- Dramatic works like Lorraine Hansberry's *A Raisin in the Sun*
- Choreographic works like the choreography in Michael Jackson's "Thriller" video
- Pictoral, graphic, and sculptural works like Jacob Lawrence's *The Blues*
- Motion pictures and other audiovisual works like *Roots*

In order to gain copyright protection, you must have created an "original work of authorship" and "fixed it in a tangible medium of expression." Perhaps you've seen something someone else created that you had already thought of and got the "took the words right out of my mouth" feeling. Well, you could just as easily think, "took the rights right out of my business." Copyright laws, and all intellectual property laws, protect *creation*, not thought. They only reward people who have actually taken the time to express their creativity in a form that can be shared with other members of society. This does not mean you need to have your work published in order for it to be protected. All it really means is that a thought, without action to turn the thought into something you can touch, is not enough. If you have original creative thought and turn it into a tangible form, even if it's a poem you scribbled on a bar napkin, you have a piece of work that is copyrighted. As one of my copyright professors reminded our class, "Creation is the hallmark of copyright protection."

There are many misconceptions about copyrights and how to "get" a copyright. Most people don't realize you don't need to do anything to "get" a copyright other than create an original work. To protect your work, however, you should state that the work is "copyrighted" or place a "©" somewhere on the work if that's possible. That's all there is to getting a copyright.

## Rights of the Copyright Owner

Now that you know how a work is copyrighted you should know just what rights a copyright owner has. Generally, copyright ownership gives an author an exclusive right to reproduce and distribute his work for his entire lifetime, plus fifty years after the author is deceased. These rights, collectively referred to as a "bundle of rights," include:

1. Right of reproduction
2. Right of adaptation
3. Right of publication
4. Right of performance
5. Right of display

For example, any of the rights Tupac didn't sell will continue to be in effect until 2045. To all y'all naysayers, Tupac is dead, and the fifty-year countdown started ticking on his rights in 1995. So if Tupac didn't sell the copyright to his work "I Ain't Mad at Cha," you could infringe on his rights by performing this song or burning it on a CD, tape-recording it, or by doing anything that could fall within the above categories. Now there are times when certain uses will not be considered copyright infringement, but these are limited to certain exceptions and "fair uses" of the work. (For more information on these exceptions and the "fair use" doctrine, contact the United States Copyright office and visit www.employers.gov.)

A more traditional example arises in the context of purchasing and using computer software. As a business owner, you will more than likely use or purchase computer software for your business. When you purchase this software, you are really just purchasing a limited license to use the software, usually on one computer. If you were to load this software on more than one computer, or fail to have this software in a safe place, thus allowing independent contractors or employees to remove it and load it on other computers like their home computers, then you may be liable for copyright infringement. Then another SBA, the Software Business Alliance, may be after you.

### ■ Case Study: Protecting Your Business's Copyrights— The Will Brent Story

Will Brent is a prominent African American photographer in the Washington, D.C., area. He carefully chooses African American men and women to model. His subject matter is tense, made even more tense by his use of black and white film. He develops his pictures and reproduces them on canvases and posters. (Artwork by Will Brent is now available on the Internet at www.willbrent.com.)

Last year, one of his friends told him that a brother on the *Jenny Jones* show had displayed one of his photographs on the show, claiming that he had been the model in the picture. He probably thought it was harmless to do that, and if y'all have ever seen Will Brent's models, who could really blame him? I don't know a sister out there that wouldn't agree that this brother had a fine body. Will, who had contacted me about copyright protection a few years earlier, contacted the *Jenny Jones* show's legal department and told them it had infringed his exclusive right to display his poster. He threatened to involve his lawyer if the show didn't compensate him. The show agreed, and the parties settled the case for a substantial amount of money. Will Brent got free advertising on a national show by this brother displaying his poster. Then he got the show to compensate him since his exclusive right to display the work had been infringed upon. This brother knows how to "keep it business."

## Trademarks ™ and Service Marks ᔆᴹ

Trademarks are words, names, devices, symbols, or a combination of these used to signify a business's products. Service marks are the same, but they signify a business's services. Trademarks and service marks are used to create what is referred to as "brand recognition." Although you can own a copyright by merely creating an original work, trademark and service mark protection is only available when the mark is used in business to signify a business's products or services.

To get and keep this protection, a business should use a "™" or "ᔆᴹ" after these marks, or a "®" after marks registered with the United States Patent and Trademark Office (USPTO). A business should also make sure slight variations of its marks are not used, and that its marks do not become associated with a type of product as a general matter and then fall into what is considered the "public domain." Kleenex was so successful with its tissues that people began to ask for a "kleenex" instead of a tissue. The same happened to Xerox when people began asking for a "xerox" to signify a photocopy. These companies had to take significant steps to protect these marks from falling into the public domain.

Another example is the widespread use of "Mickey D's" in the black community. We were using it all right, long before McDonald's ever appropriated it for its own use. But we weren't using it to sell our products or services. Therefore, none of us could have gotten trademark protection. Now, at least in black communities like Detroit, you can roll through a McDonald's and see a "Mickey D's" sign. The same thing has happened with the use of "It's All Good" by Burger King.

By using these phrases in their business to sell products, these companies can now sue others for using the same phrase to sell the same type of products. You don't have to be McDonald's or Burger King to get this protection. All you need to do is make sure you use a "™" or "SM" and use the mark to sell products or services. If you want additional protection, like having the presumption that your business is the proper owner of the mark, file the appropriate paperwork with the USPTO. You will need to complete the forms for registering a trademark. Incidentally, only businesses that have registered their trademarks can use the "®". All other businesses must use "™" or "SM". Unlike the paperwork for patent applications, this paperwork is fairly simple and can be completed without the assistance of an intellectual property lawyer. (For more information, contact the United States Patent and Trademark Office and visit www.employers.gov.)

## Protecting Your Invention with a Patent

The statute dealing with patents, 35 USC § 101, states that an inventor can seek protection whenever he or his business "invents or discovers any new and useful process, machine, manufacture or composition of matter, or any new improvement thereof." This statutory requirement has been broken down to require the following:

1. The item you want to be patented must be what is considered "patentable subject matter."
2. It must be novel.
3. It must be useful.

4. It must not be obvious, usually referred to as the "nonobvious-
   ness" requirement.
5. It must not have been patented in another country.
6. It must not ever have been described in a publication.

There are two main types of patents, a "utility" patent and a
"design" patent. Generally, patents include "articles of manufacture,"
"machines," "processes like the manufacturing of chemicals or treatment of metals," and "composition of matter" like the mixtures of
chemicals. Patentable subject matter can cover a variety of items, like a
Pentium processor in a computer.

| Patentable Subject Matter | Examples |
| --- | --- |
| Articles of Manufacture | Nike Air Jordan tennis shoes |
| Machines | Intel computer processors |
| Processes like the treatment of chemicals | Biotechnology inventions such as man-made microbes |
| Composition of matter | Prozac medication |

To protect these types of inventions, apply for a patent from the
United States Patent and Trademark Office (USPTO). The costs of
applying for these patents, coupled with the fact that the protection typically lasts for less than twenty years, makes it economically unfeasible
for many inventors to patent items that could be patentable. There is
some overlap in copyrights and patents; items that may be patentable,
like the sophisticated design of a cell phone, may also be subject to copyright laws. The particular circumstances of your business should dic-
tate whether you want to pursue a patent. Your business should hire an
intellectual property attorney to determine the best course of action for
your circumstances.

| COPYRIGHTS © | TRADEMARKS™ | SERVICE MARKS℠ | PATENTS |
|---|---|---|---|
| **INCLUDE** | | | |
| literary, dramatic, and musical works<br><br>pictures<br><br>sculptures<br><br>audiovisual works and sound recordings<br><br>architectural works | words, names, devices, symbols, or a combination of these to signify a business's products | words, names, devices, symbols, or a combination of these to signify a business's services | UTILITY PATENT: the features of a product that produce a certain function; e.g., the microchip technology found in a cell phone<br><br>DESIGN PATENT: protects what is referred to as the "ornamental" design of manufactured products; e.g., the stylish unique shape of a particular cell phone |
| **PROTECTION STARTS BY:** | | | |
| asserting rights by placing "©" or other indication, like the words "copywritten material" on "original works of authorship" | using the mark | using the mark | being granted a patent by the USPTO |
| **LENGTH OF PROTECTION** | | | |
| life of author + 50 years; or 75 years from publication or 100 years from creation, whichever is less | as long as the mark is used | as long as the mark is used | UTILITY PATENT: 17 years from the date of issue<br><br>DESIGN PATENT: 14 years from the date issued |
| **STANDARDS FOR INFRINGEMENT** | | | |
| copying and improperly appropriating for use | likelihood of confusion | likelihood of confusion | UTILITY PATENT: making, selling, using a patented invention<br><br>DESIGN PATENT: similarity of design to an ordinary observer; e.g., designing a cell phone in a way that most people would think duplicated an existing design |

## Trade Secrets

Trade secrets are considered the know-how of a business and include almost any information or processes that are generally kept confidential. One of the most famous trade secrets is the formula for Coca-Cola. While its inventors probably could have obtained a patent for the formula, patents only last for a short period of time. By keeping the formula confidential, the inventors can protect it as a trade secret indefinitely. To protect the trade secrets of your business, you must take significant steps to make sure they are divulged only to people who need to know this information. Keep such secrets on a "need-to-know" basis, and have any employees, independent contractors, and officers agree to a confidentiality agreement to protect your business's trade secrets.

# OBTAINING MORE INFORMATION

**National Urban League**
120 Wall Street, Fl. 8
New York, NY 10005
(212) 558-5300
Fax: (212) 344-5332
www.nul.org
The National Urban League has almost one hundred years
of experience fighting for the economic empowerment of
black people. It does this through local offices located
throughout the nation, which sponsor conferences and seminars specifically designed to address issues black entrepre-
neurs face.

**Small Business Administration (SBA)**
409 Third Street, SW
Washington, DC 20416
(800) 827-5722
www.sba.gov

**Copyright Office**
Library of Congress
101 Independence Avenue, SE
Room LM 401
Washington, DC 20540
(202) 707-9100

**Commissioner of Patents and Trademarks**
Crystal Park Building
2121 Crystal Drive
Arlington, VA 22202
(703) 305-8600

## CHECKLIST FOR THE BUSINESS OWNER

- Licensing and permit requirements. Research your state's requirements for licenses and permits. Many businesses need a specific type of license and possibly a permit to be "legally qualified" to engage in business in that state.
- Business certificates. You will probably need to file a "doing business as" certificate or an "assumed name certificate," which are just two different names for the same type of certificate. You can find out by contacting your local court and library. This is one of the first steps you should take.
- Insurance. Carefully consider your insurance needs. Failing to properly insure your business could lead you to be held personally responsible. You could also lose your business and personal assets.
- Written agreements. Review all written agreements you are asked to sign. There are certain protections for consumers entering into agreements. As a consumer, defined as a person purchasing products or services for personal use, it is easier to get away with not carefully reviewing consumer agreements. These types of protections are limited in the business-to-business

context since it is assumed that businesses are more sophisticated and carefully consider the terms of a written agreement. Based on this alone, carefully consider all of your business's written agreements, and carefully consider formalizing all of your business relationships by agreeing to all important terms in writing.

- Protect your intellectual property rights. To protect copyrights, trademarks, or service marks, use the appropriate mark to signify your claim. Complex intellectual property issues should be addressed by consulting an intellectual property attorney.

Keep it real and keep it business.

# 8

# IT'S ALL ABOUT THE SYSTEM

## Courts and Lawyers

■

"A fair and accessible judicial system is essential to the functioning democracy—both for redress of criminal allegations and for the resolution of civil disputes."

—Justice Thurgood Marshall

Justice Marshall knew all too well how important it is for black people to have access to the judicial system. Knowing exactly how the legal system works is key to having this accessibility. Once you grasp the basic principles, both procedurally and practically, you will have the power to choose how to use this system to work for you. This chapter provides both a brief overview of the procedural process of our judicial court system, the centerpiece of the American justice system, and an overview of practical considerations when encountering the legal system.

## The Basic Procedural Process: How Courts Are Organized

Many of us can recall the tragic story of Kemba Smith, a young black woman who was a college student at Hampton University when she was arrested for conspiracy to commit drug trafficking. BET, *Emerge*, grass-roots community activist groups, and others told how this young college student was sentenced to 24.5 years in prison for conspiracy to traffic crack cocaine. Her boyfriend was actually the target of an FBI investigation for an East Coast drug ring when he was murdered. Government officials, apparently looking for another target after his murder, proceeded against his girlfriend, Kemba, for drug trafficking. The prosecutor in the case admitted that Kemba had never used or distributed drugs. Yet this first-time "offender" was sentenced to almost a quarter of a century in prison because she pled guilty. Although the media highlighted the tragedy of what became known as "the Kemba story," they left many wondering exactly why the system worked as it did.

The Kemba story exemplifies why it is so important to figure out immediately which type of forum—whether it is a federal or state court or administrative agency—you are confronting. Kemba, who reportedly was exhausted by her situation and by the physical abuse she had suffered at the hands of her boyfriend, apparently believed that if she cooperated with the officials and agreed to their charges, she would be treated fairly.

Kemba was wrong. Because she was in the federal instead of a state system, she was subjected to mandatory sentencing guidelines. Due to these mandatory requirements, a judge would not consider any mitigating factors, like the fact that this was the first time she had been charged with any type of crime and that she had never used or distributed any drugs.

Kemba was unaware that her guilty plea could cause such horrendous consequences. Her lack of knowledge cost her more than six years of prison. Had President Clinton not pardoned Kemba in late 2000, she would likely still be in prison today.

Federal rules on how a case will proceed and the federal laws on drug trafficking are extremely different from state laws. It is therefore crucial that before analyzing any legal question you ask yourself whether you are in a *federal* or a *state* court.

## The Federal Court System

The federal court system is made up of several courts located throughout the United States. These courts have names like the Western District Court of Michigan, or the Ninth Circuit Court of Appeals. A person unfamiliar with the legal system could easily mistake a federal court like the Western District Court of Michigan for a state court.

There are three levels in the federal system: federal district courts, federal courts of appeals, and the highest court in the federal system, the United States Supreme Court. A U.S. president appointed every judge presiding over a federal court. These judges—unlike their state court counterparts, who frequently must be elected—are appointed for life and may only be removed from their positions under certain limited circumstances.

Federal courts are courts with "limited jurisdiction," which simply means that they have limited power. In other words, these courts only have authority over certain types of cases: those involving federal constitutional rights, federal statutes, federal criminal charges, and cases between residents of different states involving more than $75,000.

At least one federal district court is located in each state. Some states have more than one. States are geographically divided and a federal district court is located in each of these different geographic areas. For example, Michigan has two federal district courts—the Eastern District Court of Michigan and the Western District Court of Michigan.

When a party is unhappy with how a district court has resolved an issue, he or she may bring what is referred to as an "appeal" in a federal court of appeals. The entire country is divided along geographic lines into thirteen different "circuits." An appeal is brought in the circuit court having jurisdiction over the district court that heard the case. If the Eastern District of Michigan rendered a decision that a party wants to appeal, the party must bring an appeal in the Sixth Circuit Court of Appeals. The Sixth Circuit, which is located in Ohio, has the pleasure of having the Honorable Judge Damon Keith, one of our first black judges, on the bench.

After a Circuit Court of Appeals has rendered a decision, a party unhappy with the decision may attempt to file an appeal with the United States Supreme Court. A party does not have an absolute right to have the Supreme Court hear its case. First, it must file what is referred to as a "petition" asking the Court to hear the case, also referred to as asking the Court to "grant certiorari." The Court rejects many of these petitions, typically reserving its resources for cases that present unique issues that have been resolved differently in the lower federal courts. Remember this the next time you hear someone say, "That ain't even right. I'm taking this all the way to the Supreme Court." You'll know that his or her chances are less than favorable.

Aside from the federal district courts, the federal court of appeals, and the United States Supreme Court, there are federal courts that deal with special proceedings. These courts operate as if they were federal district courts. Among them are bankruptcy courts.

## State Court Systems

State court systems are different in many respects from the federal court system. First, unlike federal courts, which are courts of "limited jurisdiction," state courts have "general jurisdiction." This means that a state court can hear almost any type of case. Second, state court judges are not appointed for life by a U.S. president like their federal court counterparts. They are, like other high-level state officials, either elected by a popular vote or appointed by someone who has been elected by a popular vote. Third, state courts, which are also organized in a hierarchy, typically have four instead of three levels.

The first level of a state court system typically consists of district courts. Each court has different departments and the names of these departments are sometimes used instead of the district court name. For example, you may hear people say they have to go to "traffic court," "landlord–tenant court," or "small claims court," when they really mean they have to go to this section within the district court. If a claim involves a modest amount of money, usually less than $25,000, or landlord–

tenant, traffic, or criminal matters, it will usually begin in the district court.

All other cases begin in the second level of the state court system. These second-level state courts have different names depending upon the state. In Michigan, they are divided along county lines and are referred to as "circuit" courts. In North Carolina, they are referred to as "superior" courts. Even though the names vary, these courts address the same types of issues. Second-level state courts hear matters involving more money than those in the district court. They also act as the appellate court for all district courts in their jurisdiction. Like the district courts, these circuit courts have "courts" for special proceedings within the court, like "family court" and "probate court"; they also handle many administrative matters like name changes, assumed names for business purposes, marriage licenses, and birth and death certificates.

As in the federal system, a party unhappy with a decision rendered by one of the lower courts may appeal its case to the next higher court. Courts in the third level of the state court system, like the federal Circuit Court of Appeals, hear cases that have been appealed from lower state courts. If not resolved at this level, a party may then ask the highest court of the State to hear his or her case. In most states, this highest court is the state's Supreme Court.

For most cases, a state's Supreme Court is the final court capable of hearing a case. Under special limited circumstances, a case may be appealed from a state Supreme Court to the United States Supreme Court. But remember that the United States Supreme Court, like all federal courts, is a court with limited jurisdiction.

Recall the process used to resolve issues involving the 2000 presidential election. Many legal scholars believed that the United States Supreme Court would refuse to hear the case from the Florida Supreme Court involving voting rights. Because voting is primarily a state issue, scholars believed it was not the type of issue the United States Supreme Court would have jurisdiction to consider. The United States Supreme Court interpreted the U.S. Constitution to say that, although its jurisdiction was limited, it did have jurisdiction over this particular case because it involved a national issue—the election of a U.S. president. This decision was unusual, though. Under most circumstances, a case that has been resolved by a state's Supreme Court will not be subject to review by the United States Supreme Court. It is important to remember that, unlike this case, many cases cannot be appealed to the United States Supreme Court because it is a court of limited jurisdiction. In other words, a State Supreme Court is the final appellate court for most cases.

## THE PRACTICAL PROCESS: KNOWING HOW COURTS OPERATE

Do not just march down to the court when you have a legal issue. You will probably meet a salty clerk who will promptly tell you she or he cannot give you any legal advice. Save yourself some time by going to a public library or public law library and using the Internet to get the information you need, including forms you need to complete.

At this point you should start a file, much as any attorney would, and keep your papers and research in the file. The file does not need to be fancy; it could be an old notebook from your high school days. Pinpoint the name of the court or agency, locate and record its address, get its telephone number, and place this information in the file. Keep *only* information related to the issue you are addressing in this file.

Try to complete any forms prior to filing them at the court or agency. If you have any questions, contact the court or agency before completing your forms. Many forms are available, sometimes free of charge, on the Internet, at your local library, and at your local courthouse. If the forms or the court clerk states you will need certain documents, like a death certificate, make copies of these documents. Make at least four copies of any forms and documents you will be filing with the court.

If you must go to court for any reason, whether to file papers or as a plaintiff, defendant, witness, or juror, leave cell phones and pagers in your vehicle or at home and dress appropriately. One Michigan judge, who's a sister I may add, will confiscate your cell phone if it rings during her session. And sisters, don't bring any nail-care kits to court—I forgot one time and almost had mine confiscated because that itty-bitty scissor in my travel kit was considered a weapon. Fortunately, the bailiff let me leave it with her until I was finished.

It should go without saying that you should not even think about bringing a knife or gun into a courthouse. You are probably smart enough to know this, but I'll say it anyway—generally guns and knives are not permitted and attempting to bring them into a court could lead to your weapon being confiscated. You'd fare better by leaving this stuff in your ride or at the crib.

As for dress, realize that some courts have dress codes that they do not hesitate to enforce. Whether or not you agree with this practice, what you wear will determine how you are treated. If you go to court with your FUBU jeans hanging off your butt and a baseball cap on with the attitude that you're just "trying to keep it real," then it's like Chris Rock says—"you're just keeping it real dumb." Don't do it. Dress as if you expect to be respected. You don't have to dress like it's Easter Sunday, but if you stay away from jeans, shorts, T-shirts, sweatshirts, sweatpants, open-toed shoes, Spandex, and baseball caps, you should be dressed well enough to command respect. And don't forget, check the chewing gum at the door.

## WHEN TO HIRE AN ATTORNEY

"He who represents himself has a fool for a client."

—ABRAHAM LINCOLN

I have heard many people recite this quote when discussing whether someone should handle a legal matter without the assistance of an attorney. Many of us may have referred to it without considering the source of the phrase—old honest Abe, who was a lawyer himself. We may also fail to consider that "bar associations," organizations consisting of law-yers and other legal professionals, regularly use this self-serving phrase in pamphlets directed to the public. What better way to increase the use of lawyers' services than to inspire fear in those considering self-repre-sentation? I mean, who wants to be a fool? The more the public believes and relies on this quote, the more business there is for lawyers.

Interestingly, though, the American legal system was first and fore-most founded on the principle that an educated citizen could properly handle any legal matter without the assistance of an attorney. In fact the American system, based on democratic principles, was created to be accessible to the average layperson without any specialized legal train-ing. Lawyers were even banned in some colonies. Evidencing an increas-ing tolerance toward the concept of lawyers, Massachusetts passed a rule specifically permitting a person to represent another person as long as the person did so free of charge.

As America became increasingly influenced by the English system, this all changed. The American system began to resemble the English system, which was more rigid and formal and based heavily on the use of lawyers. But it was not until the 1920s and 1930s that the American Bar Association, an association of lawyers, lobbied to have states pass laws regulating the practice of law. Now, unless you have a license to practice law, you cannot engage in any activity that would be consid-ered practicing law (like giving someone legal advice or representing her in a legal proceeding). While there are exceptions to this general rule (for example, some state agencies permit nonlicensed individuals to serve as advocates in certain limited circumstances), the practice of law has become more regulated and is now almost completely monopolized by those licensed professionals we refer to as *lawyers* and *attorney*s. (At this point, it is worth mentioning that it is generally accepted that the words *lawyer* and *attorney* may be used interchangeably. Historically, *lawyer* was the general term ascribed to persons engaged in the prac-tice of law, and *attorney* indicated a person's particular lawyer. Bar associations are made up of a group of lawyers, but you hire an attorney to represent you. I suspect that with the rise in lawyer jokes, many lawyers began to refer to themselves as attorneys to distance themselves from being the all too frequent butt of these jokes.)

As this country has matured (or perhaps just gotten older) and its population increased, more laws have been passed, making the law increasingly complex. You may notice that at times I may recommend not only hiring an attorney, but hiring one who specializes in a particular area. General practitioners—lawyers who handle a wide variety of cases—are becoming an extinct breed. A good attorney in one area may not have the expertise to handle your case if it concerns an altogether different area. I have no doubt that my girl Felicia, a Dukie with me and a Harvard law grad, is a great "M&A" (mergers and acquisitions) attorney. In fact, she would certainly be able to structure a phat deal for you if you're ready to acquire BET. But she's never even argued a routine motion in front of a judge in open court. In determining whether to hire an attorney, at least consider whether you need someone who regularly handles your type of case. A graduate from the local law school who specializes in drunk driving cases may be in a better position to negotiate on your behalf than my girl Felicia. These drunk driving tickets would require your attorney to discuss your case with the local prosecutor, the attorney for the state, who may also be a graduate from the same local law school.

It should be noted that some employers, credit card companies, and independent organizations now offer prepaid legal services. The success of these ventures depends largely on the fact that almost everyone will be faced with a few legal issues sometime during their lifetime. Prepaid legal services act as a type of insurance and provide legal advice on routine matters like drafting a will. As with any product, determine exactly what you will be receiving before deciding whether it is worth the cost. These programs are still relatively new so it is hard to gauge whether they are worthwhile.

Free legal aid is also available. People charged with a crime have a right to an attorney and can get a court-appointed attorney. If you are charged with a crime and cannot afford to hire an attorney, exercise your right to a court-appointed attorney. If you have a civil rather than a criminal issue—for example, you are facing an eviction from your landlord— contact your local courthouse or bar association and ask for the number for free legal aid. These organizations, often funded by contributions by lawyers in various fields, provide free legal aid to those who qualify.

Before making a decision to hire an attorney, you should know what an attorney does and how an attorney is typically compensated. An attorney is a highly trained researcher. Because the law is constantly changing as new laws are passed, old laws are changed, and courts render decisions that alter our laws, an attorney must continually research the law. While you can ask a lawyer for an opinion on your case, as most decent lawyers will tell you, unless she has actually researched the law with your particular facts in mind, she can only provide you with a general opinion. To provide you with valuable legal advice you can rely on, a lawyer must actually turn to the law—the state statute, federal code, Constitution, and decisions from different courts—and read and analyze this material with your facts in mind to provide you with a legal opinion. Your attorney may spend only hours in the courtroom on your case, yet months and maybe years could be spent gathering factual evidence by interviewing witnesses, requesting information from the opposing party, retrieving the relevant law, reading and analyzing this law, preparing legal memoranda on specific issues, and preparing letters to your opponent.

The American Bar Association estimates that more than 51 percent of a lawyer's total revenue must be used to cover overhead expenses like the cost of conducting legal research and maintaining malpractice insurance, bar association dues, and office space and materials. To meet these demands, lawyers typically use either the contingent method or the hourly billing method. In most states, a lawyer must charge an hourly rate for domestic and criminal cases (if you're thinking what I'm thinking, yes, O.J.'s attorneys were getting *paid*). In contingency cases an attorney receives a portion of any settlement or jury award and basically works for nothing until the matter is concluded. At that time, the attorney is reimbursed all costs and receives the agreed upon contingent fee. If you agree to compensate your attorney on an hourly basis, you will likely be sent a monthly bill for the time your attorney has spent on your case. For example, your baby's momma isn't letting you see your baby girl and you hire an attorney to modify your visitation rights. If you agreed to pay your attorney $150 per hour and she spends twenty hours on your case that month, then you will be expected to pay her $3,000, plus any other costs like filing fees, when you receive your bill. A $3,000 bill for one month of legal services is no joke—that's why you may think seriously about using your own resources and handling some of your legal issues without hiring an attorney.

## Consider Representing Yourself If:

1. You are confronted with a consumer issue like a warranty on household appliances. Many times large companies have special relations departments specifically created to deal with consumer complaints. Some of these departments unfortunately use the word *ombudsman*, perhaps in an attempt to further confuse and frustrate consumers. Don't be intimidated by the fancy word. *Ombudsman* basically means an entity that investigates complaints. Many companies have ombudsmen or consumer complaint departments specifically tasked with resolving consumer issues.

2. The dispute involves less than a few thousand dollars. Small claims courts are state courts that resolve disputes between parties when the amount is less than a specified amount. This amount varies from state to state. The limit in Michigan is $1,750, while the limit in North Carolina is $4,000. Many states also forbid the use of attorneys, meaning each party must represent its own interests. This practice serves to even the playing field between individual consumers and large corporations.

3. You are the representative of an estate of a deceased person and the amount is less than $10,000 or $15,000. States provide low-cost ways for people handling small estates to file the necessary paperwork. State courts often sponsor free legal clinics to assist you in filling out the necessary paperwork. If the estate is less than $20,000, you should at least contact the local state court of the deceased and find out. It might surprise you that many cases like these can be handled in a couple of hours by simply completing a one-page form.

4. You have a routine domestic matter. Sometimes, divorced people with children later want to make changes regarding custody or parenting time. Since they likely used the services of an attorney during the divorce, they may quickly assume the matter is one that should be handled by an attorney. Typically an attorney bills on an hourly basis for domestic matters. If you have a small matter—for example, you want to change your parenting time—you may wish to file the paperwork yourself. Again, courts regularly offer free legal clinics on this topic and by filling out a form or two and attending a hearing you could have the matter resolved.

## Consider Hiring An Attorney If:

1. You are arrested for committing a crime. Listen to your Miranda rights—"you have the right to remain silent"—and keep your mouth closed. If you say anything, demand an attorney. The police can try to tempt you with a bargain and say that once your lawyer comes into the picture, "all deals are off"— I've actually heard that this is a favorite tactic of the force. Maybe the deal the police say will be off the table when your lawyer enters the picture really will be off the table. But rest assured that any deal the police made could just as easily reappear when the prosecutor and your attorney have a chance to discuss your case.

2. You get a ticket for DUI or a similar ticket like possession of marijuana. States have increased the penalties against those charged with these kinds of crimes. I asked one guy who had gotten a couple of DUIs whether he thought it was necessary to hire an attorney and he told me he'd still be locked up if he hadn't had an attorney. The problem with these charges is that to some they appear harmless, especially if it is a first offense. But driving while under the influence of drugs or alcohol is a serious crime in every state. Even first-time offenders face serious penalties, like the loss of their driving license. And repeat offenders can find themselves serving long jail sentences. If faced with such a charge, you would be well advised to enroll in a substance abuse or drug rehabilitation program on your own and hire an attorney who specializes in handling these types of cases.

3. You suffer a physical injury. You may find yourself in a minor car accident with medical expenses of a few hundred dollars. In these situations, you may want to consider handling your own case. But beware. Injuries from car accidents, even seemingly minor accidents, can sometimes take months to completely manifest themselves. If the prospect of "giving" an attorney one-third of any settlement amount from an insurance company doesn't seem fair, consider that hiring an attorney for these matters can increase your total settlement amount by more than 100 percent. While it may seem unfair, simply retaining an attorney can increase the amount the insurance company will pay. The insurance company knows that if an attorney is handling your case, there is a greater likelihood that it will be forced to get one of its attorneys on the case (frequently, insurance companies employ adjusters to handle cases when a party is not represented). It now has a greater economic incentive to offer a higher settlement figure to satisfy your attorney and keep itself from paying high attorneys' fees.

4. You suffer serious property damage. One of my clients had her home demolished by the city of Detroit. A fire had damaged her home. The city, which failed to notify her that it had scheduled her home for demolition, tore the house down right after it had its roof replaced. She promptly contacted the city and completed its paperwork to bring a complaint and seek redress for its actions. But the city never processed her complaint. After months, she retained a lawyer; she did the right thing. While it may seem unfair, had she waited and waited even after the city failed to take any action, she might have lost her ability to bring a lawsuit since it could argue that the statute of limitations period had expired. If you have already called and written a couple of letters yourself, especially in cases where you have significant losses and it has been more than a few months since the initial damage, hire an attorney to handle your case. You should never wait for more than a year before hiring an attorney.

5. You get served with legal papers. You could be getting out of your car at home and someone appears, asks you your name, then hands you some papers and says, "you're getting sued." Or you may receive notice of a divorce action through the mail. In either case, you have been served with legal papers and you will now need to take some action. Unless it is a small claims action, which you may have to handle yourself, consider hiring an attorney. More than likely, though, it is a divorce action, a personal injury case, or a case involving personal property or real estate. The paperwork should clearly state how many days you have to take action. Because the period is usually only a few weeks, contact someone as soon as possible. Do whatever you can to get over the initial shock and perhaps embarrassment of being sued. I say embarrassment because I had one client who was sued for her deceased mother's credit card bill. Her mother had listed her as a co-signer, but my client had not signed the credit card application. After looking at the credit card application her mother

had completed, it was apparent that she might have misunderstood the word *co-signer* to mean *reference*. The bill was regularly paid until my client's mother died. Instead of suing the
mother's estate, the company went after my client, alleging that
she was in fact a co-signer. My client explained that she had
always paid her bills on time and expressed that she was a little
embarrassed about being sued. Don't let any such embarrassment delay your seeking legal advice. I was able to get the company to dismiss the case before a response was even due. Had
she delayed until the last few days, this would not have been possible and more time and therefore money would have been
needed to defend the case.

6. You are dealing with other specialized matters. For example, if
   you are considering filing for bankruptcy or you are addressing
   an immigration matter, find an attorney who specializes in these
   areas to provide you with legal advice.

7. You feel too emotionally involved in the matter. Perhaps the best
   reason for considering hiring an attorney, and likely the reason
   many lawyers themselves hire attorneys to handle their own personal legal matters, is that you realize you are too close to the
   situation. An attorney often can offer a more objective opinion
   and can work with the other party so you don't have to confront
   the party yourself.

## Strategies for Hiring a "Good" Attorney

You may have seen lawyers advertising their services everywhere—on
television, on the back of telephone books, and on bus stop benches.
But if the thought of dialing 1-800-LAW-SUIT or a similar type of number makes you a little nervous, you are not alone. Finding a lawyer to
represent you can be intimidating. You may feel that because you don't
really know what you're looking for, you really won't know when you've
found the right person to take care of your issues. Here are some things
you should consider.

1. A "good" attorney for one type of case may not be a "good" attorney for another type of case. Just because your family's pastor recommends another friend who is a "good" attorney doesn't mean this attorney will be the right attorney for handling your specific case. When looking for an attorney, ask your friends and acquaintances if they know an attorney that specializes in your type of issue.

2. Don't be afraid of contacting lawyers whose advertising you've seen. Because many lawyers specialize, looking through the telephone book for lawyers who handle your type of case may be the best way to begin the process. Remember that as the client you can always "fire" your attorney, so if for some reason the relationship doesn't work, you're not stuck with this person. (You should also know that even though you can always fire your attorney, this doesn't mean you can terminate the lawyer toward the end of the case to save yourself attorneys' fees. While you can terminate the relationship, you'll remain liable for attorneys' fees and costs.)

3. If you want more information on a lawyer before hiring her, or want to see if she has ever been disciplined or suspended, contact the state bar organization, which is responsible for licensing attorneys.

4. Contact your local bar associations for referrals that will be appropriate for your specific interest. Perhaps you don't know the legal jargon or name associated with your situation. You may know that oneday, while you were delivering a package for your boss, a negligent driver hit you. But what you might not know is that this type of incident could be classified as a "workers' compensation" case. Placing a call to a local bar association and asking them for assistance can help you pinpoint what you're looking for—in this case, you'd probably be interested in a personal injury attorney who also handles workers' compensation cases.

## Should You Hire Black?

Sometimes I have been asked if a person should hire a black attorney or whether it makes any difference. Generally, the people who ask me this question have had very little exposure to the legal system beyond what they've seen on TV. All they really want to know is if the race of their attorney makes a difference.

The answer to this question is yes and no. Consider this scenario. You live in a predominantly black city like Detroit. You are the victim of racial discrimination at the hands of your employer, and you want to sue your employer for violating your civil rights. If your case ends up in court in front of a jury, the jury would likely be racially diverse and include black jurors. As in all cases, you will want an attorney the jury will find credible. Because black Americans are better able to identify with your allegations of race discrimination, the race of your attorney may be immaterial because your attorney would not have to work hard to make the jurors understand your allegations. But you may want to hire a black attorney since the jurors may find him or her more credible and trustworthy and may be able to identify with him or her better.

If, on the other hand, you were bringing the same type of case in a small, predominantly white Southern city, like Chattanooga, Tennessee, the race of your attorney would make a big and possibly decisive difference. In fact, because the jury would likely be predominantly white, and potentially all white, you may actually prefer a white attorney. As unfortunate as it may seem, the reality is that a white attorney may have more influence with the predominantly white jury and may be in a better position to advocate on your behalf. The jury may be better able to believe you were racially harassed if your white attorney, as opposed to your black attorney, says you were—remember the ABC poll that indicated most white people believe blacks exaggerate racial discrimination.

As grotesque as this may seem, the race of your attorney does matter when the allegations in the case involve race. While one of your foremost concerns should be whether your attorney makes you comfortable, you should certainly consider what type of case you are bringing, the potential racial makeup of your jury, and the overall racial makeup and climate of your geographic area when considering whether to hire an attorney based on her or his race. And know this: the other party certainly will be considering these factors. In the employer scenario above, the employer may set out to retain a black attorney to defend its racial discrimination case for similar reasons.

If you can remember how the legal system works in terms of procedure, and recognize how the system works in practical terms, you will be well ahead of the average American in understanding how to use the system to your advantage. With this general understanding of the system, you will be better able to determine whether you have a legal issue that may require the assistance of an attorney or whether you can handle the matter yourself. This general framework should serve as a backdrop for other issues addressed throughout the book.

# 9

# I'M GONNA SUE

## Representing Yourself

■

I ONCE HAD an attorney say to me, "I don't know why you're handling this case. I mean, there's not a lot of money involved." Hunh? I had to break it down for him right then and there. I reminded him that many black people before me were involved in legal battles over things like freedom and human dignity, not money, and that the principles involved in this particular case were far more important than the almighty dollar bill. What is your potential case about? Whether it be about money or human dignity, you will need to have a firm belief in your cause.

Before you rush off to court and file an action against a person or company, try to be very clear and honest with yourself about your proposed course of action. When a case is filed against someone, you have begun the "litigation" process, which is supposed to be a civilized way of doing battle.

Sometimes, though, litigation isn't too civil, and at times it can be downright ugly. What's worst is that the whole process can take years to complete. If you're frustrated now over what a person or company has done to you, try fighting over it for a couple of years. A judgment may ultimately be entered in your favor, yet you still may feel frustrated and disappointed.

This is why it is so important that you carefully evaluate what you are seeking from the process. If at some point along the way the other side decides to give you what you want, then you will know that you have in effect won and can dismiss your case and stop the process. Actually write down your answers to the following questions:

- What do you hope to achieve by suing this person or company?
- Do you need money to pay medical bills?
- Do you want a company to be punished for causing you and your family unnecessary suffering?
- Do you want to be vindicated for the pain you have suffered?

Although litigation can vindicate a person or restore his dignity, the American process tends to place a price tag on all civil disputes. This is one of the first questions I ask my clients to consider. I do this not because I expect them to know right off, but I want them to realize that if they think they are going to feel better even when all of our goals have been accomplished, then they will be sorely disappointed. Take a woman who came into my office complaining about the sexual harassment she had suffered at work. Sure, she had a case. But she needed to know that litigating against her supervisor and employer was not going to erase the pain she had suffered. When she had finally come to terms with the fact that what she really wanted was impossible, to not have been subjected to such humiliating conduct and to receive an apology from her supervisor, she was ready to take a realistic approach to her case. Only when you have reflected on your objective in this manner will you be ready to decide whether and how to proceed.

## Choosing the Right Forum

In litigation, your "forum" is the place you sue or file your complaint. There are basically two court systems in each state. State courts are courts of general jurisdiction, which means that a state court has the power to hear almost all types of disputes. Federal courts are courts of limited jurisdiction. Unlike state courts, they can generally hear only disputes involving residents of two different states when the amount disputed is over $75,000, or cases involving federal questions like an interpretation of a federal statute like Section 1983 of the Civil Rights Act. There are also agencies, both federal and state, that hear certain disputes. For example, the Equal Employment Opportunity Commission (EEOC) or your state's equivalent will be the first stop for most disputes with an employer over harassment or discrimination. Private organizations, like the American Arbitration Association (AAA), also will hear certain disputes.

To make sure you have chosen the proper forum for your action, contact the court or agency before actually preparing any paperwork to make sure you are in the right place. If you will be suing in a certain county, for example, call the clerk of the court and ask if it handles matters involving a particular city or town in that county. If you are filing a complaint at a government agency, pay close attention to the timetable for filing and ask the agency if it handles your type of complaint before you go there.

Making sure you file your case or complaint in the right forum is extremely important. To make this determination, you need to answer the following questions.

- Whom are you proposing to sue or file a complaint against?

This sounds simple, but, as many attorneys will tell you, making the right decision about whom to sue is very important when deciding where you will file your case. Are you suing your boss for unpaid overtime wages? Or your neighbor who borrowed your lawn mower and still hasn't returned it? In the first instance, you would need to file your complaint with the government agency that handles wage disputes. A minor case against your neighbor, on the other hand, should be filed in your state's local court in your area.

- What are you seeking from this person or organization?

Do you want to sue a cellular telephone service provider to get out of your contract because it is providing terrible service? Will you then ask the court to award you money? Or do you want the court to order some specific action, like "tell my neighbor to clean up his nasty yard because it's disgusting and ruining my property value"? In the first case, you'd be asking the court for "monetary damages." In the second, you'd be seeking what is referred to as "injunctive" relief, which means you are asking the court to enter an order telling the defendant to stop engaging in certain conduct.

- If you are seeking money rather than an injunction, how much money are you disputing?

Your answer will greatly influence where you should file your case. If it is only a couple thousand dollars that you are disputing, you more than likely will want to file a claim in your state's small claims court. In fact, if it is less than a certain amount, referred to as the "jurisdictional amount," you will be forced to file your action in one court as opposed to another.

- When did the incident occur?

If you file an action too soon, the court may dismiss your action because it is not "ripe," saying that you need to wait until you have actually been damaged before it will accept your suit. If you file an action too late, you could have what is referred to as a "statute of limitations" problem. This happens if the incident you are complaining about occurred years ago. If you file your action within a couple of months of the date of the incident, you should be timely enough to meet the most stringent limitations problems.

## Bringing a Small Claims Action

Small claims courts are especially suited for self-representation. These courts typically have low jurisdictional amounts, like a few thousand dollars. However, in some places, like Tennessee, the amount in controversy can be as high as $25,000. To find out the jurisdictional amount of the small claims court you are considering, either call the court clerk or locate the information on the Internet (see the Resource Guide for law-related Internet sites).

A judge or attorney may ask if "venue is proper." This means he or she is just asking if the case has been filed in the right place based on geography. If you file in a place that you believe will be convenient for all parties, more than likely you will satisfy the venue requirement. You should file your action where the defendant is living, where the firm does business, where the accident took place, or where the contract was signed. After the action has been filed, you will be scheduled for a trial. And if you've ever seen Judge Brown's court, you know what happens next. Both parties are given a chance to present their case, and then the judge renders a decision on the spot.

## Filing an Action with a Federal or State Government Agency

Often you will find that it is best to first contact the administrative agency that has been established to resolve your type of dispute. This is particularly true in cases involving an action against an employer for discrimination or against a government agency for benefits. In some instances, you need to file an administrative dispute before you can file a complaint in court. This is referred to as the requirement that you have "exhausted your administrative remedies."

Say, for example, you have been denied unemployment benefits and you want to sue your former employer because you believe it provided the agency with false information. You might think the agency arbitrarily ruled in favor of the employer and it wouldn't make much sense to file a complaint with this same agency. Wait a minute, though. Before dashing down to that court, realize that your efforts will be futile if you have not "exhausted your administrative remedies." In a case like this, you would need to appeal the denial of unemployment benefits until the administrative agency makes a final determination. Then, and only then, can you file your case in court. If you file your case in court before exhausting your administrative remedies, a court will probably dismiss your case.

There are instances, however, when a government agency will process complaints but not actually resolve disputes. Consumer complaints filed with the Federal Trade Commission (FTC) are an example. Government agencies are primarily tasked with serving the public, and they process complaints about alleged illegal conduct by an organization. Be aware, however, that filing a complaint with an agency will not have a direct impact on your case against the offending party. I have heard several people complain that they filed a complaint with a government agency, but "nothing ever happened." It is not necessarily that nothing ever happened. In your case, the agency may have just filed the information until it gets an even stronger case against the organization. At any rate, make absolutely certain when you file a complaint that you file it with the agency that actually resolves your type of dispute.

## THE LITIGATION PROCESS

Once you have pinpointed the place you need to file, here are the steps you need to take.

1. Get the right forms to file. This depends on whether you are filing in federal or state court or in a government agency. Federal courts use what is referred to as a "civil cover sheet." In most states, you will need what is called a "summons and complaint"

form to file a civil dispute unless it is a small claims matter, in which case you will likely need a special form from the clerk's office or the court's Internet site.

2. Carefully complete the forms. By answering some of the questions on these forms, you will be answering some of the questions you should have already considered when deciding to file your complaint. At this time, you might discover that you should actually file your case in another place. It is much better to make this determination before risking losing your filing fee for filing your case in the wrong place. Pay close attention.

3. Prepare what you will use as your complaint. In litigation, your complaint, as well as most other papers filed by the parties with the court, is referred to as "pleadings." Sometimes, you will be able to write on the form everything necessary to bring an action. I once defended an action brought against a company by a consumer under the federal Telephone Consumer Protection Act. His complaint was handwritten and said something like "violated TCPA by faxing without permission." It was properly served and it did its job. The complaint doesn't have to be typewritten in most states (although this will probably change given the number of people who have access to computers and word processing). Follow the court's guidelines on what is required and what is permitted. If you fail to do so, the clerk will refuse to accept your case.

4. Get the necessary documents served. This means you must have the documents provided to the defendants in a way that gives them notice that they are being sued. If you don't know what this means, just ask one of yo' cousins. I'm sure you know someone who won't go to the post office to pick up a certified letter because she thinks it's from a bill collector or someone trying to sue. For the record, ignoring certified mail will not stop a civil suit. As painful as it may be, it is always best to address legal matters head on; by doing so you can save yourself a whole lot

of drama. Sometimes, the court may offer to have the documents served for a small fee. You can also look in your local telephone book under "process servers" and have a professional serve the documents. Or you can try to serve your papers via certified mail.

What happens next depends on where you have filed your case. If you have filed a complaint in small claims court, in most states you will then receive a date for your trial. Bring all evidence, like canceled checks or receipts, that you will use to establish your case at this time. If you are in a federal or state court, the party you have served the complaint against will then file an answer. Before you ever go to trial, you will participate in several other steps. The litigation process can include "discovery," a process during which parties exchange information; mediation; status conferences; and settlement conferences. The entire process, even without any delays, can take a year or more. I've heard that a Virginia court has been nicknamed "the rocket docket" because most of its cases are completed in eight to twelve months. A case that is completed within a year is quite rare.

The litigation process is governed by the court's rules of civil procedure. These rules vary depending on the court. The court's law librarian can provide you with a copy of these rules.

## MEDIATION AND ARBITRATION: RESOLVING YOUR DISPUTE IN OTHER WAYS

Mediation and arbitration fall under what is referred to as alternative dispute resolution (ADR). Because so many people have criticized the wheels of justice for turning so slowly, mediation and arbitration were created to work with the litigation process to offer a quicker way to resolve disputes. Technically, the two are very different processes. In mediation, one neutral person works with two opposing parties to assist them in seeking a resolution. The mediator will not determine who is right or wrong. In arbitration, a neutral person actually makes a determination and renders a decision after hearing what both parties have to say about a dispute. Practically speaking, however, *mediation* and *arbitration* are sometimes used interchangeably. What might be labeled a mediation process may be more like an arbitration process.

Sometimes you will be forced to participate in ADR-type processes before actually having a trial. For example, in Michigan, parties to a petition over a child visitation matter are forced to go before a referee in what is labeled a mediation process. Michigan refers to this process as mediation even though the referee listens to both sides of the case and issues a recommended order, which is technically what an arbitrator rather than a mediator would do.

Both mediation and arbitration can lead to a quick resolution of your dispute. If you must decide whether you should use one of these processes, consider:

- The complexity of the issues involved.

If the case is complex, it might be better to submit it to an arbitrator who has expertise on that particular subject matter instead of a judge.

- How important it is for you to have your dispute heard and resolved quickly.

ADR processes typically take less time than the traditional litigation process.

- Whether you or your opponent will have an opportunity to appeal any decision to a court.

If you are agreeing to submit to "binding" arbitration, the decision of the arbitrator will be final. You will not be able to appeal the determination even if you don't agree with the decision. You can be somewhat certain that the matter will be over, and, if you are successful, the other party won't be able to appeal the decision either. (I say "somewhat certain" because parties have been known to dispute even a "binding" arbitration.)

- How much money is involved in the dispute and whether the amount is fairly definite.

If you are dealing with a contractual dispute, the total amount of your damages will not change. You will be entitled to a certain amount based on the contract. In these types of actions it is basic math; several jurors and one mediator or arbitrator should reach the same result. This is not true if the case involves more subjective issues like race discrimination. In these cases, depending on the racial composition of the geographic area where potential jurors would come from, you might be better off choosing to go to court and having the benefit of several people deciding your case.

- Whether you believe your case involves an important matter of principle that concerns the public or whether it is more of a private dispute between two parties.

Typically, an arbitrator cannot set precedent, which is legal authority that will influence the conduct of both the party you are opposing and other parties like that party. Take, for example, the civil suits that have been filed against the University of Michigan over affirmative action. If these cases had been arbitrated, the settlements would have been confidential. They would have served to resolve the dispute between the parties, but would have had absolutely no effect on other students or universities. Because the cases were filed in court, the rulings on affirmative action will have a direct impact on all public universities and their applicants.

## SELF-REPRESENTATION THROUGH LETTER WRITING

One tactic you can use to represent yourself without the assistance of a lawyer is letter writing. This can be especially effective if you have an attorney you can copy on your letters who also offers assistance and guidance. One such letter is referred to as a "demand letter": it outlines a problem, proposes a resolution, and states that additional legal action will be taken if the matter is not addressed within a set time frame (see the Resource Guide for sample demand letters).

If it is a contractual matter, you can cite a specific amount of money you would be willing to settle your claim for. However, if it involves noncontractual issues like racial discrimination, I caution you against citing any specific sum in a letter. If you ask for a figure that is too low and you later retain an attorney, it will harm your attorney's ability to handle your case. If you ask for a figure that is too high, you might be seen as a gold-diggin' plaintiff who is just trying to hit the legal jackpot. This too could hurt your case. In the demand letter, specify when you intend to take further action. And when that day comes and goes, take that action. Either retain an attorney or file your case in court. By this time, there ain't nothing left to do but to do it.

# 10

# TAKE IT TO THE POLLS

## Understanding and Exercising Your Right to Vote

■

"No Negro will vote in Georgia for the next four years."

—EUGENE TALMADGE, 1946, during his successful campaign to become the Governor of Georgia

## FROM IDEAL TO MAKING IT REAL: BLACKS DEMAND THE RIGHT TO VOTE

"The right to vote freely for the candidate of one's choice is of the essence of a democratic society, and any restrictions on that right strike at the heart of representative government."

—CHIEF JUSTICE EARL WARREN, *Reynolds v. Sims* (1964)

The essence of a democratic society might be the right to vote, but the reality is that people of color, and Southern black people in particular, have had to fight, sometimes literally to their deaths, for that right. The Constitution did not mention the right to vote until the Fifteenth Amendment was passed in 1870. The right to vote was a matter of state law, and both slavery and other restrictive laws made it impossible for blacks in many places, but particularly in the South and Midwest, to vote.

When the Civil War ended, the Military Reconstruction Act of 1867 was passed to permit Confederate states to return to the union if they agreed that all males would have the right to vote. The Fifteenth Amendment specifically made it illegal for the right to vote to be abridged based on race. Blacks, who years before could not vote, registered in significant numbers and even began to elect black officials.

Recall my insistence in Chapter 1 that just as soon as blacks enjoyed some progress, laws were enacted to curb this progress. Perhaps one of the better examples of this phenomenon is in the area of voting rights. When Reconstruction ended and federal troops were removed from the South, organizations like the Ku Klux Klan used physical violence and intimidation to prohibit blacks from registering and exercising their right to vote. These extremist groups were supported in their cause by state legislatures that actually passed laws designed to disenfranchise blacks. Literacy tests were used in conjunction with "grandfather clauses" to keep Southern blacks from voting. A person who could not pass the literacy test, like an illiterate white male, could still qualify to vote if he was a descendant of enfranchised men before the Fifteenth Amendment was enacted. Poll taxes and other means were also used to keep Southern blacks away from the polls. The gains of the Reconstruction Era were effectively nullified and Southern blacks, even though the Fifteenth Amendment provided otherwise, were once again all but disenfranchised.

By the late 1800s, beginning with the enactment of the Fifteenth Amendment, black men at least had the right to vote. By the 1960s, led by racist politics like those of Governor Talmadge, this right had been severely limited by state laws designed to prohibit blacks from voting. Civil rights activists during the mid-1960s began to focus their efforts on once again securing the right to vote for Southern blacks.

The Congress of Racial Equality (CORE), the Student Nonviolent Coordinating Committee (SNCC), the National Association for the Advancement of Colored People (NAACP), and the Southern Christian

Leadership Conference (SCLC), all civil rights organizations, joined together to form the Council of Federated Organizations (COFO) to increase the number of blacks registered to vote in Mississippi. In early 1965, protesters organized a march in Selma, Alabama, that would prove influential in securing the rights of blacks to vote. In one particular march, as the marchers prepared to cross a bridge from Selma toward the capitol, they were confronted by the Selma sheriff and state troopers. These police officers used electric cattle prods, tear gas, and bull whips, along with other devices, to deter the nonviolent protesters. Several people were hospitalized as a result. One trooper shot Jimmy Lee Jackson to death. By the middle of 1965, thousands of people had been arrested, hundreds hospitalized, and several killed as a result of attempting to secure the right of blacks to vote.

## OUR RIGHTS UNDER THE VOTING RIGHTS ACT OF 1965

The Voting Rights Act of 1965 was passed as a direct result of these events. Section two of this Act states that "No voting qualification or prerequisite to voting, or standard, practice, or procedure shall be imposed or applied by any State or political subdivision to deny or abridge the right of any citizen of the United States to vote on account of race or color." Remember, the Fifteenth Amendment provides that the " . . . right of citizens of the United States to vote shall not be denied or abridged by the United States or by any State on account of race, color, or previous condition of servitude." This section is plainly a restatement of this constitutional right.

Other sections of the Act, however, equip the federal government with powerful tools to secure the right to vote. The Act at least temporarily suspended literacy tests and provided for federal examiners who could register eligible voters. Section Five of the Act also provided that certain "covered" jurisdictions, namely Southern states that had done everything they could to deny blacks the right to vote, could only institute new procedures by seeking federal approval. The Voting Rights Act sought to accomplish what the Fifteenth Amendment should have made clear—that all adult citizens, including black citizens, have the right to vote. But the Voting Rights Act went further. It actually embodied specific means to achieve the end of racial discrimination in voting.

Many people consider the Voting Rights Act of 1965 to be the most successful civil rights legislation enacted to date. Prior to the Act, in Alabama in 1965 only 19 percent of blacks were registered to vote compared to 69 percent of whites. About twenty years after the Act was passed, approximately 68 percent of blacks were registered to vote compared to 75 percent of whites. Other Southern states, like Mississippi and Louisiana, have seen a similar increase in registered blacks. These numbers alone suggest that years after the Fifteenth Amendment was passed and the Reconstruction era ended, blacks could once again claim their right to vote without risking their lives.

An e-mail circulating around the Internet says:

> Did you know that our right to VOTE will expire in the year 2007? Seriously! The Voters Rights Act signed in 1965 by Lyndon B. Johnson was just an ACT. It was not made a law. In 1982, Ronald Reagan amended the Voters Rights Act for another 25 years. Which means that in the year 2007 we could lose the Right to vote! Does anyone realize that African Americans are the only group of people who require PERMISSION under the United States Constitution to vote!

Is this true? The short answer, if it is not already obvious, is no. The e-mail is only half true.

The Voting Rights Act, which received considerable support from both our House of Representatives and Senate (collectively referred to as "Congress"), was passed and signed into law in 1965. It is an act, but an act is a law. (The term *act* is sometimes used to indicate that a particular law is part of our body of statutory law, instead of our Constitution or laws derived from judicial opinions rendered by courts.) The Act was amended in 1982 to permit the federal government to continue to take certain steps to ensure that blacks, and other minorities as well, truly have access to the polls to cast their votes. While this amendment is set to expire in 2007, technically blacks will not lose their right to vote just because this amendment expires. This being said, however, if the federal government fails to continue to ensure that the rights of blacks to vote are protected by extending the protections of this Act, then states could once again try to disenfranchise blacks as they did after Reconstruction.

## *How* Our Vote Matters

The above-mentioned e-mail, although inaccurate, is valuable in that it cautions blacks not to sleep on our right to vote. It is probably painful for blacks who were actually part of the struggle, like SNCC leader John Lewis, who suffered a fractured skull during the March on Selma, to hear blacks complain that their vote doesn't really count. If this were true, racist Southern whites likely would not have spent so much effort to prohibit blacks from voting. Having seen the power of the black vote during Reconstruction, they moved swiftly to curtail blacks' access to the polls once the federal government left the South.

My grandmother, a lifelong resident of Mobile, Alabama, told me that her parents always paid poll taxes and voted, and that it just made her sick that one of her friends, who lives off government checks, I should add, said that she wouldn't vote "because them white folks gonna do what they wanna do anyways." I have heard several people make similar complaints.

Unfortunately, many people may recognize the importance of the right to vote but fail to understand fully just how the person you elect can have a very real impact on your daily life. Take my grandmother's friend, for example. She believes that her vote doesn't matter. But what she may not understand is that the people she could potentially have a part in electing could either directly or indirectly affect her ability to receive government assistance. This is true on both the state and federal level. Elected officials can have an enormous impact on your life.

Remember the discussion on police brutality and excessive force? There, I explained that the United States Supreme Court had ruled that a "reasonableness" standard should be applied to all excessive force cases. It must be noted that people who vote indirectly elect Supreme Court justices. The country votes for a president who in turn nominates a person to become a Supreme Court justice. The person nominated has to be approved by senators who are also elected by people who vote.

President Ronald Reagan, a conservative president, appointed several of the Supreme Court justices who currently sit on our nation's highest court. Years after he has left office, people seeking redress for police brutality and excessive force are still feeling the effect of eight years of Reaganism. The right to vote must be taken seriously.

Of course, many people have taken this right seriously. The presidential election of 2000 is proof of this. Reportedly, several of us offered rides to others who needed a way back and forth to poll booths, and we had an unprecedented turnout. But unfortunately, several people reported gross irregularities, which have led the NAACP and ACLU as well as others to file lawsuits over discriminatory voting practices.

The problems that occurred in the 2000 presidential election will hopefully lead to much needed election reform. Voting practices nationwide should be reviewed to ensure that no person is unnecessarily denied the right to vote. Florida, for example, has a law prohibiting ex-convicts from voting. What this means is that in Florida approximately 30 percent of black males are prohibited from voting by virtue of their "ex-convict" status. This law is now being scrutinized.

## Discrimination in Voting

Like the individuals who joined together to march in Selma, blacks who take action and contest discrimination in voting can make a difference. Both the Fifteenth Amendment and the Voting Rights Act of 1965 protect our right to vote. Discrimination in voting, including irregular practices or procedures that tend to dilute the black vote, should be reported.

The right to vote is not the only right that is protected by the Voting Rights Act. It protects other rights associated with the voting process, like organizing voter registration drives and campaigning for an election. If you or someone you know has been discriminated against in ways people participate in the process, report this behavior. Discriminatory practices should be reported to both your state's Attorney General office and your area's United States Attorney General office. Other organizations you should consider contacting include:

**U.S. Department of Justice**
Civil Rights Division—Voting Section
P.O. Box 66128
Washington, DC 20035-6128
(202) 307-3143
Fax: (202) 307-3961

**NAACP Legal Defense and Educational Fund, Inc.**
1275 K Street, NW, Room 301
Washington, DC 20005
(202) 682-1300
Fax: (202) 682-1312

**American Civil Liberties Union**
Public Education Department
132 W. 43rd Street
New York, NY 10036
(212) 944-9800, ext. 422
Fax: (212) 869-9065

**Southwest Voter Registration Education Project**
403 E. Commerce, Suite 220
San Antonio, TX 78205
(210) 222-0224
(800) 404-VOTE
Fax: (210) 222-1011

The right to vote is undeniably one of the most important rights we have. All of our laws result from people exercising the right to vote. An elected congressperson may support a bill that ultimately is supported by Congress and sent to the president for signature. Active participants in all of these steps are elected officials.

The same is true in state governments. State laws are a result of state legislators who have been elected to office. Some states have practices where the people directly elect their judges, so state laws are actually interpreted by people who have been elected.

The interpretation of the scope of our civil rights, the enactment of sentencing guidelines for criminal defendants, and the laws ensuring certain employee rights and consumer protections all have this in common: they are a result of people voting. If there is a regulation or law in this book you don't like, then research your candidates and in your next election vote only for those willing to make changes you deem important. Lives were lost over the right of blacks to vote. One challenge I heard during the 2000 election was that we should "vote like your life depends on it . . ."

And in fact it does. Your vote counts. My vote counts. And if we want more justice and more peace, we each must vote like our life depends on it and vote for those willing to ensure that our legal system truly becomes a justice system for all people, including black people.

# RESOURCE GUIDE

■

## GATHERING MORE INFORMATION

It is important to remember that we do live in a democracy and that the law is our law. Steps have been taken to provide the public with access to legal information. There will be times when you know you have a legal issue but have no idea where to get more information. The information contained here will provide you with basic tools you can use to address almost any legal issue.

## FINDING THE LAW ON THE INTERNET

### Federal Law

Bills, Congressional Record, Legislative History
http://thomas.loc.gov
You can use this site to research federal bills, like the one supported by Congressman Conyers to end racial profiling.

**Federal Sentencing Guidelines**

www.ussc.gov

The type of guidelines that were used in the Kemba case can be found on this site. If you or a loved one is involved in a federal criminal case, you can access this site for more information.

**United States Code**

http://law.house.gov

The United States Code is a collection of federal laws. So, for example, if you wanted to find the actual text of Section 1983 of the Civil Rights Act, you can use this site.

**Code of Federal Regulations**

www.access.gpo.gov/nara/cfr-table-search.html

The Code of Federal Regulations (CFR) contains federal regulations that change more frequently than federal statutes. These are basically federal agency interpretations of federal statute. If you file a complaint with a federal agency, you might find that its forms reference a section of the CFR. You can use this site to retrieve the actual section the agency has referenced.

## Federal Government Agencies

**Department of Education**
www.ed.gov

**Department of Justice**
www.usdoj.gov

**Department of Health and Human Services**
www.os.dhhs.gov

**Department of Labor**
www.dol.gov

**Department of State**
www.state.gov

**Department of Housing and Urban Development**
www.hud.gov

Equal Employment Opportunity
Commission
www.eeoc.gov

Federal Trade Commission
www.ftc.gov

Internal Revenue Service
www.irs.gov

Small Business Administration
www.sba.gov

Social Security Administration
www.ssa.gov

United States Copyright Office
http://lcweb.loc.gov/copyright

United States Patent Office
www.uspto.gov

United States Senate
www.senate.gov

United States Congress
www.house.gov

White House
www.whitehouse.gov

## Other Helpful Internet Sites

www.consumer.gov (FirstGov for Consumers)
www.fedworld.gov
www.findlaw.com
www.lawcrawler.com
www.lectlaw.com (The 'Lectric Law Library)
www.legaladviceline.com
www.loc.gov (The Library of Congress)
www.nationalbar.org (National Bar Association)

# SAMPLE LETTERS, AGREEMENTS, AND CLAUSES

## Sample Freedom of Information Act (FOIA) Request Letter

[This letter was actually used to request information under the Freedom of Information Act.]

■ November 1, 2002

VIA FACSIMILE (313) 555-5555 & U.S. MAIL
Port Director
United States Customs
477 Michigan Avenue, Suite 200
Detroit, Michigan 48226
Re: Freedom of Information Act (FOIA) Request for Information

Dear Port Director:

On or about October 26, 2001, an incident occurred at the United States/Canadian border on the Ambassador Bridge involving Nedra Denise Campbell. The incident began at approximately 1:00 A.M. The supervisor involved was a Ms. George. She refused to provide the names of the officers involved.

This is a Freedom of Information Act request. This request is for all documents and information, including the videotape of cars proceeding through the station involved in the incident within the hour immediately prior to the incident, and any other information, regardless of how that information is stored. This request is being made pursuant to the Freedom of Information Act, 5 USC § 552, as amended, and Part 103 of the Customs Regulations.

I am committed to paying a maximum amount of $25 US dollars for the videotape(s), documents, and other information upon receipt of these materials. Please contact me prior to proceeding in the unlikely event that my request would require a payment greater than $25. Your immediate attention to this request is required. Accordingly, I expect to receive this information as soon as possible.

Sincerely yours,
Nedra D. Campbell

## Sample Letter Concerning a Violation of Your Civil Rights

■ Date
Address

Dear Customs Director:

I was traveling from Jamaica to Atlanta on October 26, 2001. At approximately 1:00 P.M., I entered the Customs area in the Atlanta Hartsfield Airport where I was detained and subjected to extensive searches for an hour. Several other black passengers were similarly detained. I believe I suffered a violation of my civil rights and was a victim of racial profiling. Please indicate to me in writing how this situation is being addressed.

Sincerely,
[Insert Full Name and Sign]

[You may want to send a copy of your letter to other organizations that handle your type of complaint. Each time you send a letter to an organization, obtain the name and department handling your type of complaint and address your letter to its attention.]

cc: Department of Justice Civil Rights Division
National Association for the Advancement of Colored People (NAACP)
American Civil Liberties Union (ACLU)

## Sample Demand Letter

■ [Your Address]
Date
Address
Re: [Insert Your Name and, if applicable, your Account Number]
Dear [Insert Name of Company]:

On or about [Insert Date], your company agreed to repair the roof on my house. You charged me $5,000 for this project, which was to include a 10-year warranty on the job. This winter, one year after you allegedly repaired my roof, I have had severe leaking problems. These problems have caused significant damage to my home, including ruining my newly installed kitchen flooring. Your company has clearly breached your express and implied warranties.

I was forced to hire another company to repair my roof and kitchen floor. As reflected by the enclosed receipts, your breach of these warranties has caused me more than $10,000 in actual monetary damages. Presently, I am willing to forego filing a civil suit against your company for $10,000.

Please contact me within the next 10 calendar days at [Insert Your Phone Number] or the address above regarding this matter. Failure to do so will cause me to file a civil action in my local district court. At that time, I will no longer be willing to settle this matter for such a nominal amount.

Your prompt attention to this matter would be appreciated.

Sincerely yours,
[Insert Your Name]

Enclosure [if you have documentation like receipts or cancelled checks]

[The above demand letter can be used when you have entered into an agreement for a product and services and you are seeking a specified amount of money from the company. I recommend sending this type of letter via certified mail, return receipt requested.]

## Sample Demand Letter

- [Your Address]
  Date
  Address
  Re: [Insert Your Name and, if applicable, your Account Number]

Dear [Insert Name of Company]:

On or about [Insert Date], I entered into an agreement with [Insert Name of Company] for cellular telephone services. Prior to entering into this agreement, your representative indicated to me that service was available in my home area. Each time I attempt to use your services, though, I am unable to do so.

You have breached our agreement by failing to provide the agreed upon cellular services. Accordingly, I am seeking to terminate the agreement effective immediately. Please discontinue my services as soon as you receive this letter.

Should you attempt to continue to enforce any provision of this agreement, I will take legal action, which may include filing a claim in my local small claims court.

Your prompt attention to this matter would be appreciated.

Sincerely yours,
[Insert Your Name]

[The above demand letter can be used when you have entered into an agreement for services and the company has failed to deliver the promised services. I recommend sending this type of letter via certified mail, return receipt requested.]

## Sample Fair Credit Reporting Act (FRCA) Letter

[The Fair Credit Reporting Act, 15 USCA § 1681 *et seq.*, protects your right as an individual consumer to access information contained in your credit history and to have any erroneous information contained in this history deleted. The Act applies to suppliers of information, like credit card companies; users of credit information, like prospective employers or landlords; and credit bureaus that maintain information, like Experian, TransUnion, and Equifax. A consumer can sue a company for violating the Act. In most instances, such a suit can be brought in your local small claims court. The statute of limitations period for filing such a suit is two years.]

- [Your Address]
  Date
  Address
  Re: [Insert Your Name and Social Security Number or Account Number]

  Dear [Insert Name of Company]:

  Please be advised that there is erroneous information contained in my credit report. This information includes the following:

  (a) Company X, apparently a collection bureau, has reported that Account No. XXXX XXXX, is an unpaid collection account. Company A, the credit card company, reports that this account has been paid in full. This account has been paid in full and the information reported by Company X should be deleted.

  (b) Company Y reports an outstanding loan of $10,000. This amount was consolidated with other loans that are being reported by Company B. The information reported by Company Y is erroneous and incorrect, since this company no longer has this loan account.

  As you know, under the Fair Credit Reporting Act, 15 USCA § 1681 *et seq.*, you are required to conduct an investigation to ensure that only accurate information is reported. Once you have completed your investigation, I am confident that you will find that this information is erroneous and will delete it from my credit history.

  Please promptly conduct your investigation and forward your report to my attention at the address above. Failure to do so will cause me to institute an action against you under the FCRA for damages and attorneys' fees. Your prompt assistance to this matter would be appreciated.

  Sincerely yours,
  [Insert Your Name]

cc: Company X
    Company Y

## Sample Fair Debt Collection Practices Act (FDCPA) Letter

[The Fair Debt Collections Practices Act, 15 USCA § 1692(e), was primarily enacted to prohibit unfair collection practices. Generally, this Act prohibits annoying, harassing, and misleading conduct. For example, a debt collector cannot threaten you with legal action when it does not intend to take such action, nor can it induce you to pay a debt you dispute by threatening you with negative information on your credit report. You can sue a company that takes this type of action in state or federal court for actual damages or $1,000, whichever is higher, as well as your costs and attorneys' fees.]

- [Your Address]
  Date
  Address
  Re: [Insert Your Name and Social Security Number or Account Number]

  Dear [Insert Name of Company]:

  On or about [Insert Date], your company contacted me regarding Account No. XXX-XXXX. The representative called my home number and informed my teenage daughter that if this account was not paid, your company would be "taking legal action against me and that I could end up in jail." Each time your representative has contacted me in the past, I have informed her or him that I am disputing this debt.

  This letter is written notice to you under the Fair Debt Collection Practices Act, 15 USCA § 1692(e) that I am disputing this debt. You should also be advised that your comments to my daughter directly violate this Act.

  Please conduct an investigation regarding this debt. Please also refrain from contacting me by telephone.

Should you fail to take the above actions, I may institute an action against you under the Act for failure to comply with its requirements. Your prompt attention to this matter would be appreciated.

Sincerely yours,
[Insert Your Name]


## Sample Independent Contractor Agreement for Small Business

[This Independent Contractor Agreement was especially drafted to address the issues raised in Chapter 7 on small business ownership.]

- This Independent Contractor Agreement (the "Agreement"), effective as of [Insert Date], is entered into by [Insert Name of Your Company] (the "Company") and between [Insert Name of Independent Contractor] (the "Contractor").

  WHEREAS, the Company is in need of assistance in [Describe the Assignment or Work, e.g., Assistance Completing a Construction Project]; and

  WHEREAS, the Contractor has agreed to perform work for the Company;

  NOW THEREFORE, the parties hereby agree as follows:

  1. Scope of Assignment. The Contractor is being retained to perform the following services: _____ [Describe Services to Be Provided]

  2. Payment as Consideration. The Company will pay Contractor [Specify Payment Arrangement Such as an Hourly Rate or Flat Fee] on [Specify When the Payment Will Be Made, e.g. at the End of Each Month or Every Two Weeks]. Such payments shall represent the only payments that the Company shall be required to make to Contractor.

[NOTE: This clause would have protected T. J. Construction Co. because the friend the owner retained would have been stopped from claiming he was an employee.]

3. Independent Contractor Status. Contractor hereby agrees and acknowledges that s/he is an independent contractor and not an employee of the Company. Furthermore, the Contractor acknowledges that s/he is not entitled to any benefits reserved for employees of the Company and acknowledges that the Company will not withhold any amounts for payment of applicable taxes from the compensation of the Contractor. The payment of all applicable taxes shall remain the sole responsibility of the Contractor.

4. Contractor's Warranties. The Contractor hereby agrees s/he is qualified to perform the assignment. The Contractor also agrees that s/he will maintain any licenses, permits, and registrations to perform the assignment.

5. Competent work. All work will be done in a competent fashion in accordance with applicable standards of the profession and all services are subject to the final approval of [Insert Name of Supervising Agent for Company] prior to the Company's payment.

6. Representations and Warranties. The Contractor will make no representations, warranties, or commitments binding the Company without the Company's prior written consent.

7. Confidentiality. In the course of performing services, the parties recognize that the Contractor may come in contact with or become familiar with information which the Company considers confidential. This information may include, but is not limited to, information pertaining to [Specify], which may be of value to a competitor. The Contractor agrees to keep all such information confidential and not to discuss or divulge any of it to anyone unless authorized by the Company to do so. The Contractor acknowledges and hereby agrees that this agreement to maintain the confidences of the Company shall remain in effect even after the assignment has been completed.

8. Noncompetition and Solicitation. The Contractor hereby acknowledges that the Company has expended valuable resources in the development of the Company. To protect our business interest, in consideration of

the payment you shall receive under this Agreement, the Contractor hereby agrees to refrain from soliciting any of our prospective or current customers for your own benefit. Furthermore, you are prohibited from soliciting or engaging in any work, directly or indirectly, or through any corporation or association in any business, enterprise, or employment that competes with the Company within a 50-mile radius of the Company for 12 months after your relationship with the Company has ended. Both the Contractor and the Company agree that breach of this provision in the Agreement shall result in either party paying $5,000 in liquidated damages.

[NOTE: This type of provision could have protected Soccer Waza from its soccer trainers soliciting and competing with the company.]

9. Term. This Agreement shall commence on [Specify Date] and shall terminate on [Specify Date], unless terminated for any reason by either party upon thirty (30) days' prior written notice.

10. Entire Agreement. This Agreement constitutes the entire agreement between the parties. This Agreement may not be changed in any manner unless both parties agree to do so in writing by signing an amendment to this Agreement. Should a court of competent jurisdiction determine that one of the provisions in this Agreement is unenforceable, this shall not affect the enforceability of the remaining provisions of this Agreement.

11. Intellectual Property Rights. Any ideas, plans, improvements, or inventions developed by the Contractor during the term of this Agreement, including any copyrighted materials and concepts for trademarks, shall belong to the Company under the "works made for hire" doctrine.

12. Governing law. This Agreement shall be governed by the laws of the state of [Insert State].

By _____ Date _____
[Insert Name of Independent Contractor]

By _____ Date _____
Name and Title
[Insert Name of Company]

## Sample Confidentiality Clause for Small Business

■ In consideration of my working with [Insert Name of Your Business], I hereby acknowledge and agree to maintain all of the business's confidential information. Confidential information includes but is not limited to: (1) names of current and potential customers, (2) financial information, (3) plans for the future of the business, (4) marketing strategy, (5) trade secrets concerning the business's customers, suppliers, or third parties, and (6) plans for developing intellectual property like trademarks and service marks. I understand and agree that confidential information also includes personal information about the business's owners or other independent contractors or employees. The business respects that it may become privy to confidential information about me and agrees to keep this information confidential unless expressly authorized to release this information by me or required to do so by law. This agreement shall remain in effect even after our relationship terminates.

[This is a fairly simple and straightforward confidentiality clause. It can be used alone or in a standard independent contractor or employment agreement. Please be aware that it includes a clause obligating the business to maintain the confidential information regarding the independent contractor or employee. This can be helpful in building a trusting relationship between the parties.]

## Sample Noncompete Clause

■ Noncompetition or Solicitation:
You hereby acknowledge that [Insert Name of Your Company] has expended valuable resources in the development of the company. To protect our business interest and as a term of your working for the company, you hereby agree to refrain from soliciting any of our prospective or current customers for your own benefit. Furthermore, you are prohibited from soliciting or engaging in any work, directly or indirectly, or through any corporation or association in any business, enterprise or employment

that competes with [Insert Name of Your Company] within a 50-mile radius of the company for 12 months after your relationship with the company has ended.

[The above noncompetition or solicitation clause can be used in an independent contractor or employment agreement. Whether a court would enforce a clause like this depends on your state's law and on the nature of your business. At the very least, though, including such a clause in your provisions with prospective independent contractors and employees places them on notice that they should not even attempt to take business away from your company.]

## Sample Small Claims Complaint

To view a copy of the small claims form that must be completed in Michigan to file a complaint, go to http://courts.Michigan.gov/scao/ courtforms/smallclaims/dc84.pdf. The form is fairly self-explanatory. Your local small claims court will have a similar form. You can file a small claims complaint against a private individual or a large company. If you have any questions regarding how to complete the forms in your jurisdiction, ask for an instruction sheet; the court clerk usually provides it as a matter of course.

# DIRECTORY OF AGENCIES AND ORGANIZATIONS

## Bureau of Prisons—Regional Offices

Address Complaints to: Regional Director

### Mid-Atlantic Region
Area Covered: Delaware, District of Columbia, Indiana, Kentucky, Maryland, Michigan, North Carolina, Ohio, South Carolina, Virginia, West Virginia
Junction Business Park
Suite 100-N
10010 Junction Drive
Annapolis Junction, MD 20701
(301) 317-3103

### North Central Region
Area Covered: Colorado, Illinois, Kansas, Minnesota, Missouri, Nebraska, North Dakota, South Dakota, Wisconsin
Gateway Complex Inc.
8th Floor
Fourth and State Avenue
Kansas City, KS 66101
(913) 621-3939

### Northeast Region
Area Covered: Connecticut, Maine, Massachusetts, New Hampshire, New Jersey, New York, Pennsylvania, Rhode Island, Vermont
U.S. Customs House
7th Floor
200 Chestnut Street
Philadelphia, PA 19106
(215) 597-6317

### South Central Region
Area Covered: Arkansas, Louisiana, New Mexico, Oklahoma, Texas
Suite 300
4211 Cedar Springs Road
Dallas, TX 75219
(214) 767-9700

### Southeast Region
Area Covered: Alabama, Florida, Georgia, Mississippi, Puerto Rico, South Carolina, Virgin Islands
523 McDonough Boulevard, SE
Atlanta, GA 30315
(404) 624-5202

### Western Region
Area Covered: Alaska, Arizona, California, Hawaii, Idaho, Montana, Nevada, Oregon, Utah, Washington, Wyoming
3rd Floor

7950 Dublin Boulevard
Dublin, CA 94568
(510) 803-4700

## Child Support Enforcement Offices

### Alabama
Department of Human Resources
Division of Child Support
50 Ripley Street
Montgomery, AL 36130-1801
(334) 242-9300
(800) 284-4347
Fax: (334) 242-0606

### Alaska
Child Support Enforcement Division
550 West 7th Avenue, Suite 310
Anchorage, AK 99501-6699
(907) 269-6900
(800) 478-3300
Fax: (907) 269-6813

### Arizona
Division of Child Support
    Enforcement
P.O. Box 40458
Phoenix, AZ 85067
(602) 252-4045 (no toll-free number)

### Arkansas
Office of Child Support Enforcement

P.O. Box 8133
Little Rock, AR 72203
Street Address:
712 West Third
Little Rock, AR 72201
(501) 682-8398
(800) 264-2445 (Payments)
(800) 247-4549 (Program)
Fax: (501) 682-6002

### California
Office of Child Support
Department of Social Services
P.O. Box 419064
Rancho Cordova, CA 95741
(866) 249-0773 (toll-free)
in LA County: (800) 615-8858
Fax: (916) 657-3791

### Colorado
Division of Child Support
    Enforcement
1575 Sherman Street, 2nd Floor
Denver, CO 80203-1714
(303) 866-5994 (no toll-free number)
Fax: (303) 866-3574

### Connecticut
Department of Social Services
Bureau of Child Support
    Enforcement
25 Sigourney Street
Hartford, CT 06106-5033
(860) 424-5251

(800) 228-5437 (problems)
(800) 647-8872 (information)
(800) 698-0572 (payments)
Fax: (860) 951-2996

**Delaware**
Division of Child Support
    Enforcement
Delaware Health and Social Services
1901 North Dupont Highway
P.O. Box 904
New Castle, DE 19720
(302) 577-4863, 577-4800 (no toll-
    free number)
Fax: (302) 577-4873

**District of Columbia**
Office of Paternity and Child
    Support Enforcement
Department of Human Services
800 9th Street, SW, 2nd Floor
Washington, DC 20024-2485
(202) 442-9900 (no toll-free number)

**Florida**
Child Support Enforcement Program
Department of Revenue
P.O. Box 8030
Tallahassee, FL 32314-8030
(850) 922-9590 (no toll-free number)
Fax: (850) 488-4401

**Georgia**
Child Support Administration

P.O. Box 38450
Atlanta, GA 30334-0450
(404) 657-3851
(800) 227-7993 (for 706 & 912 area
    codes)
From area codes 404 & 770, dial
    code + 657-2780
Fax: (404) 657-3326

**Guam**
Department of Law
Child Support Enforcement Office
238 Archbishop F.C. Flores, 7th Floor
Agana, GU 96910
(671) 475-3360 (no toll-free number)

**Hawaii**
Child Support Enforcement Agency
Department of Attorney General
Kakuhihewa State Office Building
Kapolei, HI 96707
(808) 692-7000
(888) 317-9081

**Idaho**
Bureau of Child Support Services
Department of Health and Welfare
450 West State Street, 5th Floor
Boise, ID 83720-0036
(208) 334-2479
(800) 356-9868
Fax: (208) 334-0666

**Illinois**
Child Support Enforcement Division
Illinois Department of Public Aid
509 South Sixth
Mariott Building
P.O. Box 19405
Springfield, IL 62701-1825
(217) 524-4602
(800) 447-4278
Fax: (217) 524-4608

**Indiana**
Child Support Office
402 West Washington Street, Room
 W360
Indianapolis, IN 46204
(317) 233-5437
(800) 622-4932
Fax: (317) 233-4925

**Iowa**
Bureau of Collections
Department of Human Services
Hoover Building, 5th Floor
Des Moines, IA 50319
(515) 281-5580 (no toll-free number)
Fax: (515) 281-8854

**Kansas**
Child Support Enforcement Program
Department of Social &
 Rehabilitation Services
P.O. Box 0497
Topeka, KS 66601-0497

(785) 296-3237
(800) 432-0152 (Withholding)
(877) 572-5722 (Collections)
(800) 432-3913 (Fraud Hotline)
Fax: (913) 296-5206

**Kentucky**
Division of Child Support
 Enforcement
Cabinet for Families and Children
P. O. Box 2150
Frankfort, KY 40602
(502) 564-2285 (no toll-free number)
Fax: (502) 564-5988

**Louisiana**
Support Enforcement Services
Office of Family Support
P.O. Box 94065
Baton Rouge, LA 70804-4065
(504) 342-4780
(800) 256-4650 (Payments)
Fax: (504) 342-7397

**Maine**
Division of Support Enforcement and
 Recovery Bureau of Family
 Independence
Department of Human Services
Augusta, ME 04333
(207) 287-2886
(800) 371-3101
Fax: (207) 287-5096

**Maryland**
Child Support Enforcement
   Administration
Department of Human Resources
311 West Saratoga Street
Baltimore, MD 21201
(800) 332-6347
Fax: (410) 333-8992

**Massachusetts**
Child Support Enforcement Division
Department of Revenue
141 Portland Street
Cambridge, MA 02139-1937
(800) 332-2733
Fax: (617) 621-4991

**Michigan**
Office of Child Support
Department of Social Services
P.O. Box 30478
Lansing, MI 48909-7978
Street Address:
7109 W. Saginaw Highway
Lansing, MI 48909-7978
(517) 373-7570 (no toll-free number)
Fax: (517) 373-4980

**Minnesota**
Office of Child Support Enforcement
Department of Human Services
444 Lafayette Road, 4th floor
St. Paul, MN 55155-3846

(612) 215-1714 (no toll-free number)
Fax: (612) 297-4450

**Mississippi**
Division of Child Support
   Enforcement
Department of Human Services
P.O. Box 352
Jackson, MS 39205
(601) 359-4861
(800) 434-5437 (Jackson)
(800) 354-6039 (Hines, Rankin, and
   Madison Counties)
Fax: (601) 359-4415

**Missouri**
Department of Social Services
Division of Child Support
   Enforcement
P.O. Box 2320
Jefferson City, MO 65102-2320
(573) 751-4301
(800) 859-7999
Fax: (573) 751-8450

**Montana**
Child Support Enforcement Division
Department of Public Health and
   Human Services
P.O. Box 202943
Helena, MT 59620
(406) 442-7278
(800) 346-5437

**Nebraska**
Child Support Enforcement Office
Department of Social Services
P.O. Box 95044
Lincoln, NE 68509
(402) 471-9160
(800) 831-4573
Fax: (402) 471-9455

**Nevada**
Child Support Enforcement Program
Nevada State Welfare Division
2527 North Carson Street
Carson City, NV 89706-0113
(702) 687-4744
(800) 992-0900
Fax: (702) 684-8026

**New Hampshire**
Office of Child Support
Division of Human Services
Health and Human Services Building
6 Hazen Drive
Concord, NH 03301-6531
(603) 271-4427
(800) 852-3345 ext. 4427
Fax: (603) 271-4787

**New Jersey**
Division of Family Development
Department of Human Services
Bureau of Child Support and
   Paternity Programs

P.O. Box 716
Trenton, NJ 08625-0716
(609) 588-2915
(800) 621-5437
Fax: (609) 588-3369

**New Mexico**
Child Support Enforcement Bureau
Department of Human Services
P.O. Box 25109
Santa Fe, NM 87504
Street Address:
2025 S. Pacheco
Santa Fe, NM 87504
(505) 827-7200
(800) 432-6217
Fax: (505) 827-7285

**New York**
Office of Child Support Enforcement
Department of Social Services
P.O. Box 14
One Commerce Plaza
Albany, NY 12260-0014
(518) 474-9081
(800) 343-8859
Fax: (518) 486-3127

**North Carolina**
Child Support Enforcement Office
Division of Social Services
Department of Human Resources
100 East Six Forks Road

Raleigh, NC 27609-7750
(919) 571-4114
(800) 992-9457
Fax: (919) 881-2280

## North Dakota

Department of Human Services
Child Support Enforcement Agency
P.O. Box 7190
Bismarck, ND 58507-7190
(701) 328-3582
(800) 755-8530
Fax: (701) 328-5497

## Ohio

Office of Family Assistance and Child
 Support Enforcement
Department of Human Services
30 East Broad Street, 31st Floor
Columbus, OH 43266-0423
(614) 752-6561
(800) 686-1556
Fax: (614) 752-9760

## Oklahoma

Child Support Enforcement Division
Department of Human Services
P.O. Box 53552
Oklahoma City, OK 73152
Street Address:
2409 N. Kelley Avenue
Annex Building
Oklahoma City, OK 73111

(405) 522-5871
(800) 522-2922
Fax: (405) 522-2753

## Oregon

Recovery Services Section
Adult and Family Services Division
Department of Human Resources
260 Liberty Street, N.E.
Salem, OR 97310
(503) 378-5567
(800) 850-0228
(800) 850-0294 (Rotary)
Fax: (503) 391-5526

## Pennsylvania

Bureau of Child Support
 Enforcement
Department of Public Welfare
P.O. Box 8018
Harrisburg, PA 17105
(717) 787-3672
(800) 932-0211
Fax: (717) 787-9706

## Puerto Rico

Child Support Enforcement
Department of Social Services
P.O. Box 9023349
San Juan, PR 00902-3349
Street Address:
Majagua Street, Bldg. 2
Wing 4, 2nd Floor

Rio Pedras, PR 00902-9938
(787) 767-1500 (no toll-free number)
Fax: (787) 282-7411

**Rhode Island**
Child Support Services
Division of Administration and
    Taxation
77 Dorrance Street
Providence, RI 02903
(401) 277-2847
(800) 638-5437
Fax: (401) 277-6674

**South Carolina**
Department of Social Services
Child Support Enforcement Division
P.O. Box 1469
Columbia, SC 29202-1469
(803) 737-5875
(800) 768-5858
(800) 768-6779 (Payments)
Fax: (803) 737-6032

**South Dakota**
Office of Child Support Enforcement
Department of Social Services
700 Governor's Drive
Pierre, SD 57501-2291
(605) 773-3641 (no toll-free number)
Fax: (605) 773-5246

**Tennessee**
Child Support Services
Department of Human Services
Citizens Plaza Building, 12th Floor
400 Deadrick Street
Nashville, TN 37248-7400
(615) 313-4880
(800) 838-6911 (Payments)
Fax: (615) 532-2791

**Texas**
Office of the Attorney General
State Office
Child Support Division
P.O. Box 12017
Austin, TX 78711-2017
(512) 460-6000
(800) 252-8014
Fax: (512) 479-6478

**Utah**
Office of Recovery Services
P.O. Box 45011
Salt Lake City, UT 84145-0011
(801) 536-8500
(800) 257-9156
Fax: (801) 436-8509

**Vermont**
Office of Child Support
103 South Main Street
Waterbury, VT 05671-1901
(800) 786-3214
Fax: (802) 244-1483

**Virgin Islands**
Paternity and Child Support Division
Department of Justice
GERS Building, 2nd Floor
48B-50C Krondprans Gade
St. Thomas, VI 00802
(809) 775-3070 (no toll-free number)
Fax: (809) 775-3808

**Virginia**
Division of Child Support
    Enforcement
Department of Social Services
730 East Broad Street
Richmond, VA 23219
(804) 692-1428
(800) 468-8894
Fax: (804) 692-1405

**Washington**
Division of Child Support
Department of Social Health Services
P.O. Box 9162
Olympia, WA 98504-9162
Street Address:
712 Pear St., S.E.
Olympia, WA 98504
(360) 586-3162
(800) 457-6202
Fax: (206) 586-3274

**West Virginia**
Child Support Enforcement Division
Department of Health & Human
    Resources
1900 Kanawha Boulevard East
Capitol Complex, Building 6,
    Room 817
Charleston, WV 25305
(304) 558-3780
(800) 249-3778

**Wisconsin**
Bureau of Child Support
Division of Economic Support
P.O. Box 7935
Madison, WI 53707-7935
Street Address:
201 E. Washington Ave.
Room 271
Madison, WI 53707
(608) 266-9909 (no toll-free number)
Fax: (608) 267-2824

**Wyoming**
Child Support Enforcement
Department of Family Services
2300 Capital Avenue, 3rd Floor
Cheyenne, WY 82002-0490
(307) 777-6948 (no toll-free number)
Fax: (307) 777-3693

## Department of Education, OCR Enforcement Offices

Address Complaints to: Office for Civil Rights

### *Enforcement Division A*

**Area Covered: Connecticut, Maine, Massachusetts, New Hampshire, Rhode Island, Vermont**
J.W. McCormack Post Office and
 Courthouse Building
Room 222, 01-0061
Boston, MA 02109-4557
(617) 223-9662
TDD: (617) 223-9695

**Area Covered: New Jersey, New York, Puerto Rico, Virgin Islands**
14th Floor
75 Park Place
New York, NY 10007
(212) 637-6466
TDD: (212) 264-9464

**Area Covered: Delaware, District of Columbia, Maryland, Pennsylvania, Virginia, West Virginia**
Gateway Building
Room 6300, 03-2010
3535 Market Street
Philadelphia, PA 19104-3326
(215) 596-6787
TDD: (215) 596-6794

### *Enforcement Division B*

**Area Covered: Alabama, Florida, Georgia, North Carolina, South Carolina, Tennessee**
101 Marietta Tower
Suite 2000
Atlanta, GA 30323
Mail Address:
P.O. Box 2048, 04-3010
Atlanta, GA 30301-2048
(404) 331-2954
TDD: (404) 331-7236

**Area Covered: Arkansas, Louisiana, Mississippi, Oklahoma, Texas**
Suite 460, 06-5010
1200 Main Tower Building
Dallas, TX 75202-9998
(214) 767-3959
TDD: (214) 767-3639

### *Enforcement Division C*

**Area Covered: Illinois, Indiana, Michigan, Minnesota, Ohio, Wisconsin**
Suite 1053, 05-4010
111 N. Canal Street
Chicago, IL 60606-7204
(312) 886-8434
TDD: (312) 353-2540

**Area Covered: Michigan, Ohio (elementary and secondary schools only)**
Bank One Center
Room 750
600 Superior Avenue East
Cleveland, OH 44114-2611
(216) 522-4970
TDD: (216) 522-4944

**Area Covered: Iowa, Kansas, Kentucky, Missouri, Nebraska**
8th Floor, 07-6010
10220 North Executive Hills
    Boulevard
Kansas City, MO 64153-1366
(816) 880-4202
TDD: (816) 819-0582

**Area Covered: Arizona, Colorado, Montana, New Mexico, North Dakota, South Dakota, Utah, Wyoming**
Suite 310, 08-7010
Federal Building
1244 Speer Boulevard
Denver, CO 80204-3582
(303) 844-5695
TDD: (303) 844-3417

**Area Covered: California**
Old Federal Building
Room 239

50 United Nations Plaza
San Francisco, CA 94102-4102
(415) 437-7700
TDD: (415) 437-7786

**Area Covered: Alaska, Hawaii, Idaho, Nevada, Oregon, Washington, American Samoa, Guam, Trust Territories of the Pacific Islands**
Jackson Federal Building
Room 3310, 10-9010
915 Second Avenue
Seattle, WA 98174-1099
(206) 220-7880

## Department of Health and Human Services Regional Offices

Address Complaints to: Office for Civil Rights

**Region I**
Area Covered: Connecticut, Maine,
    Massachusetts, New Hampshire,
    Rhode Island, Vermont
Government Center
Room 2100
John F. Kennedy Federal Building
Boston, MA 02203
(617) 565-1340
TDD: (617) 565-1343

**Region II**
Area Covered: New Jersey, New
    York, Puerto Rico, Virgin Islands
Jacob Javits Federal Building
Suite 3312
26 Federal Plaza
New York, NY 10278
(212) 264-3313
TDD: (212) 264-3656

**Region III**
Area Covered: Delaware, District of
    Columbia, Maryland,
    Pennsylvania, Virginia, West
    Virginia
Gateway Building
Room 6300
3535 Market Street
Philadelphia, PA 19104
(215) 596-1262
TDD: (215) 596-5195

**Region IV**
Area Covered: Alabama, Florida,
    Georgia, Kentucky, Mississippi,
    North Carolina, South Carolina,
    Tennessee
Suite 1515
101 Marietta Street, NW
Atlanta, GA 30323
(404) 331-2779
TDD: (404) 242-2867

**Region V**
Area Covered: Illinois, Indiana,
    Michigan, Minnesota, Ohio,
    Wisconsin
105 West Adams Street
16th Floor
Chicago, IL 60603
(312) 886-2359
TDD: (312) 353-5693

**Region VI**
Area Covered: Arkansas, Louisiana,
    New Mexico, Oklahoma, Texas
Room 1360
1200 Main Tower Building
Dallas, TX 75202
(214) 767-4056
TDD: (214) 767-8940

**Region VII**
Area Covered: Iowa, Kansas,
    Missouri, Nebraska
Federal Building
Room 248
601 East 12th Street
Kansas City, MO 64106
(816) 426-7277
TDD: (816) 426-7065

**Region VIII**
Area Covered: Colorado, Montana,
    North Dakota, South Dakota,
    Utah, Wyoming

Rogers Federal Office Building
Room 1185
1961 Stout Street
Denver, CO 80294-3538
(303) 844-2024
TDD: (303) 844-3439

**Region IX**
Area Covered: American Samoa,
    Arizona, California, Guam,
    Hawaii, Nevada
Federal Office Building
Room 322
50 United Nations Plaza
San Francisco, CA 94102
(415) 556-8586
TDD: (415) 556-8586

**Region X**
Area Covered: Alaska, Idaho,
    Oregon, Washington
Blanchard Plaza Building
2201 Sixth Avenue
Seattle, WA 98121
(206) 615-2290
TDD: (206) 442-7486 here

## Department of Housing and Urban Development (HUD) Fair Housing Enforcement Centers

Address Complaints to: Director

**Region I, New England**
State Offices: Connecticut, Maine,
    Massachusetts, New Hampshire,
    Rhode Island, Vermont
Fair Housing Enforcement Center
U.S. Department of Housing and
    Urban Development
Thomas P. O'Neill, Jr. Federal
    Building
10 Causeway Street, Room 308
Boston, MA 02222-1092
(617) 565-5304
Fax: (617) 565-7313

**Region II, New York/New Jersey**
State Offices: New York, New Jersey
Area Offices: Albany and Buffalo,
    New York
Fair Housing Enforcement Center
U.S. Department of Housing and
    Urban Development
Jacob K. Javits Federal Building
26 Federal Plaza
New York, NY 10278-0068
(212) 264-1290
Fax: (212) 264-9829

**Region III, Mid-Atlantic**
State Offices: Delaware, District of
    Columbia, Maryland,
    Pennsylvania, Virginia, West
    Virginia
Area Office: Pittsburgh, Pennsylvania

Fair Housing Enforcement Center
U.S. Department of Housing and
    Urban Development
The Wanamaker Building
100 Penn Square East
Philadelphia, PA 19106-3390
(215) 656-0647
Fax: (215) 656-3449

**Region IV, Southeast/Caribbean**
State Offices: Alabama, Caribbean,
    Florida, Georgia, Kentucky,
    Mississippi, North Carolina, South
    Carolina, Tennessee
Area Offices: Coral Gables,
    Jacksonville, Orlando, and Tampa,
    Florida; Knoxville and Memphis,
    Tennessee
Fair Housing Enforcement Center
U.S. Department of Housing and
    Urban Development
Richard B. Russell Federal Building
75 Spring Street, SW
Atlanta, GA 30303-3388
(404) 331-5140
Fax: (404) 331-1021

**Region V, Midwest**
State Offices: Illinois, Indiana,
    Michigan, Minnesota, Ohio,
    Wisconsin
Area Offices: Cincinnati, Cleveland,
    and Springfield, Ohio; Flint and
    Grand Rapids, Michigan

Fair Housing Enforcement Center
U.S. Department of Housing and
    Urban Development
Ralph H. Metcalfe Federal Building
77 West Jackson Boulevard
Chicago, IL 60604
(312) 353-3303
Fax: (312) 886-2837

**Region VI, Southwest**
State Offices: Arkansas, Louisiana,
    New Mexico, Oklahoma, Texas
Area Offices: Dallas, Houston,
    Lubbock, and San Antonio, Texas;
    Shreveport, Louisiana; Tulsa,
    Oklahoma
Fair Housing Enforcement Center
U.S. Department of Housing and
    Urban Development
1600 Throckmorton Street
Fort Worth, TX 76113-2905
(817) 885-5521
Fax: (817) 885-6022

**Region VII, Great Plains**
State Offices: Iowa, Kansas,
    Missouri, Nebraska
Area Office: St. Louis, Missouri
Fair Housing Enforcement Center
U.S. Department of Housing and
    Urban Development
Gateway Tower II
400 State Avenue

Kansas City, KS 66101-2406
(913) 551-6958
Fax: (913) 551-6856

**Region VIII, Rocky Mountain**
State Offices: Colorado, Montana,
North Dakota, South Dakota,
Utah, Wyoming
Fair Housing Enforcement Center
U.S. Department of Housing and
Urban Development
Executive Tower Building
1405 Curtis Street
Denver, CO 80202-2349
(303) 672-5434
Fax: (303) 672-5026

**Region IX, Pacific/Hawaii**
State Offices: Arizona, California,
Hawaii, Nevada
Area Offices: Fresno, Los Angeles,
Sacramento, San Diego, Santa
Ana, California; Reno, Nevada;
Tucson, Arizona
Fair Housing Enforcement Center
U.S. Department of Housing and
Urban Development
Phillip Burton Federal Building and
U.S. Courthouse
450 Golden Gate Avenue
San Francisco, CA 94102-3448
(415) 436-6568
Fax: (415) 436-6418

**Region X, Northwest/Alaska**
State Offices: Alaska, Idaho, Oregon,
Washington
Area Office: Spokane, Washington
Fair Housing Enforcement Center
U.S. Department of Housing and
Urban Development
909 First Avenue, Suite 205
Seattle, WA 98101-2058
(206) 220-5170
Fax: (206) 220-5447

## Legal Aid

Free legal advice and representation
is available to low-income and elderly
people. Contact one of the
organizations below to see if you or a
loved one qualifies. The income
requirements are strict; however,
these organizations typically have
additional information available for
people who may not meet their
eligibility requirements. If an
organization is not listed in your
area, refer to the Legal Services
Corporation listing under the
National Organizations section. This
corporation is a national corporation
that sponsors legal aid agencies
throughout the country.

## Alabama

Legal Services of Metro Birmingham
Birmingham Office
1820 Seventh Avenue, North
Birmingham, AL 35203
(205) 328-3540
Fax: (205) 328-3548

Legal Services of North-Central
  Alabama
Huntsville Office
2000-C Vernon Street
Huntsville, AL 35805
(256) 536-9645
Fax: (256) 536-1544

Legal Services Corporation of
  Alabama
Mobile Office
601 Van Antwerp Building
103 Dauphin Street
Mobile, AL 36602
(251) 433-6560 or (800) 403-4872
Fax: (251) 434-2488

Legal Services Corporation of
  Alabama
Montgomery Office
600 Bell Building
207 Montgomery Street
Montgomery, AL 36104
(334) 832-4570 or (800) 844-5342
Fax: (334) 241-8683

## Arizona

William E. Morris Institute for Justice
305 South Second Avenue
Phoenix, AZ 85001
(602) 252-3432
Fax: (602) 257-8138

## District of Columbia

Legal Aid Society
666 Eleventh Street, NW, Suite 800
Washington, DC 20001
(202) 628-1161
Fax: (202) 727-2132

## Florida

Greater Orange Area Legal Services
  (GOALS)
1036 W. Amella Street
Orlando, FL 32805
(407) 841-7777

Seminole County Bar Association
Legal Aid Society, Inc.
115 Boston Avenue, Suite 2100
Altamonte Springs, FL 32701
(407) 834-1660
Fax: (407) 834-2080

## Georgia

Atlanta Legal Aid Society
151 Spring Street, NW
Atlanta, GA 30303
(404) 524-5811

Georgia Legal Services Program
1100 Spring Street, Suite 200-A
Atlanta, GA 30309
(404) 206-5175
Fax: (404) 206-5346

**Hawaii**
Legal Aid Society of Hawaii
924 Bethel Street
Honolulu, Hawaii 96813
(808) 536-4302

**Idaho**
Idaho Legal Aid Services
310 N. 5th Street
Boise, Idaho 83702
(208) 345-0106

**Illinois**
Community Law Project, Inc.
188 West Randolph Street, Suite 720
Chicago, Illinois 60601
(312) 630-9363
Fax: (312) 630-0983

**Indiana**
Indiana Legal Services, Inc.—South
  Bend
105 E. Jefferson Blvd., Suite 600
South Bend, IN 46601
(219) 234-8121 or (800) 288-8121
Fax: (219) 239-2185

**Kansas**
Kansas Legal Services
712 S. Kansas Ave, Suite 200
Topeka, KS 66603
(785) 233-2068
Fax: (785) 354-8311
TDD: (785) 233-4028

**Kentucky**
Access to Justice Foundation
400 Old Vine Street, Suite 203
Lexington, KY 40507
(859) 255-9913
Fax: (859) 231-5356

**Louisiana**
Legal Services of North Louisiana
Shreveport Central Office
720 Travis Street
Shreveport, LA 71101
(318) 222-7186 or (800) 826-9265
Fax: (318) 221-1901

New Orleans Legal Assistance
  Corporation
144 Elk Place, Suite 1000
New Orleans, LA 70112-2635
(504) 529-1000

**Maine**
Maine Equal Justice Project
126 Sewall Street
Augusta, ME 04330

(207) 626-7058
Fax: (207) 621-8148

**Maryland**
Law Foundation of Prince George's
County
P.O. Box 329
Hyattsville, MD 20781
(301) 864-8354
Fax: (301) 864-8352

Legal Aid Bureau
500 E. Lexington Street
Baltimore, MD 21202
(410) 539-5340
Fax: (410) 539-1710

**Massachusetts**
Greater Boston Legal Services
197 Friend Street
Boston, MA 02114
(617) 371-1234 or (800) 323-3205
Fax: (617) 371-1222
TDD: (617) 371-1228

**Michigan**
Legal Aid Defender Association of
Detroit
645 Griswold Street, Suite 2400
Detroit, MI 48226-4201
(313) 964-4111 or (877) 964-4700
Fax: (313) 964-1932

Michigan Legal Services
220 Bagley Avenue, Suite 900
Detroit, MI 48226
(313) 964-4130 or (800) 875-4130
Fax: (313) 964-1192

**Minnesota**
Legal Aid Service of Northeastern
MN
302 Ordean Building
424 West Superior Street
Duluth, MN 55802
(218) 726-4800 or (800) 622-7266
Fax: (218) 726-4804
TDD: (218) 726-4826

**Mississippi**
North Mississippi Rural Legal
Services
2134 West Jackson Avenue
P.O. Box 767
Oxford, MS 38655
(662) 234-8731 or (800) 898-8731
Fax: (662)236-3263

**Missouri**
Legal Services of Eastern Missouri,
Inc.
4232 Forest Park Avenue
St. Louis, MI 63108
(314) 534-4200
Fax: (314) 534-1425

Legal Aid of Western Missouri
Central Office
1125 Grand Blvd., #1900
Kansas City, MO 64106
(816) 474-6750

**Montana**
Montana Legal Services Corporation
P.O. Box 409
Poplar, MT 59255
(406) 768-3006
Eastern Part of State: (800) 999-4941
Western Part of State: (800) 666-
    6899

**Nebraska**
Nebraska Legal Services
941 "O" Street, Suite 825
Lincoln, NE 68508
(402) 435-2161 or (800) 742-7555
Statewide: (877) 250-2016
Fax: (402) 435-2171

**Nevada**
Nevada Legal Services, Inc.
111 W. Telegraph Street, Suite 200
Carson City, NV 89703
(775) 883-0404 or (800) 323-8666
Fax: (775) 883-7074

**New Hampshire**
Legal Advice & Referral Line
P.O. Box 4147

Concord, NH 03302-4147
(603) 224-3333 or (800) 639-5290
Fax: (603) 224-6067

**New Jersey**
Legal Services of New Jersey
100 Metroplex Drive, Suite 402
P.O. Box 1357
Edison, NJ 08818-1357
(888) LSNJ-LAW (576-5529)

**New York**
Bronx Legal Services
579 Courtlandt Avenue
Bronx, NY 10451
(718) 993-6250

Legal Aid Society
166 Montague Street
Brooklyn, NY 11201
(212) 577-3300

Legal Services of New York,
    Brooklyn
186 Joralemon Street
Brooklyn, NY 11201
(718) 852-8888

**North Carolina**
Legal Services of North Carolina
224 South Dawson Street
Raleigh, NC 27611
(919) 856-2564
Fax: (919) 856-2120

**Ohio**
Legal Aid Society of Greater
 Cincinnati
215 E. 9th Street, Suite 200
Cincinnati, OH 45202
(513) 241-9400
Fax: (513) 241-0047
TDD: (513) 241-6061

**Oklahoma**
Legal Services of Eastern Oklahoma
115 West Third, Suite 700
Tulsa, OK 74103
(918) 584-3338 or (800) 299-3338

**Oregon**
Lane County Legal Aid Service
376 East 11th Avenue
Eugene, OR 97401
(541) 342-6056 or (800) 422-5247
Fax: (541) 342-5091

**Pennsylvania**
Community Legal Services, Inc.
Center City Office
1424 Chestnut Street
Philadelphia, PA 19102-2505
(215) 981-3700

**Rhode Island**
Rhode Island Legal Services
56 Pine Street, 4th Floor
Providence, RI 02903
(401) 274-2652

**South Carolina**
Neighborhood Legal Assistance
 Program
438 King Street
Charleston, SC 29403
(803) 722-0107

**Tennessee**
Legal Aid of East Tennessee
502 South Gay Street, Suite 404
Knoxville, TN 37902
(865) 637-0484

**Texas**
Legal Aid of Central Texas
2201 Post Road, Suite 104
Austin, TX 78704
(512) 447-7707
Fax: (512) 447-3940
TDD: (512) 441-9487

**Vermont**
Vermont Legal Aid
264 North Winooski Avenue
Burlington, VT 05402
(800) 889-2047

**Virginia**
Legal Services Corporation of
 Virginia
1700 East Main Street, Suite 1504
Richmond, VA 23219
(804) 782-9438
Fax: (804) 648-3917

**Washington**
Legal Foundation of Washington
500 Union Street, Suite 545
Seattle, WA 98101
(206) 624-2536
Fax: (206) 382-3396

**West Virginia**
Appalachian Research and Defense
    Fund
922 Quarrier Street, Suite 500
Charleston, WV 25301
(304) 344-9687 or (800) 319-4201

**Wisconsin**
Equal Justice Coalition
P.O. Box 231
Milwaukee, WI 53201-0231
(414) 272-9305
Fax: 414-272-9304

Wisconsin Judicare, Inc.
300 Third Street, Suite 210
P.O. Box 6100
Wausau, WI 54402-6100
(715) 842-1681 (Voice or TDD),
(800) 472-1638 (Voice or TDD)
Fax: (715) 848-1885

## National Organizations

Below are just a few national
organizations dedicated to

protecting rights historically denied
to black people.

ACLU (American Civil Liberties
    Union)
132 W. 43rd Street
New York, NY 10036
(212) 944-9800
Fax: (212) 869-9065
www.aclu.org

NAACP (National Association for
    the Advancement of Colored
    People)
4805 Mount Hope Drive
Baltimore, MD 21215
Toll free: (877) NAACP-98, (410)
    521-4939
www.naacp.org

NAACP Legal Defense and
    Educational Fund, Inc.
1275 K Street, NW, Room 301
Washington, DC 20005
(202) 682-1300
Fax: (202) 682-1312
www.naacpldf.org

Rainbow/PUSH Coalition
930 East 50th Street
Chicago, IL 60615
(773) 373-3366
Fax: (773) 373-3571
www.rainbowpush.org

Southern Poverty Law Center
400 Washington Avenue
Montgomery, AL 36104
(334) 264-0286
www.splcenter.org

Free legal aid may be available in
your area if you meet the income
requirements or are a senior citizen.
The income requirements vary, but
are typically below the poverty line.
People who are over the age of sixty
usually qualify as well. The Legal
Services Corporation is a national
organization that sponsors legal aid
agencies throughout the country. You
can contact Legal Services
Corporation at the following address:

Legal Services Corporation
750 First Street NE, Tenth Floor
Washington, DC 20002-4250
(202) 336-8800

The National Bar Association (NBA)
is a national organization of African
American attorneys. You can find
your local NBA chapter by contacting
the national office at:

National Bar Association (NBA)
1225 11th Street, NW
Washington, DC 20001-4217

(202) 842-3900
Fax: (202) 289-6170
E-mail: nba@nationalbar.org
www.nationalbar.org

National Association for the
    Advancement of Colored People
    (NAACP)
4805 Mount Hope Drive
Baltimore, MD 21215
(877) NAACP-98
24-Hour Hotline: (410) 521-4939
www.naacp.org

National Legal Aid and Defender
    Association
1625 K Street, NW, Suite 800
Washington, DC 20006
(202) 452-0620

## United States Attorney's Office

Address Complaints to: United States
Attorney

**Alabama, Middle District**
One Court Square
Suite 201
Montgomery, AL 36104
P.O. Box 197
Montgomery, AL 36101
(334) 223-7280

**Alabama, Northern District**
Vance Federal Building
1800 Fifth Avenue North
Room 200
Birmingham, AL 35203
(205) 731-1785

**Alabama, Southern District**
169 Dauphin Street
Suite 200
Mobile, AL 36602
(334) 441-5845

**Alaska**
Federal Building and U.S. Courthouse
222 West Seventh Avenue, #9
Room 253
Anchorage, AK 99513-7567
(907) 271-5071

**Arizona**
U.S. Courthouse and Federal Building
230 North First Avenue,
Room 4000
Phoenix, AZ 85025-0085
(602) 514-7500

**Arkansas, Eastern District**
TCBY Tower Building
425 West Capitol Avenue
Suite 500
Little Rock, AR 72201
Mail Address:

P.O. Box 1229
Little Rock, AR 72203
(501) 324-5342

**Arkansas, Western District**
U.S. Post Office and Courthouse
Building
Sixth Street and Rogers Avenue
Room 216
Fort Smith, AR 72901
Mail Address:
P.O. Box 1524
Fort Smith, AR 72902
(501) 783-5125

**California, Central District**
U.S. Courthouse
312 North Spring Street
Los Angeles, CA 90012
(213) 894-2401

**California, Eastern District**
555 Capitol Mall
Sacramento, CA 95814
(916) 554-2700

**California, Northern District**
U.S. Courthouse
450 Golden Gate Avenue
Box 36055
San Francisco, CA 94102
(415) 556-1126

**California, Southern District**
Federal Office Building
880 Front Street
San Diego, CA 92101-8893
(619) 557-5690

**Colorado**
Rogers Federal Office Building
1961 Stout Street
Denver, CO 80294
Mail Address:
P.O. Box 3615
Denver, CO 80294
(303) 844-2081

**Connecticut**
Connecticut Financial Center
157 Church Street
Twenty-third Floor
New Haven, CT 06510
Mail Address:
P.O. Box 1824
New Haven, CT 06508
(203) 773-2108

**Delaware**
1201 Market Street
Suite 1100
Wilmington, DE 19899
Mail Address:
P.O. Box 2046
Wilmington, DE 19899-2046
(302) 573-6277

**District of Columbia**
Judiciary Center Building
555 Fourth Street, NW
Washington, DC 20001
(202) 514-6600

**Florida, Middle District**
Robert Timberlake Federal Building
500 Zack Street, Room 410
Tampa, FL 33602

**Florida, Northern District**
315 South Calhoun Street, Suite 510
Tallahassee, FL 32301
(904) 942-8430

**Florida, Southern District**
99 NE Fourth Street
Miami, FL 33132
(305) 536-4471

**Georgia, Middle District**
433 Cherry Street, Fourth Floor
Macon, GA 31201
Mail Address:
P.O. Box U
Macon, GA 31202
(912) 752-3511

**Georgia, Northern District**
Richard B. Russell Federal Building
75 Spring Street, SW, Suite 1800
Atlanta, GA 30335
(404) 331-6954

**Georgia, Southern District**
100 Bull Street
Savannah, GA 31401
Mail Address:
P.O. Box 8999
Savannah, GA 31412
(912) 652-4422

**Guam**
Pacific New Building
238 Archbishop Flores Street
Room 502-A
Agana, GU 96910
(671) 472-7332

**Hawaii**
Prince Jonah Kuhio Kalanianaole
   Federal Building
300 Ala Moana Boulevard, Room
   6100
Honolulu, HI 96813
Mail Address:
P.O. Box 50183
Honolulu, HI 96850
(808) 541-2850

**Idaho**
First Interstate Center
977 West Main Street, Suite 201
Boise, ID 83702
Mail Address:
P.O. Box 32
Boise, ID 83707
(208) 334-1211

**Illinois, Central District**
Paul Finley Building and U.S.
   Courthouse
600 E. Monroe Street, Room 312
Springfield, IL 62701
Mail Address:
P.O. Box 375
Springfield, IL 62705
(217) 492-4450

**Illinois, Northern District**
Dirksen Federal Building
219 South Dearborn Street, Fifth
   Floor
Chicago, IL 60604
(312) 353-5300

**Illinois, Southern District**
Nine Executive Drive, Suite 300
Fairview Heights, IL 62208
(618) 628-3700

**Indiana, Northern District**
1001 Main Street, Suite A
Dyer, IN 46311
(219) 322-8576

**Indiana, Southern District**
Federal Building/Courthouse
46 East Ohio Street, Fifth Floor
Indianapolis, IN 46204
(317) 226-6333

**Iowa, Northern District**
The Center
425 Second Street, SE, Suite 950
Cedar Rapids, IA 52401
Mail Address:
P.O. Box 74950
Cedar Rapids, IA 52407-4950
(319) 363-6333

**Iowa, Southern District**
U.S. Courthouse Annex
110 East Court Avenue, Suite 286
Des Moines, IA 50309-2053
(515) 284-6257

**Kansas**
Epic Center
301 North Main, Suite 1200
Wichita, KS 67202-4812
(316) 269-6481

**Kentucky, Eastern District**
110 West Vine Street, Room 400
Lexington, KY 40507
Mail Address:
P.O. Box 3077
Lexington, KY 40596-3077
(606) 233-2661

**Kentucky, Western District**
Bank of Louisville Building
510 West Broadway, Tenth Floor
Louisville, KY 40202
(502) 582-5911

**Louisiana, Eastern District**
Hale Boggs Federal Building
501 Magazine Street, Second Floor
New Orleans, LA 70130
(504) 589-2921

**Louisiana, Middle District**
Russell B. Long Federal Building and
  Courthouse
777 Florida Street, Room 208
Baton Rouge, LA 70801
(504) 389-0443

**Louisiana, Western District**
300 Fannin Street, Suite 3201
Shreveport, LA 71101-3068
(318) 676-3600

**Maine**
100 Middle Street
East Tower, Sixth Floor
Portland, ME 04101
(207) 780-3257

**Maryland**
Garmatz Federal Courthouse
  Building
101 West Lombard Street, Room 604
Baltimore, MD 21201
(410) 962-4822

**Massachusetts**
McCormack Post Office and U.S.
  Courthouse
Room 1003
Boston, MA 02109
(617) 223-9400

**Michigan, Eastern District**
Federal Building
211 West Fort Street, Suite 2300
Detroit, MI 48226
(313) 226-9501

**Michigan, Western District**
330 Ionia, Suite 501
Grand Rapids, MI 49503
(616) 456-2404

**Minnesota**
U.S. Courthouse
110 South Fourth Street, Room 234
Minneapolis, MN 55401
(612) 348-1500

**Mississippi, Northern District**
Mail Address:
P.O. Drawer 886
Oxford, MS 38655
(601) 234-3351

**Mississippi, Southern District**
One Jackson Place
188 East Capitol Street, Suite 500

Jackson, MS 39201
(601) 965-4480

**Missouri, Eastern District**
U.S. Court and Custom House
1114 Market Street, Room 401
St. Louis, MO 63101
(314) 539-2200

**Missouri, Western District**
1201 Walnut Street, Suite 2300
Kansas City, MO 64106-2149
(816) 426-3122

**Montana**
Western Federal Savings Bank
2929 Third Avenue North, Suite 400
Billings, MT 59101
Mail Address:
P.O. Box 1478
Billings, MT 59103
(406) 657-6101

**Nebraska**
Edward Zorinsky Federal Building
215 North Seventeenth Street, Room
  7401
Omaha, NE 68101
Mail Address:
P.O. Box 1228, DTS
Omaha, NE 68101
(402) 221-4774

**Nevada**
701 East Bridger Avenue, Suite 800
Las Vegas, NV 89101
Mail Address:
P.O. Box 16030
Las Vegas, NV 89101
(702) 388-6336

**New Hampshire**
55 Pleasant Street, Room 312
Concord, NH 03301-3904
(603) 225-1552

**New Jersey**
Peter Rodino Federal Building
970 Broad Street, Room 502
Newark, NJ 07102
(201) 645-2700

**New Mexico**
625 Silver Street, SW, Fourth Floor
Albuquerque, NM 87102
(505) 766-3341

**New York, Eastern District**
U.S. Courthouse
225 Cadman Plaza East
Brooklyn, NY 11201
(718) 254-7000

**New York, Northern District**
James M. Hanley Federal Building
100 South Clinton Street, Room 900

Syracuse, NY 13261
Mail Address:
P.O. Box 7198
Syracuse, NY 13261-7198
(315) 448-0672

**New York, Southern District**
One St. Andrews Plaza
New York, NY 10007
(212) 791-0008

**New York, Western District**
138 Delaware Avenue
Buffalo, NY 14202
(716) 551-4811

**North Carolina, Eastern District**
Federal Building
310 New Bern Avenue, Suite 800
Raleigh, NC 27601-1461
(919) 856-4530

**North Carolina, Middle District**
324 West Market Street
Greensboro, NC 27402
Mail Address:
P.O. Box 1858
Greensboro, NC 27402
(910) 333-5351

**North Carolina, Western District**
U.S. Courthouse
227 West Trade Street, Suite 1700

Charlotte, NC 28202
(704) 344-6222

**North Dakota**
655 First Avenue, North
Fargo, ND 58102
Mail Address:
P.O. Box 2505
Fargo, ND 58108
(701) 239-5671

**Ohio, Northern District**
Bank One Center
600 Superior Avenue, East, Suite
  1800
Cleveland, OH 44114-2600
(216) 622-3600

**Ohio, Southern District**
Two Nationwide Plaza
280 North High Street, Fourth Floor
Columbus, OH 43215
(614) 469-5715

**Oklahoma, Eastern District**
101 North Fifth Street, Room 333
Muskogee, OK 74401
(918) 687-2543

**Oklahoma, Northern District**
Page Belcher Federal Building
and U.S. Courthouse
333 West Fourth Street, Room 3460

Tulsa, OK 74103
(918) 581-7463

**Oklahoma, Western District**
First Oklahoma Tower
210 Park Avenue, Suite 400
Oklahoma City, OK 73102
(405) 231-5281

**Oregon**
888 Southwest Fifth Avenue, Suite
  1000
Portland, OR 97204-2024
(503) 727-1000

**Pennsylvania, Eastern District**
Philadelphia Life Building
615 Chestnut Street, Suite 1250
Philadelphia, PA 19106-4476
(215) 451-5200

**Pennsylvania, Middle District**
Federal Building, Suite 309
Washington Avenue and Linden
  Street
Scranton, PA 18501
Mail Address:
Federal Building
228 Walnut Street, Room 1162
Harrisburg, PA 17108
(717) 348-2800

**Pennsylvania, Western District**
U.S. Post Office and Courthouse
   Building
700 Grant Street, Room 633
Pittsburgh, PA 15219
(412) 644-3500

**Puerto Rico**
Federal Office Building
Carlos E. Chardon Avenue, Room
   452
Hato Rey, PR 00918
(809) 766-5656

**Rhode Island**
Westminster Square Building
10 Dorrance Street, Tenth Floor
Providence, RI 02903
(401) 528-5477

**South Carolina**
First Union Building
1441 Main Street, Suite 500
Columbia, SC 29201
(803) 929-3000

**South Dakota**
230 South Phillips Street, Suite 600
Sioux Falls, SD 57102
Mail Address:
P.O. Box 5073
Sioux Falls, SD 57117-5073
(605) 330-4400

**Tennessee, Eastern District**
Plaza Tower
800 South Gay Street, Suite 700
Knoxville, TN 37901
Mail Address:
P.O. Box 872
Knoxville, TN 37901
(423) 545-4167

**Tennessee, Middle District**
110 Ninth Avenue South, Suite
   A-961
Nashville TN 37203-3870
(615) 736-5151

**Tennessee, Western District**
Davis Federal Building
167 North Main Street, Room 1026
Memphis, TN 38103
(901) 544-4231

**Texas, Eastern District**
350 Magnolia Avenue, Suite 150
Beaumont, TX 77701-2237
(409) 839-2538

**Texas, Northern District**
Earl Cabell Federal Building
1100 Commerce Street, Third Floor
Dallas, TX 75242
(214) 767-0951

**Texas, Southern District**
910 Travis Street, Suite 1500
Houston, TX 77002

**Texas, Western District**
601 Northwest Loop 410, Suite 600
San Antonio, TX 78216
(210) 308-3500

**Utah**
Frank E. Moss U.S. Courthouse
350 South Main Street, Room 478
Salt Lake City, UT 84101
(801) 524-5682

**Vermont**
Federal Building
11 Elmwood Avenue, Third Floor
Burlington, VT 05401
Mail Address:
P.O. Box 570
Burlington, VT 05402
(802) 951-6725

**Virgin Islands**
Federal Building and U.S. Courthouse
5500 Veterans Drive, Room 260
St. Thomas, VI 00802-6424
(809) 774-5757

**Virginia, Eastern District**
1101 King Street, Suite 502
Alexandria, VA 22314
(703) 706-3700

**Virginia, Western District**
Thomas B. Mason Building
105 Franklin Road, Southwest,
   Suite 1
Roanoke, VA 24011
Mail Address:
P.O. Box 1709
Roanoke, VA 24008-1709
(703) 857-2250

**Washington, Eastern District**
Federal Courthouse
920 West Riverside Avenue, Room
   300
Spokane, WA 99201
Mail Address:
P.O. Box 1494
Spokane, WA 99210-1494
(509) 353-2767

**Washington, Western District**
Seafirst Fifth Avenue Plaza
800 Fifth Avenue, Room 3600
Seattle, WA 98104
(206) 553-7970

**West Virginia, Northern District**
Horne Building
1100 Main Street, Suite 200
Wheeling, WV 26003
Mail Address:
P.O. Box 591
Wheeling, WV 26003
(304) 234-0100

**West Virginia, Southern District**
P.O. Box 3234
Charleston, WV 25332
(304) 345-2200

**Wisconsin, Eastern District**
Henry S. Reuss Federal Building
517 East Wisconsin Avenue, Room
530
Milwaukee, WI 53202
(414) 297-1700

**Wisconsin, Western District**
660 West Washington Avenue, Suite
200
Madison, WI 53703
(608) 264-5158

**Wyoming**
J.C. O'Mahoney Federal Building
2120 Capitol Avenue, Room 4002
Cheyenne, WY 82001
Mail Address:
P.O. Box 668
Cheyenne, WY 82003-0668
(307) 772-2124

# United States Commission on Civil Rights

**Regional Offices**
Address Complaints to: Regional
    Director
Complaint Referral System
United States Commission on Civil
    Rights
(800) 552-6843 or (202) 376-8513

**Eastern Regional Office**
Area Covered: Connecticut,
Delaware, District of Columbia,
Maine, Maryland, Massachusetts,
New Hampshire, New Jersey, New
York, Pennsylvania, Rhode Island,
Vermont, Virginia, West Virginia
624 Ninth Street, NW, Suite 500
Washington, DC 20425
(202) 376-7533
TDD/TTY (202) 730-2481

**Southern Regional Office**
Area Covered: Florida, Georgia,
Kentucky, North Carolina, South
Carolina, Tennessee
100 Alabama Street, SW, Suite 1840T
Atlanta, GA 30303
(404) 562-7000
TDD/TTY (404) 562-7004

## Midwestern Regional Office

Area Covered: Illinois, Indiana,
Michigan, Minnesota, Ohio,
Wisconsin
55 West Monroe Street, Suite 410
Chicago, IL 60603
(312) 353-8311
TDD/TTY (312) 353-8362

## Central Regional Office

Area Covered: Alabama, Arkansas,
Iowa, Kansas, Louisiana, Mississippi,
Missouri, Nebraska, Oklahoma
400 State Avenue, Suite 908
Kansas City, KS 66101
(913) 551-1400
TDD/TTY (913) 551-1414

## Rocky Mountain Regional Office

Area Covered: Colorado, Montana,
North Dakota, South Dakota, Utah,
Wyoming
1700 Broadway, Suite 710
Denver, CO 80290
(303) 866-1040
TDD/TTY: (303) 866-1049

## Western Regional Office

Area Covered: Alaska, Arizona,
California, Hawaii, Idaho, Nevada,
New Mexico, Oregon, Texas,
Washington
3660 Wilshire Boulevard, Suite 810
Los Angeles, CA 90010
(213) 894-3437
TDD/TTY: (213) 894-3435

# GLOSSARY OF LEGAL TERMS

■

**accumulative sentence.** This means you're going to be in jail for a long time, plus some. It's a sentence that is imposed, in addition to other sentences imposed at the same time, which will begin after you have completed the other sentences. Unlike concurrent sentences where you can serve time for two sentences at one time, accumulative sentences follow one another.

**action in personam.** An action against a person based on personal liability. Most civil actions, like actions against a negligent driver in an automobile action, are in personam actions.

**action in rem.** An action for the recovery of a specific object, usually an item of personal property such as an automobile.

**adjudication.** Means that an issue has been addressed and ruled on by a court. An attorney may ask, "Has there been an adjudication of the issues?" When a court renders a judgment or decree, it is said to have "adjudicated" certain issues.

**adversary system.** The type of legal system we have in the United States. In this system, two parties oppose each other in a process called litigation to resolve disputes between the parties.

**allegation.** An assertion usually made by one of the parties about facts involving a dispute.

**answer.** A statement that must be filed by a party who has been served with a summons and complaint by the plaintiff. In most jurisdictions, this party, the defendant, will need to answer each of the allegations the plaintiff has made in the complaint.

**appearance.** The way a person introduces and submits herself to the jurisdiction of a particular court. Your attorney may enter an appearance on your behalf, or you may enter an appearance on your own behalf by merely showing up to court at the designated time or by filing the necessary paperwork at the designated time.

**appellant.** The name given to a party appealing an unfavorable decision or judgment to a higher court.

**appellate court.** A court having jurisdiction of appeal and review over lower courts. These are not "trial courts," like Judge Brown's court, but are higher courts, like the United States Supreme Court. They can overturn the decisions of the lower courts. The United States Supreme Court is the highest appellate court in our system.

**appellee.** The name given to the party in an appeal who is not appealing the lower court's decision. This party has won in the lower court and must now defend against the attack of the appellant.

**arraignment.** A term used in the criminal context; the arraignment is when a person accused of a crime is brought to court to be informed of the charges against him or her and asked to answer to these charges.

**bail.** The amount of money imposed by the court in order for a person who has been arrested or imprisoned to be set free until a later court hearing.

**bail bond.** A monetary agreement between three parties—the accused, the state, and a "surety," a bond company—executed to ensure that a person who has been set free on bail will actually appear in court as required.

**bailiff.** The "security guard" for the court. This person is tasked with keeping order in the courtroom. The bailiff can answer your questions, like "Am I in the right place?" "Who is the prosecutor?" or "When is the judge expected to take the bench?"

**bench warrant.** A document that has been signed by a judge directing that a person be arrested. Because the judge signs it, it is considered to have been issued by the court itself and therefore "from the bench."

**binding instruction.** A jury instruction that directs the jury to render a decision for the plaintiff or the defendant if they find certain factual conditions exist.

**bind over.** To hold a person on bail until trial.

**brief.** A document that a party must prepare to submit to the court at certain stages during the litigation process. The document must adhere to the court's rules of procedure, which set forth various criteria like the maximum number of pages permissible. The document typically provides both facts and case law in support of the party's case.

**burden of proof.** The term used to designate which party must provide enough evidence to prove facts in dispute in order for the jury to render a decision in its favor. In criminal cases, the government has the burden of proof to establish a person committed a crime beyond a reasonable doubt.

**burglary.** A serious crime that involves a person both breaking into a building and entering the building. It is a felony and is frequently referred to as a B&E charge.

**chambers.** Private office of a judge.

**circumstantial evidence.** Indirect, as opposed to direct, evidence. A jury could base its entire verdict on substantial circumstantial evidence that it will rely on to infer that the disputed conduct occurred.

**commutation.** The process whereby a criminal charge is changed from a greater sentence to a lesser sentence, for example from capital punishment to life in prison.

**complainant.** The person who has started the lawsuit or judicial proceeding.

**complaint.** The first document or "pleading" filed with the court clerk that will begin a lawsuit.

**concurrent sentence.** Sentences for more than one crime to be served simultaneously rather than successively. Say you are charged with two crimes and are sentenced to five years for one and seven years for the other. If your sentences were to run concurrently, you would only need to serve seven years.

**contempt of court.** The act of being held responsible by a court, usually through a judge, for obstructing or hindering the judicial process.

**contract.** A written or oral agreement between two parties that is enforceable by law. Parties can enter into an agreement, but technically it is not a contract. An agreement is not a contract unless it is enforceable. An agreement to murder someone is not a contract because it is an illegal and unenforceable agreement.

**corpus delicti.** Literally means the body on which a crime has been committed, for example, the corpse of a person who has been murdered.

**court reporter.** A person responsible for recording testimony during court proceedings.

**costs.** The expenses that are incurred in filing and prosecuting a case, like the filing fee, deposition expenses, and so forth.

**counterclaim.** A claim that is made by a defendant against the plaintiff after being served with the plaintiff's complaint.

**criminal insanity.** The inability to distinguish between right or wrong due to diminished mental capacity. Or, as C-Rock would say, it means you're *Crazy.*

**cross-examination.** Questioning at trial or during a deposition by the party who did not ask for this person's testimony.

**damages.** The monetary value a person is entitled to receive by law for injuries suffered.

**decree.** A decision or order of a court, as in a divorce decree.

**default.** A type of judgment that is entered against a party that fails to appear at the specified time and place.

**deposition.** A tool typically used by trial attorneys to discover information about a case by requiring a person, the "deponent," to appear at a set time and place to answer questions under oath.

**direct evidence.** Unlike circumstantial evidence, this type of evidence directly establishes a case, for example, eyewitness testimony.

**direct examination.** The process of calling a witness and asking the witness to answer certain questions, as distinguished from cross-examination, where the attorney asking questions has not called the witness to testify.

**directed verdict.** An instruction by the judge to the jury that it should enter a verdict in favor of one party over another. Usually, an attorney will request that the judge makes such an instruction after the plaintiff has "rested" by ending its introduction of evidence and after the close of trial.

**discovery.** The process during litigation whereby the parties exchange evidence and discover the strengths and weaknesses of their case prior to trial.

**dissent.** The word used to indicate that a judge or group of judges have disagreed with the majority opinion of the court.

**domicile.** A legal term used to describe the place that is truly a person's home. A person may have more than one residence; they may reside on the East Coast and West Coast, but can only have one domicile. If a person does have two residences, then the person should choose one to be considered her place of domicile.

**double jeopardy.** The doctrine that prohibits a government from prosecuting a person twice for the same crime.

**due process.** The right to a fair trial.

**eminent domain.** The power of the government to take private property for the benefit and use of the public.

**enjoin.** A request to a court typically by filing an injunction to ask that it order the defending party to stop engaging in certain conduct.

**entrapment.** The act of law enforcement officers soliciting and inducing a person to commit a crime that the person would not have otherwise committed. It is a defense used by defendants in a criminal case to defeat the charges filed against them.

**exhibit.** A document that is used during a hearing, deposition, or trial to help establish a particular point.

**expert evidence.** Testimony given by a person who has special training and understanding about the subject matter which she will be called upon to testify. For example, a mechanic may be an expert on brakes and a physician an expert on the human body.

**extenuating circumstances.** Circumstances that can be used by a defendant in a criminal case to demonstrate that the alleged criminal conduct was not as bad as it would seem; these are typically considered mitigating factors.

**false arrest.** An unlawful restraint of a person's liberty.

**felony.** A serious crime that is generally punishable by being imprisoned for more than a year, as opposed to a misdemeanor, which is a less serious crime punishable by being jailed for less than a year.

**full faith and credit.** The doctrine provided by the United States Constitution that requires a judgment of a court to have the same faith, credit, and effect in all states regardless of where the judgment was obtained. Under this doctrine, a divorce obtained in one state is as effective as a divorce obtained in any other state.

**gag order.** A court order requiring participants in a court proceeding to not discuss the proceeding with others. These orders are typically used in highly publicized criminal proceedings like the O. J. Simpson trial.

**garnishment.** A process used by creditors to take the property of a debtor, like the debtor's wages, to satisfy a judgment.

**guardian ad litem.** An adult appointed to ensure that the interests of a minor are protected.

**habeas corpus.** Literally means, "You have the body." The name given a variety of writs whose object is to bring a person before a court or judge. In common usage, it is a document directed to the official or person detaining another, commanding him to produce the body of the prisoner or person detained so the court may determine if this person has been denied his liberty without due process of law.

**harmless error.** In appellate practice, an error committed by a lower court during a trial, but not prejudicial to the rights of the party and for which the court will not reverse the judgment.

**hearsay.** Evidence not proceeding from the personal knowledge of the witness.

**holding.** Ruling of a court upon specific issues of law raised in a case.

**impeachment of witness.** Attacking the credibility of a witness by offering evidence to show that the witness is wrong.

**imputed negligence.** Negligent conduct a person or organization might not directly have been involved in, which will be attributed to the person or organization because of a special relationship, like an employer–employee relationship, between the person or organization and the one directly responsible for the negligence. For example, a pizza company could be liable under the doctrine of "imputed negligence" for the accident of one of its pizza delivery drivers.

**inadmissible.** Evidence that cannot be admitted or considered by a court under the rules of evidence, for example hearsay or "he said, she said" evidence.

**indeterminate sentence.** A sentence that is indefinite in nature. Instead of being sentenced to a certain amount of time, the sentence is for at least X amount of time but less than Y amount of time, with the exact length of time to be determined afterward by the parole authorities.

**indictment.** A written document submitted by a grand jury after it has considered the government's evidence finding that a person who has been accused of committing a crime should be forced to stand trial.

**information.** An accusation by a law enforcement officer, instead of a grand jury, that a person should be forced to stand trial for the commission of a crime.

**injunction.** An order issued by a court demanding that a party cease taking certain action. "Injunctive relief" was sought in several civil rights cases where lawyers demanded that institutions stop engaging in racial discrimination.

**instruction.** A direction from the judge to the jury explaining how it should treat evidence it has ruled and how it should reach a verdict based on the evidence.

**interlocutory.** A temporary ruling, order, or decree made by a court.

**interrogatories.** A tool used during the discovery phase whereby a party directs written questions to the opposing party to help the party obtain evidence about a case.

**intestate.** The act of dying without a will. The law in each state decides how the property of a person who has died without a will shall be disposed of; these laws are called "intestate laws."

**irrelevant.** Evidence that is inadmissible because it does not relate to an issue in dispute.

**jurisprudence.** The philosophy or science of law that studies the relationship of legal principles.

**jury.** The group of individuals selected from the list of potential jurors who is tasked with making factual determinations and deciding whose case is more credible based on all the evidence. A grand jury is a jury that is typically impaneled by a prosecutor when the prosecutor cannot decide whether a case should proceed. This type of jury must then look at all of the evidence and determine if a person should be indicted and forced to stand trial. A petit jury is the standard group of twelve or fewer jurors who serve as the fact-finding body for a court in a criminal or civil trial.

**leading question.** A manipulative question that instructs, either directly but more than likely indirectly, how the question should be answered. These types of questions, with the exception of background questions, are prohibited on direct examination.

**limitations period.** The time period designated by statute or another rule within which a person is required to bring his or her case.

**malicious prosecution.** An action instituted by someone with the intention of harassing someone else when the person who institutes the action knows the person did not commit the alleged act.

**manslaughter.** The killing of another human being without malice.

**material evidence.** Evidence that is relevant and helps establish an issue in dispute.

**misdemeanor.** A crime less serious than a felony that is generally punishable by a fine and/or imprisonment for less than one year.

**mistrial.** A trial that is deemed invalid because an important legal requirement has been disregarded. For example, a trial that proceeds until it is discovered that the jurors were wrongfully impaneled can be declared a mistrial.

**mitigating circumstances.** Factors that can serve to reduce the degree of a crime a defendant in a criminal case may be charged with; these factors do not serve to justify or excuse the conduct, but can have the effect of reducing a sentence. A "cracked-out" criminal defendant could use this factor to mitigate a finding that she committed burglary.

**moot.** An issue that need not be settled in the case that a court has been called upon to decide because it is no longer an issue.

**moral turpitude.** Conduct that is contrary to ordinary concepts of decency; crimes of moral turpitude are those that involve poor morals like prostitution.

**murder.** Unlawfully killing another person without legal justification or excuse.

**next of friend.** An adult who is acting for the benefit of a minor or other legally incompetent person.

**nolo contendere.** A plea made by defendants in criminal cases that literally means "I will not contest it."

**notice to produce.** A notice prepared during the discovery phase of litigation that demands that the other party produce certain papers or documents.

**objection.** A formal statement to the judge usually made by an attorney that the court rules are not being followed in some manner by the other side.

**parole.** The release of a person from prison on certain conditions.

**parties.** The people or organizations directly involved in a case, such as a plaintiff or defendant.

**peremptory challenge.** A challenge that a lawyer may use to reject a person from a panel of jurors without having a reason for doing so.

**plaintiff.** A person who causes a case to be filed against another.

**pleading.** The name given to several written documents filed with the court and exchanged between parties in a lawsuit.

**power of attorney.** A written document that gives a person the ability to represent another for certain purposes.

**prejudicial error.** "Reversible error"; the type of error that provides the appellate court with a reason to reverse the judgment of the lower court.

**preliminary hearing.** A "preliminary examination"; when the person charged with a crime is asked to appear in court to determine whether the action should proceed any further.

**preliminary injunction.** An injunction granted near the time of filing of a suit to restrain a party from doing or continuing some act.